LONE STAR CHAPTERS

NUMBER SEVENTEEN

Tarleton State University

Southwestern Studies in the Humanities

William T. Pilkington, General Editor

Texas A&M University Press
College Station

LONE

STAR

CHAPTERS

The Story of

Texas Literary Clubs

✤

Betty Holland Wiesepape

For Sybil, a sister
Texas writer

Betty Wiesepape

The paper used in this book meets the minimum requirements
of the American National Standard for Permanence
of Paper for Printed Library Materials, z39.48–1984.
Binding materials have been chosen for durability.
∞

Library of Congress Cataloging-in-Publication Data

Wiesepape, Betty Holland, 1941–
      Lone star chapters : the story of Texas literary clubs / Betty
Holland Wiesepape.—1st ed.
            p. cm. — (Tarleton State University southwestern
studies in the humanities; no. 17)
Includes bibliographical references (p.) and index.
      ISBN 1-58544-324-7 (cloth : alk. paper)
1. American literature—Texas—History and criticism. 2.
American literature—Texas—Societies, etc. 3. Authors,
American—Homes and haunts—Texas. 4. Literature—
Appreciation—Texas. 5. Texas—Intellectual life. 6. Texas—In
literature. I. Title II. Series
PS266.T4W54 2004
810.9′9764—dc22

                                                            2003018571

This book is dedicated to all the writers
who have gone before me and,
in so doing, have made this book
and my own creative
writing possible.

CONTENTS

ILLUSTRATIONS

ACKNOWLEDGMENTS

The archival research that preceded the writing of this book would have been impossible without the help and cooperation of a number of individuals and research institutions: Dawn Letson of the Woman's Collection of Texas Women's University in Denton; Kay Bost and Francisco Garcia at the DeGolyer Library of Southern Methodist University in Dallas; John Sutsin of the Southwest Collection at Texas Tech University in Lubbock; Ellen Brown of the Texas Collection at Baylor University Library in Waco; Stephanie Wittenbach of the Center for American History at the University of Texas at Austin; Cecilia Aros Hunter of the South Texas Archives & Special Collections at Texas A&M University in Kingsville; Betty Bustos of the Panhandle-Plains Historical Museum and Archives at West Texas A&M University in Canyon; Marge MacElhaney of Alumni Records at Southern Methodist University in Dallas; the staff of the Amarillo Public Library; Jonathan Jeffery of the Manuscripts and Special Collections at Western Kentucky University in Bowling Green; William Erwin, Jr., and Linda McCurdy of the Rare Book, Manuscript, and Special Collections Library at Duke University in Durham; the staff of the History and Archives Department of the Dallas Public Library; Kathy Toon, director of the Children's Department at the Dallas Public Library; Tara Wenger and the staff of the Harry Ransom Humanities Research Center at the University of Texas in Austin; Dan Gorman of KGNC-AM Radio in Amarillo; Dorsey Wilmarth of the *Amarillo Globe-News;* and Linda Snow at McDermott Library at the University of Texas at Dallas.

The following individuals granted interviews and/or provided valuable information about the clubs in this study: Nova Bair, Mildred Bond, Robert Bond, Jerry Bradley, Paul Christensen, Margaret Dvorken, Carol Finch, Elizabeth Goodwyn, Frank Goodwyn, Mary Gordon, Claudia Harold, Jr., Jenny Louise Hindman, Sara Johnson, Rosemary Kollmar, Allen Maxwell, Doris Meredith, Emerett Sanford Miles, Charlotte Baker Montgomery, Robert Rhode, Ellen Richardson, Helen Sanford, Jim Scarborough, Peggy Schachter, and Bret Kruger Smith.

Dr. Lou Rodenberger encouraged my research and made her personal files on Texas women writers available to me. Dr. Rodenberger, Dr. Paul Christensen, and Dr. Tom Pilkington read all or portions of the manuscript and encouraged me to turn the material into a book. Dr. Clay Reynolds edited a version of the manuscript and made valuable suggestions for revision. Catherine Simpson Mitchell, Pat Michaelson, Joan Chandler, and Robert Nelsen proofed and edited an earlier version, and my husband, Floyd Wiesepape, spent many hours proofreading and correcting the final version. Gene Blankenship and Floyd Wiesepape applied their expertise in digital photography to make acceptable photocopies of photographs that appeared in deteriorating newspaper copy.

My deepest appreciation to Dr. Joan Chandler, who directed my doctoral dissertation at the University of Texas at Dallas, and to Dr. Frederick Turner, Dr. Robert Nelsen, and Dr. Pat Michaelson, who served on my dissertation committee. These individuals have shared my interest in Texas literary clubs, offered sound advice, and encouraged my work throughout this project.

Finally, I must thank George Ward, who accepted my original article, "The Manuscript Club of Wichita Falls, A Noteworthy Literary Club," for publication in the April, 1994, issue of *Southwestern Historical Quarterly*. It is reprinted in this book in a revised form, courtesy of Texas State Historical Association in Austin.

LONE STAR CHAPTERS

INTRODUCTION

I would here correct one erroneous impression
in regard to the character of the early settlers of Texas. . . .
There were in the early history of Texas
more college bred men in proportion
to the population than now.

T. J. Pilgrim, as quoted in Davis Foute Eagleton,
Writers and Writings of Texas

In *A Journey through Texas on Horseback,* New York landscape architect Frederick Law Olmsted portrays the Texas frontier of the 1850s as a region where rowdy adventurers and backward people coexisted in near-primitive conditions, a place where books were scarce and where interest in educational and artistic pursuits were almost nonexistent. For more than a century and a half, the public perception, fostered by Olmsted's account of a trip he made across the region on horseback in 1850, has persisted that frontier Texas was populated by debtors, drifters, desperados, and uneducated ruffians.

Yet evidence abounds in the statements of eyewitnesses, such as T. J. Pilgrim, that individuals of superior intellect, education, and refinement were also among those early immigrants. Philosophers, teachers, poets, painters, sculptors, and skilled craftspersons left cultural centers in Europe, in the Northeast, and in the Old South to make their way to the Texas frontier. Some came in search of adventure, some to escape political tyranny, and some to avail themselves of economic opportunities that were no longer available in their former homelands. Others, propelled by the romantic spirit of the age in which they lived, believed they could achieve a utopian life-style in the region's natural setting.[1]

Life on the Texas frontier was primitive and demanding, and artisans and philosophers were not as suited as farmers and common laborers to the task of survival. Separated from institutions that had supported their intellectual interests, some of these refined individuals became discouraged. They soon abandoned their dreams and returned to their former homelands, but some remained and found new ways to sustain their intellectual interests in the wilderness. Evidence that such individuals resided on the frontier can be found in anthologies of early Texas writing as well as in accounts by a number of historians and scholars, but this weight of scholarly evidence has proved ineffectual in countering popular myth. The figure of the rowdy adventurer, which captured the artistic imagination and shaped the public's perception of Texas residents early on, eventually took on mythical proportions that obscured this second, equally valid, narrative.[2]

In fact, Texas residents who do not fit the commonly accepted stereotypes have been meeting in locally organized literary clubs to read, discuss, and write literature since at least the 1850s. Members of Prairie Blume, a writing club composed of young men and women of the German settlement Das Lateinische, met in rural Fayette County from 1857 until the beginning of the Civil War. This group came together twice a month to read original poems, stories, and essays and to exchange criticism. Members of this club wrote primarily in the German language, but they utilized images from the Central Texas landscape and celebrated freedoms afforded them by their newly adopted homeland. A group of Norwegian, Swedish, and Danish immigrants began meeting at approximately the same time at Four Mile Prairie in North Texas. This reading club, made up of representatives of sixteen family groups, met primarily to share books and to engage in literary discussions.[3]

Five literary societies met in Independence throughout the

1850s. Two of these clubs were composed of males associated with Baylor College, and three were made up of females at Mary Hardin Baylor. Philomathesian, the oldest of these five clubs, was organized in 1851. In Salado, the Amasavourien Society was organized shortly after the close of the Civil War. Made up of individuals associated with Salado College, this club was modeled after Sorosis, the first recorded women's club in New York. Members of Amasavourien engaged primarily in the study of literature, but some members produced original compositions that were read or performed at club meetings.[4]

Locally organized clubs such as these made possible the continued existence of individuals of culture and refinement on the Texas frontier. However, these organizations exerted only minimal influence on the general cultural development of a sparsely populated region where a majority of residents were preoccupied with survival. When the Civil War ended and Indian hostilities no longer demanded the full attention of Texas residents, the society was, at last, ready for cultural advancement.

This state of readiness just happened to coincide with a popular education movement that swept the United States in the last quarter of the nineteenth century. Lyceums, chautauquas, and the General Federation of Women's Clubs of America, all manifestations of this movement, precipitated interest in clubs as a means of popular education all across the country. The number of clubs in Texas multiplied rapidly during this period; by the turn of the century, Texas residents' appetite for education, literature, and fine arts had precipitated literary societies, writing clubs, and other fine arts groups in communities throughout the state. These clubs had a much greater impact on cultural development of the region than clubs that met during the frontier period.[5]

Reports of club meetings and of work accomplished by literary clubs and their members appeared regularly in Texas newspapers throughout the early decades of the new century. This quickening of interest in fine arts on the part of Texas citizens was, at first, applauded by scholars and journalists, but by the latter part of the 1930s, a dramatic change had taken place in the attitudes of Texas literati toward members of literary clubs. Work that had once been applauded began to be denigrated, and terms like "pink tea poets," a derogatory term commonly attributed to J. Frank Dobie, began to be applied to members of literary clubs. The stereotypical image generally associated with pink tea poets was one of middle-aged women dressed in hats and gloves, assembling to drink tea and read, what one literary club member referred to as "kitchen poetry."[6]

Close inspection of the activities of literary clubs and the accomplishments of individual members of these groups reveals something quite different. Clubs organized between World War I and World War II served a more important function in the development of regional writing than most scholars have realized. As the narrative histories of the four organizations presented in this book will demonstrate, literary clubs operating during this period aided the development of a community that would eventually be able to sustain and encourage the creative work of ensuing generations of writers.

Many of these clubs met informally and kept no written accounts of club activities. Records of other groups have long since been destroyed, or they reside in closed collections that have not been catalogued and are not available for research. But even if information on all these clubs could be recovered, the total number is so great that a discussion of all of them could not be contained in a single volume.[7]

Texas literary societies and writing clubs, composed of both professional and nonprofessional writers, encompassed individuals of a variety of ages, occupations, and social classes. Organizations such as the Young Men's Literary Society and the Shakespeare Club of Dallas were made up of socially elite citizens, and some groups, such as the Bluebonnet Club of Richardson, were composed of rural farm wives. Other clubs, such as the Ladies Reading Circle of Dallas, the Shakespeare Club of Lancaster, Pathfinders of Austin, and the Jewish Literary Club of Houston, served the needs of minority groups whose members were excluded from socially elite clubs composed primarily of Anglo-Americans. Any number of these organizations would make worthy subjects of study.

Many interesting groups met in Texas between 1890, when a statement by the superintendent of the Census of 1890 signaled the official close of the American frontier, and the advent of World War II in 1941. Four groups from this period have been selected as subjects of study: the Manuscript Club of Wichita Falls, the Makers of Dallas, the Panhandle Pen Women of Amarillo, and the Border Poets of Kingsville. The following factors influenced the selection of these particular clubs: geographical location, time and duration of club activities, availability of historical materials, amount and quality of literary production, and the influence of the organization on the surrounding area. The selection of four clubs located in different areas of the state and operational in the same general time period facilitated comparisons and provided a broad picture of statewide activity.

Another consideration in the selection of these four clubs was the composition of membership as it relates to gender. In the initial stages of research, evidence materialized that many Texas citizens of both genders met together in literary clubs in the early decades of the twentieth century. However, some clubs that were represented as having all-male memberships turned out, on closer inspection, to have included both genders. And in clubs where the membership was composed of both genders, females generally outnumbered males. This evidence indicates that although both genders participated in literary club activities, females did so in much greater numbers.

Twenty-one literary clubs registered with the Texas Federation of Women's Clubs in 1897. By 1901, this number had grown to 132, and by 1941 the 1,200 clubs registered with the state Federation included more than 60,000 female members. Theodora

Penny Martin, Karen Blair, and other historians of the women's club movement in the United States estimate that the total number of clubs registered with Federated Women's Clubs of America accounted for only 10 to 15 percent of the total number.[8]

Scholarly writing about the activities of literary clubs anywhere in the United States is limited, and writing centered on Texas clubs is almost nonexistent. The predominance of female membership in these organizations may account, in part, for this gap in the historical record, for the activities of Texas women writers traditionally have not received as much attention as the activities of their male counterparts.[9]

Two clubs whose histories are included in this study were made up entirely of female members. The memberships of the two remaining groups were mixed in gender. Comparisons between all-male and all-female writing clubs were impossible because groups composed solely of male members were limited and those few groups that did exist failed to meet other criteria in this study. Nevertheless, this book does make limited comparisons of the activities and accomplishments of male and female writers who were members of the same group.

In chapter 1, the story of the Manuscript Club of Wichita Falls is set within the context of the women's club movement of the late-nineteenth and early-twentieth centuries. The student club known as the Makers of Dallas is the subject of chapter 2. Jay B. Hubbell organized this group during the early years of his illustrious academic career. The club's history is presented in relation to a flurry of literary activity, particularly poetry writing, that erupted throughout the southern region of the United States in the early decades of the 1900s. Members of this club played a major role in shaping and defining what later became known as the Southwestern literary movement.

In chapter 3, a narrative account of the Panhandle Pen Women of Amarillo (PPW) connects this club to two early professional organizations that existed for the benefit of Texas journalists: the Texas Press Association and the Texas Women's Press

Association. PPW, the only club in this study that is still in existence, is one of the oldest continuously meeting writing clubs in the United States.

The Border Poets, a writing club that drew poets from the entire South Texas valley region to Kingsville, Texas, for meetings, is the subject of chapter 4. The story of this group is set within the historical context of the King Ranch and the racial unrest that existed in the southern region of Texas for many years.

In the conclusion, the activities of these four writing clubs are compared and contrasted, and the findings of this study are detailed. Because human memory of events is often unreliable and because published reports of accomplishments by literary club members are sometimes exaggerated, a variety of research methods have been employed in this study. These methods include archival research, personal interviews, and examination of literature produced by literary club members. Club histories presented in this book are the result of careful examination of newspaper articles, anthologies of Texas writing, yearbooks of individual clubs, and the published literature and private papers of members of these organizations, as well as interviews with club members, their relatives, and their associates.

This initial research into the activities of Texas clubs could have been presented from a number of theoretical perspectives. A deliberate attempt has been made to present this information in the form of historical narratives rather than to couch it in accordance with any current philosophical debate or theoretical argument.[10]

This decision was influenced by Leonore Hoffmann and Deborah Rosenfelt, who write in *Teaching Women's Literature from a Regional Perspective* that the first job of scholars is to describe what they find. The choice of the historical narrative over a theoretical approach was influenced also by the concepts of Natalie Zemon Davis, Margaret Ezell, Dominick LaCapra, and other historians who contend that history should be a dialogue with the past in which historians refrain from imposing present-day values and issues upon the participants of a former period. These historians believe that participants in those events should be allowed to speak for themselves whenever possible. An attempt has been made in the following chapters not only to allow these participants to speak but also to place their statements in a position of primary importance within the text.[11]

This study uncovers no great undiscovered works of genius, but it does illuminate writing by a few individuals that merits an opportunity to be reintroduced to readers. No attempt has been made to rank these works as to their literary quality. In the place of literary analysis, a brief description of selected works appears along with some accounts of how these works were received by readers and critics at the time they were published.[12]

Variations from club to club and from region to region make rigid comparisons between the four clubs in this study both difficult and inadvisable. These clubs were autonomous organizations, each operating in a region of the state with a unique history. The formation of each group was stimulated by a different set of circumstances, and each organization was created to fill the needs of particular individuals. Although all four clubs were organized within the same ten-year period, the length of time each organization was active varied from seven to more than seventy-eight years. Nevertheless, this investigation of the activities of these clubs has revealed a number of striking similarities.

Literary societies and writing clubs did indeed play a major role in the development of writing in the state of Texas. Local literary societies and writing clubs enabled educated citizens to preserve their interests in cultural and literary pursuits and to pass these values on to future generations. The activities sponsored by these organizations encouraged the development of future young writers. Most members of these four clubs were not professional writers, and their writing did not provide their major source of income. In fact, a majority of these individuals had never sold any of their work before they joined these clubs, but through participation in club-sponsored activities, some of them acquired writing skills and gained confidence that enabled them to place their writing in some of the best regional and national publications of the period. A few of these individuals even went on to become authors who gained national recognition.

Through club-sponsored activities and events, literary societies encouraged the growth of a community of readers, and as this community of readers increased, so did the demand for regional publications. As more avenues for publication became available to writers within the state, the reputation of Texas writing increased, and even more opportunities for Texas writers were created both within and outside the state. A number of these club members became purveyors of culture, some as leaders of statewide organizations for the promotion of literary arts, some as teachers of creative writing, and some as editors and publishers of regional and national publications.

This narrative of four Texas literary clubs fills a gap in the historical record of literary development in the state. It also replaces popular stereotypes with useful models and provides valuable information about the types of communities and the kinds of activities that foster learning and nurture the growth of creative arts. In addition, this study illuminates the important role of colleges and universities in this developmental process.

CHAPTER ONE

The Manuscript Club of Wichita Falls

"What's the matter with them?"
A friend drew me cautiously aside and spoke in a confidential
undertone. "Are they dead beats on the town?"
I shook my head. . . .
"Bolsheviks? KuKluxers?" she continued.
I shook my head again. . . .
"Have they leprosy or cancer or smallpox?"
"No of course not," I answered quickly.
"Well then, what makes them so undesirable?"
"They are club-women."

Ruth Laughlin Barker,
"Club-Women," *Southwest Review*

With all the activity taking place on the streets of Wichita Falls in 1922, the seventeen women who converged on the red brick building on Lamar Street that mid-September day would have attracted no more than a passing glance from local residents. Encounters with stylishly dressed women who were rushing off to attend a club meeting were not uncommon, not even in a region as remote and underdeveloped as West Texas. With husbands busy at work and school-age children back in the classroom for the fall semester, women all across the country were turning their attention to club work. September was the beginning of the club calendar year, the time when existing clubs reconvened and new clubs that would better facilitate the needs and interests of local club women were being organized.

The seventeen women who gathered at the Kemp Public Library in Wichita Falls on September 14, 1922, had come together to organize a writing club. No one knows who initiated the idea to organize the Penwomen's Club, but the group assembled at the request of Mrs. Walter Robinson, president of the District Federation of Women's Clubs. Mrs. Robinson's purpose for calling the meeting was clear. Wichita Falls needed a club where women who had an interest in writing could share that interest with others and further develop their writing skills through joint association.[1]

The women meeting at the Kemp Public Library that day were a diverse group. They differed in age, personality, background, education, financial circumstances, and marital status and had little in common other than their shared interest in writing. No one was a professional writer, but a few women in the group had made earlier attempts at writing. One or two had a publication to their credit, and these individuals were interested in producing work for publication. The others had been writing only in the privacy of their homes and had responded to Mrs. Robinson's summons because they were interested in trying their hand at writing and wanted to improve their writing skills. A few women in the assembled group had neither writing experience nor aspirations to produce anything original. They were what the daughter of one club member called "literary appreciators." They loved literature, enjoyed activities that provided mental stimulation, and had enough knowledge of literary techniques to supply helpful criticism, but they had no literary aspirations. Some, if not all, of the women must have approached the meeting with a mixture of anticipation and trepidation. Writing in the privacy of their homes was one thing. Sharing their innermost thoughts with people they barely knew was something only a few of them had experienced.[2]

Mrs. Robinson convened the meeting, and the assembled group set to work organizing the club that would serve the needs of Wichita Falls women. Displaying a high degree of organization that was common to clubs associated with the General Federation of Women's Clubs, they selected a full slate of officers at that first meeting. Mrs. May Marshall McGee was elected president. Mrs. J. M. F. Gill and Mrs. Wayne Somerville agreed to be vice presidents; Mrs. G. H. Abbott and Irene Davidson shared secretarial duties, one recording and the other corresponding. Mrs. F. V. McMordie agreed to perform the duties of treasurer, and Mrs. Mabel Carter, Mrs. J. C. Berney, and Louise Williamson assumed the duties of auditor, parliamentarian, and custodian, respectively. Other charter members who attended the organizational meeting of the club but did not assume an office included Frances Coffin Boaz, Winifred Sanford, Mary E. Weldon, Marie Engle Johnson, Clare Dillon Holt, Virginia Sherrod, Katherine Henricle, and Lucille Sherrod. Fourteen of the seventeen women in attendance that day appear to have been married, and three were single.[3]

Former club members' accounts of the requirements for membership differ, and it is likely that membership requirements were different at various points in the club's history. In the beginning, the organization was open to all women in the Wichita Falls area who shared a serious interest in writing. Later on, membership in the group was not so easily attained. As Manuscript Club members became increasingly successful in terms of published work, membership requirements became more stringent. Early on in the club's history, an applicant for membership had to present samples of published work along with proof that she was actively seeking publication. Later, applicants were required to submit complete lists of published works, and their application for membership was accepted or rejected by a majority vote of existing members on the basis of these lists. Only the daughters of present or former club members were exempt from these requirements.

Membership in the Penwomen's Club soon became a recognized achievement among would-be writers in the community, and in the fourth year of the club's existence, the women changed the name of the club from Penwomen to Manuscript Club so that men who had expressed an interest in joining the group might be admitted. Only one man joined the group at that time, and former members could not recall any other male members joining the club in the group's twenty-plus-year history.

Early meetings took place in a public facility, usually in the Kemp Public Library or the YWCA building, at a regularly scheduled time and place. These early gatherings were conducted according to strict parliamentary procedure, but as members of the club became increasingly successful in their writing endeavors, this formality was discarded. It was replaced by informal critique sessions in which club members engaged in serious discussions of new literary offerings.

Former members and daughters of deceased members used the following words to describe the mood during these critique sessions: "charged," "exciting," "democratic," "intellectually stimulating." These women stressed the informality of the atmosphere, the intelligence of participants, and the excellence of the criticism. One Manuscript Club member said, "[They were] extremely bright women with active minds and definite convictions."[4]

Manuscript Club members may have dispensed with formalities, but they continued to maintain proper decorum. While engaging in lively debates, they were careful to exercise good manners and deliver their criticisms in proper grammatical form. Displays of anger, profanity, or other behavior deemed unacceptable by the group could, and on at least one occasion did, result in the expulsion of a member. Members tried to be honest in their evaluations of literary offerings, but they were also careful to deliver their opinions in a "kindly manner." In general, such criticisms were well received because the individual receiving them was usually very aware of their value. If the recipient did not agree with the suggestions made by other members, she simply rejected those suggestions and did not allow them to crush her spirits.

The following quotation from an undated newspaper article attests to the effectiveness of the group's methods: "Manuscript is conspicuous in the volume of its delivery of literary products to publications of high standing, for its . . . unorthodox procedures . . . and for the free-for-all, outspoken criticism . . . which is directed in open meetings at any manuscript which any member may submit. Members of writers' groups in other cities of Texas have expressed frank wonder and admiration of . . . reciprocal criticisms among the members. . . ."[5]

Manuscript Club member Winifred Sanford alludes to benefits she received from club meetings in a letter she wrote to Margaret Cousins in 1945: "A group of that sort is of much more value to a writer than an outsider would suppose. It is so much more than a mere giving and taking of criticism. The air seems thick with ideas whenever you get together. You are put on your mettle; the old competitive spirit rises . . . and you find yourself writing in spite of yourself."[6]

But the greatest testimony to the effectiveness of the Manuscript Club's methods is the high rate of success achieved by club members in terms of published work. Within two years of the club's organization, these women began a history of publication that would have been exceptional for any group of writers. This record was especially remarkable for a group composed primarily of novice writers. A short story by Winifred Sanford was the first piece to be approved for publication. "Wreck" was accepted on receipt by H. L. Mencken for publication in the *American Mercury,* one of the top literary journals in the United States in the 1920s. Mencken's acceptance of Sanford's story began a streak of publication by Manuscript Club members that would continue for more than twenty years.[7]

Winifred Sanford and at least three other Manuscript Club members went on to earn national recognition in the 1920s, 1930s, and 1940s. Three short stories by Sanford were listed by J. O. O'Brian in *The Best Short Stories of 1926,* and one story by Fania Kruger was included in Martha Folle's *Best American Short Stories* in 1952. Two poems by Fania Kruger and one by Laura Faye Yauger won first-place awards in American Poetry Society competitions, and Anne Pence Davis produced a popular novel that earned a Pulitzer prize nomination. Work produced by these four women earned praise from literary notables such as Joseph Auslander, Paul Engle, and H. L. Mencken. All were selected for membership in the Texas Institute of Letters (TIL). They gave readings, participated in seminars, taught writing classes, spoke at writers' groups, and wrote articles on the craft of writing for writers' periodicals. In the Manuscript Club's heyday, these four women writers were more than amateur scribblers.[8]

Other members of the club achieved success to a lesser degree, but as their reputations in the regional and national literary community increased, the respect they were accorded in their own homes did not change. One former member related that even those husbands who gladly consented to their wives' participation in club activities did not regard the women's writing or their participation in Manuscript Club activities as having any "real value." Perhaps the attitudes of the women themselves were partially responsible for their spouses' underestimation of the value of their writing. With only one or two exceptions, the married members of the club never represented themselves as professional writers. In fact, many of them went out of their way to deny that they were "professional writers" even at the time that their work was being nationally acclaimed. Like most women of the period, Manuscript Club members placed family responsibilities and household duties ahead of their writing and continued to look to their husbands for financial support. One former member explained that to do otherwise would have reflected unfavorably on the men, something most of these women would not allow to happen.[9]

Winifred Sanford is the Manuscript member whose work is

best known today, although all that remains of her literary output is a single volume of short stories. Sanford published fourteen stories in leading literary and popular magazines between 1925 and 1932, and nine of those stories appeared in the *American Mercury*. Mencken's acceptance of "Wreck" initiated a warm and friendly correspondence between Mencken and Sanford that continued until he resigned as the magazine's editor in the early thirties. Mencken greatly admired Sanford's work and wrote a number of encouraging letters about it.[10]

Six of Sanford's published short stories are set in Texas, and three in Minnesota where she lived before she married Wayland Sanford and moved to Texas. The settings of five other stories cannot be determined from their context, but events and characters in these stories were probably inspired by Sanford's observations of contemporary people she encountered in Texas landscapes. Her realistic portrayals, based on current events and present-day people, were a departure from the romantic style favored by many Southwestern writers of the period. Her Midwest background and her preference for realism prevented her from becoming entrapped in sentimental expressions. Sanford accomplished the realism, so favored by H. L. Mencken, through her use of irony, a method she discovered when she wrote "Wreck." In earlier, less successful stories, she took a sympathetic view of her characters and was, by her own admission, their press agent. But in "Wreck" and later work, Sanford adopted an unsympathetic narrative stance that enabled her to maintain emotional distance from working-class characters who struggle to survive tragic events.

At the time that this work was published, Sanford's starkly realistic portrayals received mixed reviews. Approximately fifty years later, when Sanford's stories were rediscovered, assembled in a collection, and reissued by Southern Methodist University Press, critics and reviewers declared the short stories collected in *Windfall and Other Stories* to be some of the finest written in Texas before 1940.[11]

Winifred Sanford, a member of the Manuscript Club, wrote short stories about Texas during the oil-boom days. H. L. Mencken published her stories in the *American Mercury. Photograph courtesy of the Sanford family*

These short stories are, indeed, finely crafted, but part of their value lies in the fact that they provide insight into a fleeting historical moment in the state's history. Sanford's depictions of life in the early days of the Burkburnett and East Texas oil booms provide rare glimpses of a Texas culture in transition, as traditions and values of an agrarian society were being threatened by the rapidly developing technology of the oil industry.

The literary achievements of Winifred Sanford and other members of the Manuscript Club were due, no doubt in part, to historical and economic circumstances that existed in West Texas in the early decades of the twentieth century. These circumstances brought this diverse group of women together and precipitated the conflicts and transitions in society that fueled their writing.

As early as 1900, residents of the Wichita Falls area had observed oil seeps. Oil production actually began in 1902, when drillers digging a water well struck oil. A major oil strike occurred in Electra in 1911, but it was the advent of World War I that increased the demand for fossil fuel and precipitated the frenzy of drilling activity that led to a major discovery in the Burkburnett field in 1918.[12]

An oil well called "Fowler's Folly" by local residents erupted with a flow of twenty-two hundred barrels per day. Within three weeks of this discovery, fifty-six oil derricks were erected, and oil field equipment, vehicles, and tents littered the landscape. Real estate values doubled and then tripled in a short period of time. Workers who could not find housing in Burkburnett secured accommodations in Wichita Falls and commuted daily to the oil fields by rail. Wichita Falls, now surrounded by oil fields, became headquarters for the region's oil production.[13]

Even before this oil boom occurred, Wichita Falls had encompassed more diversity within its population than most West Texas communities. A major rail line passed through Wichita Falls, and people traveling between Dallas and Oklahoma City stopped off there. The construction of a military airfield in World War I increased the diversity within the population even more, but when the Burkburnett oil boom occurred, hundreds of people from all over the world flocked to Wichita Falls within a very short period of time.[14]

Local residents as well as newcomers enjoyed increased prosperity, but along with this prosperity they had to endure the invasion of what one former Manuscript Club member called "kooks, drifters, and practicing eccentrics." A carnival atmosphere prevailed, as hustlers, prostitutes, and bootleggers mingled both with uneducated farmers and individuals of superior intellect and education. Conflicts were inevitable in such a setting as strangers with liberal ideas moved into an area formerly dominated by religious conservatives.[15]

Very few charter members of the Manuscript Club were natives of West Texas. A majority of the women had moved to Wichita Falls from other regions of the United States and from Europe with husbands who were attracted to the area by the economic opportunity that accompanied the oil boom. Like other newcomers to West Texas, most of these women did not hold traditional agrarian attitudes toward religion, and their more liberal attitudes alienated them, somewhat, from the local society. One former member explained, "The first question asked of a new resident was — what church do you attend? Everyone was expected to fit into an established group, and people looked askance at anyone who did not attend religious services." Another former member said quite simply, "These women were ladies of the 1920s."[16]

Early members of the Manuscript Club may have been unconventional in their thinking, but outwardly they conformed to accepted behavioral norms for married women of the time period. Former members explained that the women were concerned about their families and the welfare of their children and therefore would never have acted in any way that would bring reproach on their husbands. They would not have attempted the lifestyle of the Algonquin group, but they admired that kind of independence. One former member explained, "They were liberated in their souls."[17]

Undoubtedly, the women's unorthodox attitudes contributed to the feelings of isolation and alienation that they expressed in their conversations with others and in their writing. Some spoke openly with their friends and their children of the difficulties they encountered in adjusting to the Texas terrain, to the vast emptiness of the plains, to the extremes of Texas weather, and to a society that was more conservative than any they had experienced previously. Others encapsulated these feelings in original poems and stories. One Manuscript Club member told her daughter that only in the beauty of West Texas sunsets did she find a sense of serenity and acceptance.

Certainly Fania Kruger, a Manuscript Club member whose work received worldwide recognition in the 1940s and 1950s, held religious views that were very different from those of the majority of the West Texas population. Kruger was born to Jewish parents who immigrated to the United States when she was fifteen years old. Her life was so deeply rooted in Jewish tradition that in 1912 she consented to an arranged marriage and moved to Wichita Falls with her husband to operate a jewelry store and raise a family. Kruger had composed poems in the Russian language early in her life, but after her marriage, she quit writing and directed her energies to raising a family and helping her husband in the family business. She resumed writing after she became associated with the Manuscript Club, but Fania Kruger did not achieve publication quickly. She worked for ten years to master the English language and studied writing techniques in summer writing courses at the University of Colorado, Brandeis, and Harvard before she published her first American poem. Once begun, her production of written work continued until the end of her life.[18]

Kruger lived in Texas for sixty-eight of her eighty-three years, but she wrote only a few poems that originated from her Southwestern experience. Dominant images in her poetry were from her childhood in Sevastopol, Russia, a childhood that Kruger called "paradoxical" because her memories of that period were a mixture of terror and beauty. Kruger translated those experiences into intense, dramatic verses. Jewish themes and images of Cossacks, pogroms, ominous shadows, and swaying figures dressed in black are dominant elements in her poetry, but her portrayals

Fania Kruger, a Russian Jewish immigrant to Texas, wrote poems about the Jewish experience that attracted an international readership in the years surrounding World War II. *Photograph courtesy of Bert Kruger Smith*

of human suffering are remarkably free of bitterness. She wrote from a Jewish perspective, but the brotherhood of humankind is a major theme threaded throughout her work. The artistic quality of Kruger's poetry varies from poem to poem, but the emotional intensity and the humanitarian spirit she exhibits are consistent throughout the body of her work.[19]

Poems and short stories by Kruger appeared in many publications between 1930 and 1970, including the *New York Times, Prairie Schooner, Lyric, Contemporary Poetry, Redbook,* and *Southwest Review.* She published three volumes of poetry, the first in 1937, the second in 1949, and a third in 1973. Two of her poems won first-place awards in the American Poetry Society's annual contest in 1946 and in 1947, and other Kruger poems received prizes in a number of regional competitions. Aesthetically, this body of work is uneven, but Kruger's poetry achieved wide distribution and favorable critical comments at the time it was written. No doubt world sympathy for the plight of European Jews in the years surrounding two world wars accounts, in part, for the popularity of Kruger's writing and for the fact that few scholars know her work today.[20]

The Krugers, the Sanfords, and the families of other members of the Manuscript Club prospered greatly during the oil-boom years, but social position and family income were never emphasized among club members. Unmarried members, of necessity, worked at jobs or pursued professional careers, but the majority of members were married women who did not seek work outside their homes. Their husbands engaged in a variety of occupations, ranging from blue-collar work to professions such as medicine and law. The women formed warm and lasting personal relationships with one another, but as couples they rarely socialized with other members and their husbands.

Manuscript Club members' low-key attitudes toward wealth and social position were not the norm in West Texas during the oil-boom years. The region's newly rich quickly became class conscious. In a town where tent revivals had recently provided a major source of entertainment, a variety of cultural activities began to flourish, as the newly rich sought ways to spend their fortunes. One former member said, "If someone said that something was a big deal in New York in those days, the newly rich would have to have that person come here to perform."[21]

Consequently, between 1920 and the onset of the Great Depression, an inordinate amount of cultural activity took place in Wichita Falls for a town with a population of approximately fifty thousand. Touring companies such as the Columbia Artist Series brought famous singers, musical groups, European ballet companies, and Russian pianists to perform at the local opera house. Fashionably dressed men and women made their way down unpaved and sometimes muddy streets to attend imported cultural events. Other residents formed a symphony and a ballet company that featured local talent. A number of literary clubs were organized during this period as well. Among them were the

Shakespeare Club, the Browning Club, and an association of women's clubs known as the Women's Forum. In fact, so much cultural activity was taking place in Wichita Falls in the 1920s and 1930s that one local newspaper had to engage a full-time arts editor to cover the multiplicity of cultural events. This was an uncommon occurrence in a West Texas town in the 1920s.

The club that eventually became known as the Manuscript Club organized under the auspices of the Women's Forum. The activities of most clubs in this association were primarily social, with programs that centered on travel, bridge, dances, and luncheons. Former members of the Manuscript Club stated emphatically that, from its inception, the Manuscript Club was not a social club that served as entertainment for prominent Wichita Falls matrons. Manuscript Club members had little interest in belonging to an organization where the primary goal of attending meetings was to show off the latest fashions in one's wardrobe and to engage in casual gossip. One former member said, "These were serious writers, not kitchen poets."[22]

Throughout the club's history, some members pursued the study of writing with greater enthusiasm and intensity than others, enrolling in workshops, university courses, and writers' seminars to master new forms and currently popular writing techniques. Others felt, just as emphatically, that the ability to write was a natural gift and that instruction in popular techniques was neither necessary nor advisable. Lively discussions between proponents of these respective positions erupted from time to time at Manuscript Club meetings.

One Manuscript member who entered the most fervently into these discussions and pursued new forms and new methods of writing with great vigor was Anne Pence Davis. Davis utilized some of these modern techniques in the writing of a popular adult novel entitled *The Customer Is Always Right*. The novel is set in a department store in Plainstown, Texas, in 1938. Industrialization has come to West Texas via the oil industry, and descendants of pioneers are embracing free enterprise. Davis assembles divergent elements of West Texas society and confines their actions to the interior of a modern store. She conveys regional setting through the sale of particular merchandise, the celebration of local holidays, and the speech and mannerisms of local characters. The structure of the novel is circular, with material divided into sections that correspond to the four seasons of the calendar year. While store employees from night watchman to marketing manager engage in the business of doing business, the omniscient narrator moves from the mind of one character to another as Davis skillfully propels the novel to a conclusion without allowing any one character to draw the novel's focus away from the main character, the store. *The Customer Is Always Right* received mostly favorable reviews and a nomination for a Pulitzer prize. The book did not advance into the final round of competition for the Pulitzer, but it later became a Book-of-the-Month Club selection.[23]

Davis had established a reputation as a writer of children's books several years before *The Customer Is Always Right* was published in 1940. She began to write books for adolescent girls in 1935, after Winifred Sanford's ten-year-old daughter Helen complained that the only books available to girls her age were "old fashioned, unnatural, and unrealistic." Davis's first book, *Mimi at Camp,* filled a void in the juvenile book market and became an instant commercial success. Davis eventually wrote two more books in the Mimi series and three other books for adolescents. The books she wrote for children became so popular that copies of the first printing of *Wishes Were Horses,* published in 1938, sold out in advance of publication.[24]

Davis's commercially successful books for adolescents and her one popular adult novel established her reputation as a writer of note, and the demand for her services as a writer, speaker, and writing teacher grew. She later went on to publish an advice book to writers of juvenile fiction and a how-to book about breaking into a juvenile market, in addition to poems, book reviews, short stories, and many articles that appeared in magazines and newspapers. But without the companionship, encouragement, and inspiration afforded Davis by other members of the Manuscript Club, it is unlikely that she would have achieved this level of success as a writer or as a teacher of writing.[25]

The Manuscript Club played an even greater role in the achievements of Fania Kruger, Winifred Sanford, and Laura Faye Yauger. In a feature article in the *Dallas Journal,* Hilton Greer explains that Kruger's childhood interest in poetry writing had to be revived after years devoted to the roles of wife and mother. This renewal of interest in writing on the part of Fania Kruger coincides with the initiation of her association with the Manuscript Club.[26]

Sanford wrote most of the short stories collected in *Windfall and Other Stories* during the years she was associated with the Manuscript Club. Her productivity declined sharply after the Sanford family moved from Wichita Falls to Dallas in the early 1930s, and she eventually stopped writing altogether. A combination of factors contributed to the decline of Sanford's writing career, but one of the major factors was her separation from the Manuscript Club. Fifteen years after her family's move to Dallas, Sanford wrote the following to Margaret Cousins: "I am particularly interested in what you had to say about the incentive one receives from meeting with a group of fellow writers. . . . [Without] the Manuscript Club . . . I should never have begun my own somewhat limited career."[27]

Without the influence and encouragement of Manuscript Club members, Laura Faye Yauger might never have tried her hand at writing poetry. In an article that featured Yauger's poetry writing, Greer tells how the club served as catalyst for her writing: "Her first efforts at writing verse were made . . . when she was assigned the task of composing . . . a poem before the writers' club of Wichita Falls. . . . She had never written a line of verse, has always believed that she could not master rhythm and rhyme, and her first thought was to resign from the organization."[28]

Yauger composed her first eight-line poem to fulfill the membership requirements imposed on active members of the

Laura Faye Yauger, whose poem "Planter's Charm" won regional and national awards, wrote her first poem to satisfy an assignment for Manuscript Club membership. *Photograph courtesy of Bert Kruger Smith*

Manuscript Club. The poem was accepted for publication in the poetry magazine *Kaleidograph* almost immediately. Later that same year, *Kaleidograph* awarded Yauger's ballad "County Fair" first prize in the publication's annual contest for the year 1929. In 1932, "Planter's Charm" won a Poetry Society of Texas first-place award. In 1935, the same poem was awarded first place in the American Poetry Society's annual competition, and sometime later, a book of poems by the same title won the Kaleidograph Press Fifth Annual Book Publishing Contest.[29]

This slim volume contains verses that are insightful, spirited, and poignant. The experience at the center of Laura Faye Yauger's poetry is Southwestern. Chokecherry trees, barbedwire fences, water tinted red by desert sand, and abandoned farmhouses serve as major images. As the daughter of pioneers who lived, for a time, in a lean-to in the Sierra Nevada, Yauger knew the joys and the hardships of living a pioneer lifestyle. She translated her impressions of southwestern vistas into lyrical verses that are often reminiscent of folk songs. As a child, she observed firsthand the difficulties that the family's nomadic existence caused her mother, and she drew on these bittersweet memories in the writing of several poems in her only collection.[30]

Alienation, unrealized dreams, and disappointment in love are major themes in Yauger's work. Her poems closely parallel the difficult, disappointing, and often tragic events of Yauger's own life, but she avoids sentimentality through the use of humor and irony. The female characters who are the focus of most of her poems almost always experience disappointment, as is the case in her highly acclaimed poem "Planter's Charm." The central image in this poem — a farm woman broadcasting corn seed — is dated today, but a majority of the poems in *Planter's Charm* are surprisingly relevant to contemporary human existence more than seventy years after she wrote them.

Today, only a few literary historians know that the poems in this slim volume exist, but in the 1930s, Laura Faye Yauger's poems were highly acclaimed by both regional and national critics. When members of the newly formed Texas Institute of Letters were asked to name ten outstanding writers to be Fellows of the Institute in 1936, Laura Faye Yauger was named among the ten. She was nominated by J. Frank Dobie, who said in his letter to William H. Vann that Yauger's ballad "Planter's Charm" was the most powerful and original poem ever written in Texas. Dobie stated that, in his opinion, if work of that caliber went unrecognized, the TIL's selections would appear ridiculous.[31]

Like Winifred Sanford, Laura Faye Yauger was never a prolific writer. She was not able to sit down and write on command, and like most other members of the Manuscript Club, she placed her many family responsibilities and her domestic duties ahead of her writing. As circumstances in her personal life became more complex, Yauger devoted less and less time to writing, and finally, she ceased to write for publication entirely.[32]

In her letter to William Vann, written in response to his invitation to become a charter member of the Texas Institute of Letters, Yauger provides insight into the factors that contributed to the termination of her brief, highly successful career. She tells Vann that she thinks she should have postponed publication of the book *Planter's Charm,* for now that the book is completed, she lacks incentive to write another. She expresses the following doubts about her future writing: "As long as I haven't tried — and failed — I can have the joy of assuring myself that I shall write my own 'Now in November.' But if I should try and find that I lacked the skill what should I do then?"[33]

Publication was always more important to some Manuscript Club members than to others, particularly to women who were unmarried or to those who had no children, such as Anne Pence Davis. Some members found that in order to achieve publication in popular magazines, they had to write to prescribed formulas, but the entire membership admired and respected members such as Sanford, Kruger, Davis, and Yauger, who managed to gain publication without adhering to specified conventions.

Members of the Manuscript Club were acutely aware of the distance that separated them from major literary markets in the North and Northeast. They recognized the difficulty of achieving publication while living in a remote area of Texas, and they helped one another by sharing information about publication opportunities at bimonthly club meetings. If a member received some communication from an editor or a publisher, she brought the letter to the next club meeting and read it aloud to the rest of the members at the earliest opportunity.

Despite these women's perceived difficulties in getting their work published, they achieved a remarkable rate of publication success for a period of more than twenty years. In addition to the accomplishments of Davis, Kruger, Sanford, and Yauger, Charlene Underwood published poetry in *Life* and other magazines and newspapers, and she published a book of children's verses that was illustrated by another Manuscript Club member, Mrs. Walter Achning. Frances Coffin Boaz published work in poetry magazines, household journals, and newspapers. She conducted a radio program entitled "Poetry for Children" over station KTAT in Fort Worth and edited an anthology of children's poems. She also published one book of poetry and received a citation from *American Magazine* as a patron of child poets of America. Ione Parfet wrote articles for interior decorating magazines and published poems and stories in other publications. Marie Engle Johnson won a prize for her one-act play, *Echoes,* and her poems were accepted in various publications. Ollie Roediger won an award from Poetry Society of Texas in 1949, and Mary Beth Little published two volumes of poetry and became an editor for *Mademoiselle.*

Former members credit this success, in part, to the fact that the women were, as a group, supportive of one another's endeavors. They were not highly competitive among themselves, and the entire group rejoiced at the success of each individual member. One former member attributed the lack of competitiveness among members to the variety of interests, writing styles, and subject matter encompassed within the membership.

Former members could not remember the exact date when the Manuscript Club ceased to exist. The consensus of surviving members was that the club began a gradual decline in the early 1940s. The Great Depression of the 1930s appears to have had little effect on the literary production of the group. One former member explained that only in retrospect did the women realize just how bad the situation had been. Another member said, "All one needed to write was a pencil and a few sheets of paper, and those things didn't cost much."[34] Conversely, the country's entrance into World War II had a devastating effect on the organization. Some of the younger members left Wichita Falls and moved to other regions of the country to be near their husbands who had entered the armed services. Some elderly members stopped writing altogether and descended into a depression from which they never fully recovered. These women had experienced the emotional upheaval of one major world war when they were in their teens and early twenties, and when the United States entered the Second World War, they were older and less resilient. The thought of a conscripted army staffed by sons and grandsons was difficult for them to accept.

The Manuscript Club disbanded altogether sometime in the 1950s. By that time, some of the club's most illustrious and productive writers had moved away from Wichita Falls. Others were deceased or had grown so old that they no longer had an interest in writing. Some, such as Fania Kruger and Anne Pence Davis, continued to write and to seek publication throughout their lives, but the literary production of other members, such as Winifred Sanford and Laura Faye Yauger, ceased many years before their lives ended.

For a period of approximately twenty years, members of the Manuscript Club produced work that gained the respect of the local and national literary communities, but in 1991, when Wichita Falls was selected to receive a National Endowment for the Humanities Award and to host a five-week study series on American poets, no one employed by the Kemp Public Library in Wichita Falls was aware that a successful writers' group called the Manuscript Club had ever held meetings there. The only evidence of the group's operation within the city was a single newspaper article in the files of the local newspaper office and notices of club meetings that appear in microfilm copies of newspapers from the twenties, thirties, and forties.[35]

Even when this club was active, when members of the group were publishing their work and receiving awards, little public attention was given to the role the club played in the achievements of individual members. As one former member explained, "This was a working group. These women met for the purpose of writing. They neither desired nor sought publicity." But evidence uncovered in this study illuminates the important role that the Manuscript Club played in the development of these four illustrious members.[36]

Many other women's literary clubs were also operating in Texas in the first half of the twentieth century. Evidence located in obscure newspaper articles and in the biographies of some Texas women writers indicates that a relationship between these clubs and the production of writing by Texas women does indeed exist.[37]

By 1912, the General Federation of Women's Clubs was the largest association of women's clubs in America, with 1.7 million members. This national association was composed of thousands of "culture clubs," and some of these clubs were penwomen's groups. The Manuscript Club was but one of a number of chapters of penwomen meeting regularly in Texas cities throughout the 1920s and 1930s.[38]

Perhaps the high rate of success enjoyed by Manuscript Club members was atypical. Perhaps no other group of writers associated with the National Association of Penwomen of America or with the Texas Federation of Women's Clubs produced a comparable amount of published material. A comparison of the Manuscript Club to other Texas literary clubs would be helpful in determining if this is the case, but no such studies exist. Members of a few women's clubs have preserved accounts of the social and service activities engaged in by these groups, but the contributions these organizations made to the developing culture and their influence on the development of an intellectual community that could sustain regional arts have not been addressed by scholars.[39]

The construction of a model that can be used for the purpose of comparison is also difficult, for as both Karen Blair and Eleanor Flexner note, making steadfast generalizations about the composition of [women's] literary clubs is difficult due to the large number of clubs, the variety within the membership of clubs, and the diverse interests of club members. The only comparison that is possible, then, is a comparison of the attributes and activities of the Manuscript Club to a set of generalizations about women's literary clubs that emerges from the writings of feminist scholars Karen Blair, Theodora Penny Martin, and Sheila Rothman.[40]

As a general rule, literary clubs were made up of middle-aged, middle-class matrons whose children were no longer a constant daily responsibility. Members usually shared a common background — the same point of origin, the same alma mater, or the same religious affiliation. Class, economic status, or husbands' occupations were often the common factor that drew these individuals together. Most clubs were made up mostly of married women and did not serve the needs of single and professional women.

Meetings were held in public facilities or in individual homes from one to four times per month. These gatherings took place at a time when they did not interfere with members' domestic responsibilities, and they generally lasted approximately two hours. Club meetings were genteel affairs that did not require members to depart from what society perceived to be the proper role of a married woman. Membership in literary clubs allowed these middle-class women to acquire education and to participate in intellectual, service, and/or social activities without making a radical commitment to feminism that was required of suffrage groups. In general, women's clubs reinforced established values of society regarding the home and the place of women in society.

In most groups, members themselves prepared papers and presented programs that were related to a yearly theme. Presenters were serious and energetic in their preparations and presentations, but most lacked the skills necessary to perform scholarly research and rarely acquired these skills from participation in club activities.

Membership in most literary groups was restricted, but a strong emphasis on family ties superseded stringent membership requirements when relatives of current members were nominated. Men were excluded from membership, as a general rule. Some husbands saw the literary club as a threat to domestic tranquility, but most were tolerant of their wives' participation as long as the domestic routine of their homes was not disturbed.

When the Manuscript Club is compared to these generalizations, a number of differences become apparent. Members of the Manuscript Club did not share a common place of origin, alma mater, or religion. The membership varied in age, marital status, income, and social position. The format of Manuscript Club meetings was informal. The acceptance of Manuscript Club members' work by the national literary community indicates that members of this club attained a high level of skill. Finally, men were not excluded from membership in the club.

When the Manuscript Club is compared to this set of generalities, the following similarities become apparent. Manuscript Club meetings were held in public meeting places and in private homes. Club affairs were conducted in a "ladylike" manner, and members engaged in intellectual activities that bolstered their self-confidence without causing them to neglect domestic duties or family responsibilities. Manuscript Club members shared the spirit of women activists, but their personal conduct fell within the acceptable pattern of behavior. Membership requirements were relaxed when relatives applied for membership, and finally, most husbands of the Manuscript Club did not object to their wives' participation, but they did not view club activities as serious efforts.

Certainly, enough similarities exist between the Manuscript Club and scholars' generalizations about women's clubs to merit additional study of individual clubs whose members were engaged in writing. If the Manuscript Club is a reliable example of what members of literary clubs in Texas were accomplishing in the first half of the century, some of the best writing produced in the state during that period may have taken place in conjunction with club activities. When career opportunities for women in Texas were severely limited, women's literary clubs may have been the primary creative outlet for some of the region's most intelligent citizens.

Individuals Who Are Known to Have Been Members of the Manuscript Club

Mrs. G. H. Abbott
Mrs. Walter Achning
Mrs. J. W. Akin, Jr.
Mrs. J. C. Berney
Frances Coffin Boaz
Mabel Carter
Irene Davidson
Anne Pence Davis
Margaret Dvorken
Mrs. R. A. Faver
Mrs. E. E. Fisher
Josephine Fisk
Mrs. J. M. F. Gill
Katherine Henricle
Anne Francis Hill
Jenny Louise Hindman
Mary Hindman
Clare Dillon Holt
Marie Engle Johnson
Berta Mae Kruger (Smith)
Fania Kruger
Mary Beth Little
Mrs. L. H. McCullough
May Marshall McGee

Mrs. F. V. McMordie
Joy Micheau
Baldwin Montgomery (male)
Ione Parfet
Mrs. J. B. Pitman
Mrs. H. N. Roberts
Ollie Roediger
Winifred Sanford
Lucille Sherrod
Virginia Sherrod
Phylura Skalinder
Mrs. Wayne Somerville
Francis Lee Tolbert
Mrs. C. B. Toney
Mrs. E. J. Tschabold
Charlene B. Underwood
Frieda Van Emden
Dorah McConnico Wade
Mary E. Weldon
Dorothy Whiting
Louise Williamson
Peggy Williamson (Schachter)
Mary Elizabeth Weldon
Laura Faye Yauger

CHAPTER TWO

The Makers of Dallas

Poets are a strange tribe — and a numerous one.
It has gotten so that one cannot shake a bush
without a poet or two falling out.

W. E. Bard, *Fountain Unsealed:*
A Collection of Verse by Texas Writers

By the first weekend in April, the landscape in North Dallas had turned a vibrant shade of green. All around the newly constructed red brick buildings, plants were putting out tender shoots of new growth, and the night air was fragrant with the scent of blossoms and freshly turned earth, as the group of Southern Methodist University students made their way from the campus to the nearby home of Professor Jay B. Hubbell. They were in high spirits, for they had been invited to the home of one of their favorite professors to participate in the organization of a poetry club.

Just how many students Dr. Hubbell invited to his house that evening is unclear, but seven undergraduates responded to his invitation: George D. Bond, Loia Magnuson, Edyth Renshaw, Jeanne Calfee, Sherwood Gates, Sam Hilburn, and Faye Lemmon. In Hubbell's opinion, these seven students were some of the most talented individuals in his classes, but on that April evening in 1922, they were far from the serious writers they would become under Hubbell's direction. Edyth Renshaw recalled the mood of the group that evening in a videotaped interview in 1983: "We wanted to be freaky and wear sandals and

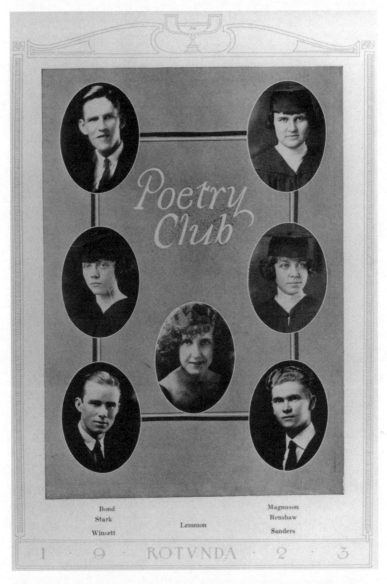

Members of the Makers as they appeared in the 1923 SMU annual, the *Rotunda*. Counterclockwise from top left-hand corner: George D. Bond, Elsie Marie Stark (later Harry), Marvin D. Winsett, Faye Lemmon, Ottys Sanders, Edyth Renshaw, and Loia Magnuson. *Photograph courtesy of the DeGolyer Library, Southern Methodist University*

39

be far out, but he suggested that it would be better to imitate the ancients . . . instead of imitating Greenwich Village."[1]

Dr. Hubbell suggested that the students call themselves "the Makers." He told them that the term was a modern English translation of the Saxon word *scop,* the equivalent of a poet or minstrel in the Middle Ages. The students submitted to Hubbell's guidance and named the club the Makers. No one, including Jay Hubbell, could have foreseen then the contribution that this club, started by a group of immature college students, would eventually make to Texas letters.[2]

The students who attended the organizational meeting of the Makers and those who joined the club later were, for the most part, Texas natives. Their families lived in rural communities in the vicinity of Fort Worth and Dallas, where their parents worked as ministers, schoolteachers, and owners of small businesses. Few, if any, of these families were wealthy, but the occupations the parents engaged in indicate that many had received college training. Once again, the facts of Texas history do not support the commonly accepted myth that early Texas was a cultural wasteland. All seven of the young Texas natives who attended the organizational meeting of the Makers had previous experience in poetry writing, and four were, in Hubbell's opinion, "exceptionally gifted."[3]

Dr. William Carry Crane commented on Texas residents' affinity for poetry writing as early as 1887, when he called Texas a "land of poetry" and said that poetry was embedded in the heart of Texas people. This interest in poetry on the part of Texas residents did not originate within the state. It was transported to the region by immigrants who brought the interests, manners, customs, and leisure activities of older and more sophisticated societies along with them. In North Texas, the intersection of two railroads in Dallas in the 1850s brought an influx of individuals of superior intellect, education, and culture to the area to assume managerial positions in the new and rapidly developing center of commerce.[4]

By the turn of the century, poetry writing had become a popular form of entertainment among North Texas residents. In an interview with the author, Mildred Bond, wife of Maker George Bond, recalled parties in Hillsboro, Texas, in the first decade of the new century: "Everyone was writing poetry. . . . They weren't writing it very well, but everyone was writing it, and all the newspapers were publishing it. . . . You went to someone's home, and someone read poetry or . . . played the piano, and that's what you did for entertainment back then."[5]

With the organization of the Poetry Society of Texas in 1921, poets who previously had been isolated from one another began to have contact. Most Texas poets whose work was being published in national magazines were members of the Poetry Society during the organization's early years. The society not only put poets and would-be poets in touch with one another but also provided many Texas residents their first opportunities to hear presentations by leading American literary figures.[6]

By the 1920s, Texas colleges began to nurture local residents' interest in verse writing, and literary societies and writers' clubs began to be organized in most towns where colleges and universities were located. The Makers of Southern Methodist University (SMU) quickly emerged as one of the most important of these college groups. This club's importance was due, in part, to its location in the city of Dallas. With a group of talented visual artists in residence and with a rapidly developing little theater movement, Dallas was emerging as an important center of cultural activity in the Southwest.

Hubbell describes the intellectual awakening that was taking place in the region in a 1925 editorial in the *Southwest Review*. He personifies the new Southwest and speaks of its insatiable cultural appetite for science, literature, ideas, and all forms of art. He tells that it devours the finest literary magazines and newspapers and still will not be satisfied until it has magazines of its own. He lists five regional magazines that have already been founded, and he offers the Poetry Society of Texas and the little theater movement as evidence that Texas in the mid-twenties had developed interests other than those of the founders of the republic. Hubbell suggests in this article that although athletic events were drawing large crowds, more students may have been interested in writing poetry than in playing football. Whether or not this statement is accurate, Hubbell and his young Makers were in an ideal position at SMU to play key roles in the cultural awakening that Hubbell describes in this editorial.[7]

By all accounts, Hubbell was the key figure in the success of the poetry writing club known as the Makers. From an early age Hubbell had dreamed of becoming a poet, but as an adult he realized that the poems he wrote were imitative and lacked imagination. He eventually abandoned his dream of becoming a poet and focused his energies on an academic career, but Hubbell's early experience in poetry writing had a positive effect on his method of teaching literature. Throughout his long and distinguished academic career, he placed higher value on the making of literature than he did on the criticism of literature.[8]

John McGinnis recruited Jay Hubbell to the position of assistant professor in the SMU English Department in October, 1915. The college had been in operation for only thirty days when a greater-than-expected enrollment precipitated an acute need for additional faculty, and Hubbell, who had not yet completed requirements for his doctoral degree, accepted the position McGinnis offered. Hubbell was young and ambitious, and he expected his stay at the new Texas college to be brief. He had no way of knowing that his tenure at SMU would span a ten-year period and that the position at the relatively unknown Texas college would provide him opportunities for career advancement that probably would not have been available to him at a more prestigious East Coast university.[9]

When Hubbell came to SMU, he was one of a small number of young scholars who were determined to make the study of work by American authors respectable, for universities were

Jay B. Hubbell, organizer of the Makers, enjoys a moment of retreat from his adoring students and hectic academic duties at Southern Methodist University in 1923. *Photograph courtesy of Duke University Library*

not offering courses in American literature at that time. While Hubbell and his colleagues were developing a curriculum for the new English Department, they were also experimenting with new methods of teaching literature. Unable to find a suitable text for their sophomore English classes, Jay Hubbell and John Beaty coedited *An Introduction to Poetry*. This textbook, published by the Macmillan Company, included works by contemporary American poets such as Robert Frost, Carl Sandburg, and Vachel Lindsay, along with poems by Henry Wadsworth Longfellow, Edgar Allan Poe, Robert Browning, and Alfred Tennyson. The book soon became a best-selling college text that carried the names of the two young professors and Southern Methodist University into classrooms in prestigious universities all across the country. The name recognition and the contacts that Hubbell made while working on the book enabled him to persuade well-known contemporary writers to come to Dallas to give readings and lectures. Hubbell's reputation as a scholar continued to increase, and while he was on the faculty at SMU, he chaired the first American Literature Group of the Modern Language Association. Later in his career he would go on to found *American Literature: A Journal of Literary History, Criticism, and Bibliography,* an important scholarly publication devoted to the study of American literary history, criticism, and bibliography.[10]

Another of Hubbell's accomplishments involved the transfer of the *Texas Review* from the University of Texas at Austin to SMU in 1924. He renamed this publication the *Southwest Review.* With the help of John McGinnis, George Bond, and Herbert Gambrell, Hubbell turned it into an outstanding literary journal that became an important organ for the developing field of Southwestern life and literature. Like the textbook he coauthored with Beaty had done earlier, the *Review* carried the names of the journal's editors, Southern Methodist University, and emerging Texas writers into major literary centers.[11]

The poetry writing club known as the Makers was another

of Hubbell's experiments. Inspired by a new era of poetry that had begun in Chicago in 1915 with Harriett Monroe's publication of *Poetry, A Magazine of Verse,* he was seeking new ways to encourage students to study the work of contemporary American poets. He also wanted to create a venue where talented students could be encouraged to try their hand at composing poetry, for creative writing courses were not taught in American universities at that time.[12]

The objective of the Makers, as that objective was stated in an article in the SMU college newspaper, the *Campus,* was to stimulate student members' interest in poetry and to improve the quality of their writing through a process of mutual criticism. In reality, Hubbell had an ulterior motive for encouraging the organization of the student club. He needed a venue where he could train promising student poets and then encourage them to submit their compositions to a national poetry contest that was soon to be sponsored by the SMU English Department. Dallas businessman Louis Blaylock, Jr., had given an anonymous donation of $175 to SMU, and the staff of the English Department had decided to use this money to sponsor a poetry contest that would be open to undergraduates in colleges and universities all over the country. Years later, journalist Hilton Greer would refer to this student contest as "an interesting item in the history of the literary awakening of the Southwest."[13]

Under Hubbell's kind but firm direction, the Makers soon evolved into a community of serious writers who met at the Hubbell home every other Wednesday evening to read original compositions and exchange criticism. In a tribute to Hubbell, written shortly after his death, former Makers George Bond and Ottys Sanders recall what took place at these gatherings: "We were indeed 'makers,' learning the fusion of ingredients that make poetry good and understandable. . . ."[14]

Each participant was expected to produce at least one original poem for critique. These poems were typed, unsigned, and handed in anonymously when students arrived at the meeting. Submissions were then read to the group by a designated reader, and a discussion ensued in which each poem was discussed, analyzed, and evaluated. The poems presented for critique usually dealt with one of two subjects, the prairie or the city, but the compositions varied in form, style, and type. Some members of the group experimented with the new free verse, while others preferred to write in traditional forms like the triolet, the sonnet, and the ballad.

Hubbell encouraged diversity, for he recognized that a variety in poetic forms reflected individual differences in the participants' temperaments and points of view. He impressed on the students that poetry should never be conventional and that it should always have some relationship to human lives. He reiterated this message in his introduction to the 1924 anthology of the Makers' poems, entitled *Prairie Pegasus:* "Today the fortunate undergraduate knows that poetry is not the mere stringing together of pretty phrases, but a way of looking at the changing procession of life, a variety of experiences. . . ."[15]

Meetings of the Makers were informal gatherings with no order of business and no regularly elected officers. No attendance records or minutes of these meetings could be located. Given the informal nature of club proceedings, it is doubtful that such records ever existed. Membership in the group was easily obtained in the club's beginning. Prospective candidates submitted their names along with three or four samples of their work to Hubbell, who then presented these poems at club meetings. The poems were read aloud to the group, and following the reading of each poem, its merits were discussed in open forum. The only real requirements for membership in the club were a genuine interest in poetry, a desire to receive helpful criticism, and the ability to write decent verses. Each applicant's acceptance or rejection was determined by a majority vote of assembled members. In later years, after the club's reputation was established and applicants for membership were numerous, unanimous approval by the membership was necessary before an individual's name could be added to the list of active members.[16]

The group was constantly being infused with the energy of youth as older members graduated and left the university and new students entered and sought membership in the club. The number of students who attended the Makers' meetings appears to have varied from seven or eight to fifteen or sixteen. Guests were often in attendance, for SMU professors, graduate students, and interested members of the community met with the club from time to time. Former student members who remained in the Dallas area after their graduation often continued to participate in club activities, and some alumni who moved out of the area after graduation later returned and rejoined the organization. Other former members returned from time to time to give talks and readings and to share information about markets in the Northeast.[17]

In their tribute to Jay Hubbell, Bond and Sanders recall that Jay and Lucinda Hubbell were gracious hosts who welcomed students into their home. Professor Hubbell listened to their compositions and made helpful comments about their writing. Lucinda, who was herself one of Hubbell's former students, preferred to stay out of sight until the end of the meetings, when she appeared to serve refreshments. The couple's gentle demeanor and caring approach to students set a pleasant tone for club proceedings. Bond and Sanders used the phrase "not so subdued" to describe members' comments during the critique sessions, but they stressed that the atmosphere was "never raucous." Hubbell himself described the exchange that took place as "frank and often severe," but he noted that he had never seen a group more able to receive criticism without taking offense.[18]

An interesting report of a Makers meeting by an outsider who attended as a guest appeared in an editorial in the November, 1924, issue of the *Buccaneer*. In this editorial, the unidentified reporter tells that upon entering, he felt as if he had entered a mutual admiration society. Most of the poems were technically unfinished, and some "fairly gushed from the spouts of undeveloped fountains." But as each poem was analyzed and commented on, "streamers of gold festooned in the mesh of calico and gingham." As the evening progressed, this reporter became increasingly impressed with club proceedings and especially with Jay Hubbell's "cautiously sanguine criticisms."[19]

When the winners of the first national student poetry competition sponsored by the SMU English Department were announced, the time and effort Jay Hubbell had invested in the student group did not go unrewarded. In the 1921–22 contest, a cash prize was offered in each of three divisions. The first division, with a prize of one hundred dollars, was open to undergraduates enrolled in American colleges or universities. Entries in this division were submitted by college and university English departments rather than by individual students. The second division, with a prize of fifty dollars, was open to all residents of Texas; and the third division, with a prize of twenty-five dollars, was open only to SMU students. Notices of the contest appeared in national publications such as the *Bookman,* the *New York Times,* the *Editor,* and the *Student Writer.* In response to these notices, the SMU English Department received 155 entries in the first division. These entries came from some of the most prestigious universities in the country, including Yale, Columbia, Stanford, Radcliffe, Wheaton, Randolph-Macon, William and Mary, Johns Hopkins, Smith, Cornell, Emory, Wesleyan, Mount Holyoke, and the Universities of Chicago, Michigan, California, and Nebraska. Tucked inside envelopes with the entry forms came notes from various professors congratulating the faculty for their efforts on behalf of student poets. When winners in the three divisions were announced by three separate panels of judges, a poem by SMU sophomore George Bond won first place in all three categories.[20]

Like many of the poems written by members of the Makers during their college years, George Bond's winning poem reflects the concerns of an agrarian population in a period of advancing industrialization. Today, few scholars know of the existence of the poem that won the first U.S. collegiate poetry competition. The poem is reproduced below, with the permission of the Bond family, as it appears in *Prairie Pegasus*.

Sketches of the Texas Prairie

I. In Winter

All winter long the prairie lies remembering;
Old, old, and gray, and blurred with drifting mist,
Silent and listening, hearkening to the rain,
Hearing the wind scream in its desert places.
The cotton rows stretch long and brown and lifeless,
The stubble fields are still and sad as death;
The prairie lies defeated, broken-hearted,
Conquered by winter, brooding in the cold —
Pining for fields where the tall, green grass is waving,
Longing for flowers that the springtime brings,
Brooding on other springs that are long since gone,
Brooding, and thinking of its endless past,
In the rain and the mist.

II. In Early Spring

Silent upon the prairie falls the warm rain,
Slow-dropping, dropping from the low, dull clouds.
An old, old pain, long frozen in the gloom,
Tears at the bare earth's heart.
The prairie's bosom stirs; the wild, green, tender
        blades of grass come forth,
Piercing the wet, black earth where the raindrops fall
Slowly and softly like big, splashing tears.
Out of the travail and the age-old pain, the spring is
        born.
In tears and sacred joy, the prairie gives it birth.

III. April Rains

There is a magic in the April rains
That fall day-in, day-out upon the prairie
Silver the big drops fall through the gray day,
And silver at night they gleam on the long grasses
When the dim stars show.
Soft is the music of their silver-clinking,
And soft their patter on the lone, dwarf trees;
Over the prairie grasses and the flowers,
They drop a veil of music and of color,
A silver veil that sings a silver song.
And through it breaks the purple and the gold
Of vivid Texas flowers.

IV. A Summer Night

Only the locusts cry in the black midnight,
Only the wind stirs in the lonely grass.
No light, no other life, no other sound,—
Only the vast, black prairie and the dim, limitless space
    where the worlds revolve.
And in the dark, the prairie lies awake and restless,
Impatient of man's control, hating his cities and his
    fences and himself,
Waiting for him to join the mammoth and the laelaps,
Knowing his time will come, and waiting, waiting,
    waiting,
Biding her time to rise and cover him up;
Dreaming a dream of cities, silent, deserted,
And of prairie grass creeping slowly over their ruins;
Dreaming a dream of a tyrant overcome, and of many,
    many bones beneath the thick, wild flowers;
Dreaming a dream of many years of silence, broken
    only by the song of the wind and the cry of the
    locust.

V. The Gift of the Prairie

I am sick unto death of sin and of talking of sin,
And I long for the cleansing touch of the wholesome
        earth;
O, I want to be clean as the wind-swept prairie is,
Or a rock that is washed by the rain and dried by the
        sun.
I will go lay me down in the sun-drenched field,
With my face to the earth, among the weeds and the
        flowers,
Where the tall dog-daisies wave in the prairie wind.
There I will feel the warm steam rise from the damp
        earth,
And the white-winged moths will flutter about my head,
While the grasshopper's song will throb through the
        Noon-day stillness.
Yes, I will go and lay me down on the prairie,
As a child at a mother's breast: and lo, she will give me
Peace and forgetfulness and care-free strength.

The prize money awarded the young SMU sophomore proved to be a good investment on the part of the university. Throughout the 1920s, poems by George Bond appeared in national and regional publications such as *Poetry,* the *Literary Digest,* and the *New York Times,* but it was as editor of the *Southwest Review* and as a teacher of literature and creative writing classes that George Bond made his greatest contribution to Texas arts and letters. Bond, who was assistant editor of *Southwest Review* when he was still a student, left Dallas to take a position as editor for McFadden Publications in New York, but he returned to Hillsboro two years later to assist his family in running the family farm in the aftermath of the Great Depression. Eventually, he enrolled in graduate school, earned a doctoral degree, and returned to SMU to assume a full-time teaching career. Dr. Bond taught English, journalism, and creative writing classes, and he served for many years as chair of the SMU English Department. In addition to his academic duties, Bond served as editor of the *Southwest Review* and as associate editor of the *Dallas Morning News* Book Page. Following the pattern set previously by Jay Hubbell, Bond became an important mentor for SMU student writers. Like Hubbell, he sponsored informal meetings of talented students whom he encountered in his courses. Also like Hubbell, he inspired many SMU students to submit work for publication to regional and national journals and magazines. Because of George Bond's influence, a number of SMU students pursued literary careers after graduation. William Humphrey, author of the highly acclaimed *Home from the Hill,* and James Hoggard, the poet laureate of Texas in the year 2000, are among the students who studied with Dr. Bond at SMU.[21]

George Bond was not the only Maker to win the national student poetry competitions sponsored by the SMU English faculty. In succeeding years, a different member of the club won the national prize four out of six times. Ottys Sanders, whose poem placed second to George Bond's in the 1923 contest, won first place in 1924. Maker member Isaac Wade won the competition in 1925, and Dawson Powell, in 1926. All three of these young men were, at one time, on the editorial staff of the regional poetry magazine the *Bard.* Wade and Powell also served as editors of another important regional poetry magazine, the *Buccaneer.* Eventually, all three men left the state to pursue graduate studies and to assume careers in scientific or technological fields.[22]

Even in years when members of the Makers did not take first place in the national student contest, their poems ranked among the top ten entries. Makers whose poems achieved this high ranking include Jeanne Calfee, Mattie Lou Frye, Ruth Maxwell, and Aubrey Burns. Their names and poems, along with the names and poems of the contest winners, appeared in an annual *Bulletin,* published by the SMU English Department and distributed to every college, university, and public library in the country. The distribution of this publication further increased the reputation of Southern Methodist University and the Makers.[23]

Jay Hubbell recruited well-known writers whom he had met while working on *An Introduction to Poetry* to serve as judges of these student contests. When these notable writers and scholars came to Dallas to judge the contests, they gave readings and lectures to enthusiastic audiences that sometimes numbered in the hundreds. Hubbell involved the Makers in these events in such a way that the students felt as if they were sponsoring these prestigious literary gatherings. Members of the club helped to select featured speakers and served as hosts at social functions arranged in each speaker's honor. One year the student club assumed full financial responsibility for the contest. Through participation in these events, individual members of the Makers established important contacts with some of the most distinguished literary minds in the United States. Only in retrospect did these individuals realize that such famous writers and scholars would not have come to SMU except for the efforts of Jay Hubbell.[24]

The list of individuals recruited by Hubbell to judge the student contest includes Witter Bynner, president of the American Poetry Society; John Erskine, editor of the *Cambridge History of American Literature;* William Rose Benet, poet and editor of the *Literary Review;* Bliss Perry, Harvard professor and former editor of the *Atlantic;* Harriet Monroe, editor of *Poetry: A Magazine of Verse;* author Louis Untermeyer; poets Sara Teasdale, John Hall Wheelock, and Carl Sandburg; John Farrar, editor of the *Bookman;* Heyward DuBose, poet and president of the Poetry Society of South Carolina; John Crowe Ransom, a member of the Fugitive Poets and a Southern Agrarian; authors Lizette Woodworth Reese and Hervey Allen; and poets Joseph Auslander, Donald Davidson, David Morton, and Robert Frost.[25]

As a result of Hubbell's promotion of the student contests

and the Makers, additional avenues of opportunity became available to these students. Their work was accepted for publication in national journals and anthologies, and because their work was widely published, it was reviewed and evaluated by some of the county's leading critics. In his introduction to *Prairie Pegasus,* Witter Bynner comments that SMU has "developed a number of young poets well worth watching [whose work] . . . exhibited a quickening sense of the live importance of poetry." In that same publication, Jay Hubbell quotes Carl Sandburg's statement that he "would not be surprised at any sort of work of genius that might issue from this group; the feeling is there; it has the rebel yell, the lone wolf howl, and the yellow rose of Texas in it." Sandburg also expressed surprise at finding a talented group of poets and a healthy literary atmosphere in the city of Dallas.[26]

The Makers had regional and local opportunities, as well, for publication of their work. Some members of the Makers served as editors, assistant editors, and staff members of the SMU student newspaper, the *Campus.* Through their efforts, a "Poetry Page" was added to the student newspaper in 1922, and poems by Makers appeared there on a regular basis. Other members of the club served on the staffs of *Southwest Review,* the *Bard,* and the *Buccaneer,* and work by the Makers appeared in all these publications. The Poetry Society of Texas held monthly and yearly contests, and poems by various members of the Makers were included in the society's annual yearbook. Some of the Makers had opportunities to travel about the state and give readings of their work to audiences on other college campuses while they were still students.[27]

Jay Hubbell's sponsorship of the poetry club ended in 1927 when he accepted a position at Trinity College, soon to become Duke University, in North Carolina. Hubbell hated to leave his students, his many friends, and his associates at SMU, but he had become increasingly unhappy with internal strife at SMU that, in Hubbell's words, took the form of "athletic rows and ecclesiastical politics."[28]

The commercially successful novel *Pigskin,* written by Maker member Charles Ferguson soon after he graduated from SMU, was based on conflicts between higher education, sports programs, and religion that closely parallel the situation at SMU at the time Jay Hubbell resigned his position. Written in a witty, irreverent, and caustic style that marked Charles Ferguson's early writing, this highly entertaining book portrays the difficulties that the chancellor of the fictitious Seaton College encounters as he attempts to utilize one Texas community's worship of football to achieve his own personal and religious goals. In this popular novel, Ferguson exposes the underbelly of academic life in the modern period in a manner that is reminiscent of the *Devil and Daniel Webster.* This book was a commercial success when it was first released, but it was not well received by the SMU administration.

Hubbell reveals other factors that contributed to his resignation from SMU in the following passage from *Lucinda, A Book of Memories:* "The Dean was almost incompetent and the autocratic President . . . had little understanding of the functions of a university. I was overworked. I was editor of the *Southwest Review,* chairman of the English department . . . I was teaching summer as well as winter, and I was trying to find time to write a book."[29]

Hubbell's tenure at SMU lasted approximately twelve years, but his contribution to Texas literature and culture via individual members of the Makers was to continue for over half a century. By the time Hubbell left Texas, he had launched some of his most promising students on productive literary careers. He and his associates in the English Department had brought favorable attention to Southern Methodist University and had established the college as a center for Southwestern life and literature. A 1925 article in the *Semi-Weekly Campus* credits

Hubbell with having done "more to put SMU on the literary map" than any other person connected with the university. In "A Tribute to a Giant among Men," former Makers George Bond and Ottys Sanders write: "How could one man do so much in so little time to bring favorable attention to a new, penurious university, struggling to stay alive, out in the hinterlands? We, his former students . . . cannot answer the question. We only know that this man had an abundance of intelligence, good taste, good humor, civilization, and grace and shared those scarce commodities with everyone whose life he touched."[30]

Jay Hubbell achieved a long and distinguished academic career at Duke University, but he never lost interest in the Makers or ceased to be proud of their many accomplishments. He continued to mentor and encourage them individually and to recommend their work to his many acquaintances in various literary fields. As late as 1965, in an essay entitled "The Creative Writer and the University, with Special Reference to the 1920s," Hubbell tells of his plans to write a book about the accomplishments of a remarkable group of young poets at SMU who called themselves the Makers.[31]

Jay Hubbell's innovative methods, his youth, and his enthusiasm had made him a favorite with SMU students. Because of his influence, many of his students aspired to literary or academic careers. Throughout their lives, the Makers recalled their favorite professor with fondness and acknowledged the role that their association with him had played in the establishment of their successful literary and academic careers. In an interview conducted at her retirement from SMU, Irma Herron tells of SMU students' admiration for the professor they called "the Judge" and comments that a list of Hubbell's SMU students who achieved distinction in American literature "reads like a miniature version of Who's Who. . . ."[32]

Just how long the Makers continued to meet actively after Jay Hubbell left SMU is unclear. Allen Maxwell, brother of

Maker Ruth Maxwell and editor of the *Southwest Review* from
1946 to 1963, was of the opinion that the student club began its
decline soon after Hubbell's departure. But Mildred Bond, wife
of Maker George Bond, recalled attending club meetings after
she and her husband returned to Texas from New York a full two
years after Hubbell left SMU.

By 1928, the *Southwest Review* had assumed responsibility for
the annual student poetry contest, and in February of that year,
an article in the *Campus* reported that Henry Nash Smith, who
replaced Hubbell as the club's sponsor, stated that the club's
membership had dwindled significantly. In this article Smith offers the following explanation for the club's decline: "The poetry movement which arose in 1912 seems to be reaching its end,
perhaps dying out. People are not as interested in poetry now as
they were a few years ago." Smith made an appeal for individuals who had benefited from the club's activities to step forward
and aid in reorganizing it. In another article on November 14,
1928, the newspaper quotes Smith as saying that unless more
students show an interest in the poetry club, it will cease to exist. Smith explains that in the past year faculty and alumni have
composed most of the membership and have taken much of the
responsibility for a club that was supposed to be a student organization. No additional articles about the Makers appear after
that date.[33]

Mildred Bond was of the opinion that by the time the student club ceased to meet, former members of the Makers were
already so intertwined with the Poetry Society of Texas that the
two groups were inseparable. Certainly, writings of early leaders
of the Poetry Society leave little doubt that, even as students, the
Makers made a significant contribution to the Poetry Society. In
"Dallas Poets" Vaida Montgomery writes, "The earlier meetings
of the Society were enlivened by a talented group from Southern Methodist University." Making reference to the Makers,
Hilton Greer said, "For twenty years I wrote with the feeling
that no one in the entire Southwest cared anything about po-

etry; and now when I hear young people talking about poetry as a normal interest of the human race, I rub my eyes to see if I am awake."[34]

The Makers was active as a student club on the SMU campus for approximately ten years, but for many student members, the activities and associations afforded them during this period were life-changing events. One member of the editorial staff of the *Semi-Weekly Campus,* in an unattributed article, "The Makers," chronicles the kind of change that took place: "At the onset, the writers were unsure of themselves and of what they could do. Now they are confident of becoming figures in literature."[35]

The acclaim that the Makers had received from their participation in club activities and national contests, the publication of their work in prestigious national journals, and the praise that was bestowed by leading literary figures did, indeed, heighten the students' expectations for literary careers. But for a majority of them, these dreams were never realized. For those individuals who took up residence within the state of Texas, authorship remained an avocation, an activity they engaged in for pleasure rather than as a major source of income. An economic base for the support of the arts was not fully developed. Only a few regional publishing houses existed, and the state's most important poetry magazines were not income-generating operations.

Some of the most talented and ambitious members of the Makers migrated to the Northeast where opportunities for lucrative literary careers were more promising. Another factor that contributed to the drain of this young talent from the state was the general feeling of restlessness prevalent among artists and intellectuals in the 1920s. Jay Hubbell commented on this period of unrest in *Who Are the Major American Writers?* by explaining that a generation gap occurred in the 1920s that was similar, in many ways, to what took place in American society in the 1960s. As artists from the East Coast were taking up residence in Paris and London, aspiring young Texans were heading north and east. The following statement by Mildred Bond,

The Makers

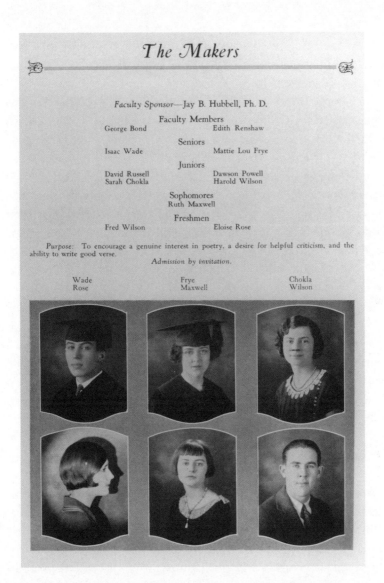

Faculty Sponsor—Jay B. Hubbell, Ph. D.

Faculty Members

George Bond   Edith Renshaw

Seniors

Isaac Wade   Mattie Lou Frye

Juniors

David Russell   Dawson Powell
Sarah Chokla   Harold Wilson

Sophomores
Ruth Maxwell

Freshmen

Fred Wilson   Eloise Rose

Purpose: To encourage a genuine interest in poetry, a desire for helpful criticism, and the ability to write good verse.

Admission by invitation.

Wade   Frye   Chokla
Rose   Maxwell   Wilson

Members of the Makers as they appeared in the 1925 SMU annual, the *Rotunda.* Top row: Isaac Wade, Mattie Lou Frye, Sarah Chokla; bottom row: Eloise Rose, Ruth Maxwell, and Harold Wilson. *Photograph courtesy of the DeGolyer Library, Southern Methodist University*

59

taken from an interview with the author, illustrates the impetus: "Everyone was going East in those years. Everyone was doing it, and so we went."[36]

George Bond and Charles Ferguson moved to New York to work as editors. Ottys Sanders went to Chicago to work with Harriett Monroe on the staff of *Poetry, A Magazine of Verse.* Isaac Wade, Mattie Lou Frye, and Sarah Chokla enrolled in graduate studies at Columbia University; and Madeline Roach, a few hours short of a master's degree, left SMU to work for poet and essayist Porter Sargeant. Loia Cheaney moved east to pursue an unspecified literary career, and David Russell traveled to Europe to study theater.[37]

Although it might appear that members of the Makers who left the state soon after their graduation from SMU ceased to have an effect on the Texas literary community, this was not the case. Makers who became editors of leading magazines and major publishing houses provided important contacts for Texas writers in the publishing world of the Northeast, and with the advent of the Great Depression, some of the individuals who had left the state returned to Texas and took up permanent residence.[38]

Like George Bond, whose contributions to cultural life in Texas have already been noted, David Russell also returned to Dallas and became a member of the SMU faculty. Russell, along with Mary McCord and Maker Edyth Renshaw, turned the Dallas Little Theater into one of the most prominent little theater groups in the United States. In his work with the SMU drama and speech program, Russell composed original plays and operettas and produced English translations of foreign productions. He continued to compose poetry as well. Individual poems by Russell appeared in the *Saturday Evening Post,* the *New York Times,* the *New York Herald Tribune,* the *Southwest Review,* and the *Bard.* Russell published four collections of poetry. His second volume, *Sing with Me Now,* received the Texas Institute of Letters book award, and a third volume, the *Incredible Flower,* won the Kaleidograph Book Publication Contest in 1953. Russell was active in the American Educational Theater Association, the Theater Library Association, the Texas Folklore Society, and the Texas Institute of Letters. David Russell served as president of the Poetry Society of Texas for ten years, and from 1941 to 1947, he was poet laureate of Texas.[39]

Sarah Chokla returned to Texas to teach at the University of Texas at Austin after a year of graduate work at Columbia University. She married Benjamin Gross in 1938 and returned to New York, where she wrote book reviews for the *New York Times* and the *Dallas Morning News* and held editorial positions at *Publishers Weekly* and *Library Journal.* In the 1960s and 1970s, she served as assistant editor of children's books for Franklin Watts Incorporated, where she edited *Every Child's Book of Verse.* Mattie Lou Frye and Madeline Roach also returned to Dallas. Frye taught creative writing classes at the YWCA, served as associate editor of *Texas Weekly,* and was a special feature writer for the *Dallas Times Herald.* After her marriage to Dr. Raymond S. Willis, Frye took a job as a publicity writer and later as a teacher of journalism and business English at Hockaday School for Girls. She continued to write and to publish poetry and short stories in Texas newspapers and journals for many years. Madeline Roach wrote award-winning plays that were performed by the SMU Drama Department. One of Roach's plays won an award, but no reviews of this play or any additional information about Roach could be located.[40]

Obtaining information about Chokla, Frye, and Roach was a difficult task, and locating data about other female members of the Makers after their graduation from SMU proved to be impossible. A large part of this difficulty resulted from name changes that occurred when female members married and took their husbands' last names. Another factor that made the tracking difficult was the expectation of a conservative, Christian-oriented society that married women of the 1920s and 1930s should confine their activities to the private rather than the public domain, especially after the birth of children.

When the Makers were still students, the general opinion that female students were not serious students was so widespread that S. J. Hay, SMU dean of women, addressed this issue in an article in the *Campus* in 1925. Hay disclosed the results of an informal survey of 208 female coeds currently enrolled at the college. When asked what practical use they intended to make of their education, 118 females stated their intent to become teachers; 1 to become a lawyer; 1, a banker; 1, a doctor of medicine; 1, a cotton buyer; 4, bacteriologists; 6, journalists; and 6, secretaries or stenographers. Fourteen women were undecided, and only 4 of those surveyed indicated that they were attending college to learn to enjoy the "finer things of life." Hay's survey shows that most female students enrolled at SMU in 1925 aspired to professional careers. However, evidence that emerged from this study indicates that except for Sarah Chokla Gross, the only female members of the Makers club who achieved professional careers were those individuals who did not have children, or in the case of Sarah Chokla, whose children were deceased.[41]

For whatever reasons, female members of the Makers who did achieve professional careers did not receive the same amount of public recognition as their male counterparts. Both Mattie Lou Frye and Elsie Marie Stark continued to write, to publish poetry, to work as journalists for local newspapers, and to serve as editors of magazines and journals, but no biographical information on either of these women could be located in the Texas/Dallas History and Archives Department of the Dallas Public Library. In contrast, information about several male members of the Makers was on file in that department. Both Edyth Renshaw and David Russell served on the faculty of the SMU drama and speech program, and Renshaw rather than Russell eventually was named to head the program. Yet more than fifty newspaper clippings of Russell's poems, five feature articles about his writing, and a book of quotations from noted literary figures who praised his work are located in his biographical file in the Dallas Public Library. By contrast, Edyth Renshaw's biographical file contains only a single article that appeared in a local newspaper at the time of her death. This death notice is much shorter than the death notices of George Bond, Ottys Sanders, and David Russell. Of all the obituaries of female members of the Makers that have been located, only Ruth Maxwell Sanders's is equal in length to that of her husband. Half of Mattie Lou Frye Willis's obituary is devoted to the accomplishments of her husband, Dr. Raymond Willis, founder of Lakewood Hospital. In contrast, the obituaries of George Bond, David Russell, and Ottys Sanders mention their spouses only as survivors.[42]

All of the Makers whose lives could be traced appear to have maintained an interest in poetry throughout their lives, and many continued to be involved in literary and cultural pursuits in some manner. A few members of the club were already serving on the editorial staffs of regional literary journals before they left SMU. Others assumed editorial positions after graduation. Marvin Winsett and David Russell filled extended terms as presidents of the Poetry Society of Texas, and both men served the state as poet laureates. George Bond, Charles Ferguson, and David Russell became active members of the Texas Institute of Letters. Elsie Marie Stark, Mattie Lou Frye, Sarah Chokla, and Christopher O. Gill worked as journalists, book reviewers, and editors for Texas newspapers and magazines. David Russell, Edyth Renshaw, and Madeline Roach participated in the little theater movement in Dallas. Bond, Russell, Ferguson, Renshaw, Frye, and Wilson taught classes in Texas schools and/or colleges. George Bond headed the SMU English Department, Edyth Renshaw headed the SMU drama and speech program, and Charles Ferguson served a term on the SMU Board of Trustees. In their positions as teachers and directors of education, these Makers became mentors for succeeding generations of Texas writers.[43]

Today, even the most highly praised poems, stories, and novels written by the Makers have been relegated to dark corners of rare bookstores or dusty shelves in the back rooms of university libraries. Their lesser works exist only on the age-yellowed and crumbling pages of old journals and magazines stored in various university archives. One exception is a biography by Charles Ferguson published in 1958, *Naked to Mine Enemies: The Life of Cardinal Wolsey.* In this book, Ferguson begins his panoramic sweep of British history with the murder of Thomas à Becket several hundred years before Wolsey's birth and traces Wolsey's life through his roles as judge, reformer, educator, and diplomat to his banishment from the court of Henry VIII. Ferguson presents carefully documented historical facts in an artful and dramatic manner that combines his skills as a storyteller and a scholar. The result is a spellbinding story that appeared on the *New York Times* best-seller list at the time the book was first published. This volume continues to be an important source of information about the Tudor period.

Charles Ferguson probably gained more national recognition for his writing than any other member of the Makers. In a letter to Jay Hubbell dated March 29, 1965, Ferguson writes, "I have no doubt that it was the fellowship in the early days . . . that set the mood of expectancy that has not left me. Certainly the long line of luck that has been my lot can be linked directly to the day . . . you asked me to write on Jim Ferguson. . . ."[44]

The satirical essay about Jim Ferguson that Charles Ferguson mentions in his letter to Hubbell appeared in *Southwest Review* when Charles Ferguson was still a student at SMU. The essay captured the attention of then-powerful New York editor H. L. Mencken, who invited Ferguson to submit some of his work to the *American Mercury.* After his graduation from SMU, Ferguson worked as a Methodist preacher in the Northwest Texas Conference for only eighteen months. He resigned this position to attend Union Theological Seminary and the New School for Social Research, but Charles Ferguson never returned to the ministry. Instead, he became an editor of religious books for Doran, Doubleday and later for publishers Ray Long and Richard Smith. In 1932, he assumed the presidency of Round Table Press, and in 1934 he became one of the first senior editors at *Reader's Digest,* where he worked until his retirement in 1968. After the publication of *Naked to Mine Enemies,* Ferguson served a two-year term as cultural ambassador at the U.S. embassy in London.

Charles Ferguson published thirteen books of fiction and nonfiction, along with reviews, newspaper columns, and feature articles that appeared in national publications such as *Harper's,* the *American Mercury,* the *New York Times,* and *Saturday Review.* Among his most notable works are *Confusion of Tongues,* a book about religious cults in America; *Pigskin,* a novel about the problems of a football program at a religious college; *Fifty Million Brothers,* a book on the contribution of clubs and lodges to American life; *Naked to Mine Enemies;* and *Organizing to Beat the Devil,* a book about the social development of Methodism in the United States. Ferguson was selected for membership in the Texas Institute of Letters and received TIL awards for *Naked to Mine Enemies* and *Organizing to Beat the Devil.* Charles Ferguson was born in Quanah, grew up in West Texas, attended college at Southern Methodist University, and returned to Texas on many occasions to give readings, make appearances, and teach classes. But he spent so much of his adult life in the Northeast that few Texans today know that this successful author was, at one time, a native of the state.[45]

In contrast to Ferguson's prolific publication record, only a few published poems by Christopher O. Gill could be located. Nevertheless, Gill's contribution to Southwestern literature as the editor of the poetry magazine the *Bard* is significant. During the three years that Gill edited this magazine, work by some of the leading poets in the United States appeared on the journal's pages. Like other young intellectuals of the 1920s and 1930s, Gill was caught up in a spirit of restlessness. He terminated his work on the *Bard* to travel about the country living the life of a hobo. Eventually, he returned to Dallas and took a job in newspaper advertising. Poetry writing became for Gill, as it did for many of the Makers, an avocation that he engaged in mostly for his own pleasure.[46]

In a poem entitled simply "Sonnet," Gill utilizes the traditional form of the English sonnet to express the frustrations of a poet who seeks to attain the perfection of artistic expression. The frustrations Gill represents in this sonnet were shared by other members of the Makers who pursued careers as poets after they left SMU. Allen Maxwell, retired editor of the *Southwest Review* and brother of Maker Ruth Maxwell Sanders, is of the opinion that, as a group, the Makers did not fulfill their initial promise as poets. In a telephone interview with this author, Maxwell said, "It is as if they peaked in their college years."

Certainly, statements made by Allen Maxwell's brother-in-law Ottys Sanders in the later years of his life indicate that he did not attain the level of literary success to which he aspired. Sanders developed a friendship with Harriet Monroe after he won the SMU student poetry contest, and he moved to Chicago soon after his graduation to work with her on the staff of *Poetry Magazine*. Poems by Sanders were published extensively for a time, but in 1925 he returned to Dallas where, according to his brother-in-law Allen Maxwell, the young poet peddled his poetry for meals and a place to sleep. In time, Sanders set his dreams of becoming a poet aside and achieved success in the field of biology. He founded the Southwestern Biological Supply Company and eventually sold this business to devote more time to scientific research. Sanders published numerous articles in scientific journals and one very important book on the evolutionary biology of toads.[47]

After his retirement from business, Sanders once again turned his attention to poetry writing. He self-published a single volume of verses in which he included poems written by his deceased wife, former Maker Ruth Maxwell. His disappointments as a poet are evident in his letter to former Maker Aubrey Burns, written in 1978, following the publication of Sanders's volume of poetry: "Your kind letter praising my poetry touched me, for aside from my dear wife, Harriett Monroe, Dr. Hubbell and yourself, I have never had any encouragement so far as I can recall. . . . none of it has ever appeared in any of the anthologies nor have I ever been called on to recite it for English classes. . . . Because of your letter I wondered if I still had the touch. . . ."[48]

Aubrey Burns was another member of the Makers who did not achieve the level of success as a writer that he envisioned. Burns expressed the disappointment he and other Makers felt in the following poem.

For the Makers

Are they all broken, the bows that once we drew
Across the strings of life and the young earth?
It is true the notes were weak, and a little mirth
Was our only answer; but the fresh morning dew
Was mingled with our music, and the world was new.
Whatever must be said of it, it was worth
All that it cost us; and what was fit for birth
Would have been sound worth hearing when it grew.

They are broken, lost, and covered with the dust
Of long disuse. We have found other tools
More needful to our hands, and dig for gold
Whether we will and no, because we must.
But for all our need we know that we are fools
To let the strings slacken while our hearts grow cold.[49]

Even David Russell, a prolific writer of verses who received a large measure of regional acclaim, indicates feelings of regret and disappointment in the title poem of his Texas Institute of

Letters award-winning volume *Sing with Me Now.* In one poem in this collection, a mature narrator looks backward and forward at the same time and addresses a younger man, who may or may not be another poet, in the following manner, "The earth is yours. We who have tried and failed, turn prayerfully to you."[50]

As Jay B. Hubbell and John Beaty stated in the introduction to the freshman textbook they coauthored before the Makers was ever formed, "Great poets are the rarest of nature's productions."[51] Whether or not the Makers fulfilled their dreams and achieved greatness as writers is not the chief concern of this study. This project is concerned primarily with what these authors and the writing club to which they belonged contributed to the development of a literary community and to the establishment of a literary tradition that could support the production of future literary arts. When these standards are used to evaluate the Makers, this writing club achieved a greater measure of success than any other club included in this study. Members of the Makers served for many years in leadership roles in organizations that promoted statewide literary arts, such as the Poetry Society of Texas, the Texas Institute of Letters, and the Dallas Little Theater Center. As publishers, editors, journalists, and book reviewers, they promoted Texas writing and Texas writers, both inside and outside the state; as teachers and college professors, they served as mentors for succeeding generations of Texas writers.

Individuals Who Are Known to Have Been Members of the Makers

Francis Alexander	Jeanne Calfee
Dorothy Amann	John Chamberlin
Beth Bryant	Loia Cheaney (Magnuson)
George D. Bond	Sarah Chokla (Gross)
Aubrey Burns	S. Lloyd Cowen

Charles W. Ferguson
Irene Flake
Mattie Lou Frye (Willis)
Sherwood Gates
Christopher O. (Ottie) Gill
Wynona Guest
Irma Herron
Sam Hilburn
Judith Joor
Faye Lemmon
Smythe Lindsay
Mary Francis Lloyd
Ruth Maxwell (Sanders)

Dawson Powell
Edyth Renshaw
Madeline Roach
Eloise Rose
David R. Russell
Ottys E. Sanders
Marie Stanbery
Elsie Marie Stark (Harry)
Marsha Todd
Isaac W. Wade
E. Roland Wilkinson
Fred Wilson
Harold Wilson
Marvin Davis Winsett

CHAPTER THREE

The Panhandle Pen Women of Amarillo

*"Own your own typewriter" has become the slogan of
women's club executives. . . . if it comes to a choice
between a new gown and a typewriter, the true executive
will choose the latter.*

Charles W. Ferguson, *Fifty Million Brothers:
A Panorama of American Lodges and Clubs*

Spring had arrived in the Texas Panhandle by the twentieth of April, but a strong wind was blowing and the morning air held enough chill to raise goose bumps on unprotected skin. Gentlemen paused in the lobby of the Amarillo Hotel to button their jackets and secure their hats before passing through the door into the wind. Most male members of the Panhandle Press Club had already departed when Laura Hamner and Phebe Warner arrived. Fighting to keep their hats atop their heads and their skirts below their knees, the two women passed through the front door into the hotel lobby where the smell of tobacco, aftershave, and saddle-soaped leather lingered. Massive couches, brass spittoons, and ashtrays filled to overflowing signaled to all who entered the front door that the lobby of the Amarillo Hotel was a male domain. Laura Hamner and Phebe Warner must have been acutely aware of this as they selected seats where they could see the front door, smoothed the backs of their skirts, and sat down to wait.

They had no idea how many women would respond to the invitation they had extended. After years of dreaming and

Laura Hamner, at the extreme left, appears in this 1949 photograph with officers of the Texas Women's Press Association. Ms. Hamner was a charter member and an officer of the Texas Women's Press Association, founder of the Panhandle Pen Women, and poet laureate of Texas. Other officers, from left to right: Mrs. A'Dele Steed and Mrs. Joe O. Naylor, both of San Antonio; Mrs. Barclay Megarity of Waco; Mrs. Lucy H. Wallace of Mission; Mrs. Florence Fenley of Uvalde; and Ms. Margaret Young of Beaumont. *Photograph courtesy of the* Amarillo Globe-News

months of planning, the two women were prepared to carry forth their plan even if the turnout was small. The spring meeting of the Panhandle Press Association was in session at a location a short distance down the street, but Hamner and Warner, who were both members of that organization, would not be in attendance. It was doubtful that any of the men journalists would miss them or any of the other female members of the Press Association who decided to respond to the invitation. In fact, that was one of the reasons the two women had scheduled the organizational meeting of the Panhandle penwomen's club to coincide with the annual meeting of the Panhandle Press Association. As Laura Hamner later explained, they were counting on the fact that male members of the Press Association would welcome "an admirable place to park their wives while they met in solemn consultation. . . ." This was not the first women's club that Laura Hamner and Phebe K. Warner had organized. They knew from experience the kind of resistance a women's club could generate, and they hoped to avoid the kinds of objections that had arisen when they organized the Wednesday Afternoon Club of Claude ten years earlier.[1]

In an article that appeared in *Panhandle Pen-Points* on March 9, 1922, Laura Hamner tells how the idea to organize a club that would serve the needs of women writers of the Panhandle came about:

> For years I had in mind the need for association of those who write or try to write or who wish to write. I did not wish to issue the call for organization lest the public say, "'Laura Hamner.' Who is 'Laura Hamner?' What has she done?" . . .
>
> Finally I realized that I was cheating myself and others out of fun and help by delaying, and so, with no small degree of trepidation, in the spring of 1919 I issued a call through the Panhandle press of all women interested in writing to meet me at Amarillo at the time the Panhandle Press Association was to meet there.[2]

Hamner's hesitancy to move into the public domain with her writing appears to have been shared by other women writers in the area. According to Mildred Cheney, another charter member of Panhandle Pen Women (PPW), "There were . . . plenty of potential 'pen women' in the Panhandle but any women so inclined were wont to write only when they were sure no one was looking"[3]

In other parts of Texas, women had been recording their experiences for many years. Some of the earliest writers on the Texas frontier were women who helped their husbands operate newspaper presses in sparsely settled areas. In an 1893 article that appeared in the *Galveston Daily News* in two installments, Birdie Taylor alludes to the difficulties of earlier female writers and enumerates the professional frustrations experienced by Texas women journalists at the turn of the twentieth century. Taylor states that all these women writers, past and present, had "put forth their efforts timidly with little expectation of any recognition . . . unseen and generally unhonored."[4]

Just six weeks before Birdie Taylor's article appeared in the Galveston newspaper, Aurelia Hadley Mohl had issued an invitation for Texas women journalists to meet to form the Texas Women's Press Association. Mohl, who had worked as a journalist in Texas since 1856, moved to Washington, D.C., after the death of her husband to work as a correspondent for Texas newspapers. While she was in Washington, she served as corresponding secretary for the Woman's National Press Association, and while doing so, she became convinced that Texas women writers could benefit from a similar association. When Mohl later returned to Texas, she issued a call for women writers who were in Dallas for the meeting of the Texas Press Association to meet with her to organize a Women's Press Association. Among the thirty-eight women who responded to Mohl's invitation was a woman named Laura Hamner.[5]

She was a young woman in her twenties who had been a resident of the Texas Panhandle for only two years. She had come to Texas from Tennessee to teach school. As the youngest daughter of a respected Tennessee family, Hamner led a sheltered life. She grew up on a family-owned plantation near Memphis where domestic servants were employed to do household chores. She attended Miss Higbee's School for Young Ladies and went on to study at Peabody College, where she earned a teaching degree. As Hamner later confessed, she had never so much as washed a handkerchief before she moved to the Panhandle to be near her older sister Mary, whose husband had set up a medical practice in Armstrong.[6]

Like a majority of the pioneers who settled in the Panhandle, the young schoolteacher was confident about her future in the new location. When she boarded the train in Tennessee, she was filled with optimism and eager for new experiences, but when she disembarked in Amarillo, experienced the blowing wind, and observed the coarseness of Panhandle residents, she considered breaking her teaching contract and purchasing a return ticket to Tennessee. Amarillo, the commercial center of the last region in Texas to develop as the frontier moved from east to west, was only four years old when Hamner arrived. Life in the Panhandle was primitive compared to the patrician life Hamner had known in Tennessee, but she adapted quickly to her new surroundings. Hamner soon came to admire the stark beauty of the barren landscape and to appreciate the courageous people who dared to make their homes in such a setting.[7]

Within a year of Hamner's arrival in the Panhandle, her parents, who were then experiencing poor health and financial reversals, also moved from Tennessee to Claude, Texas, to be nearer their daughters. Hamner's father had worked for many years for the *Memphis Appeal,* and soon after the family moved, he purchased the *Claude News.* In addition to her teaching duties, Hamner began to help her father put out a local newspaper. It was this work that brought her into contact with Aurelia Mohl and led to her membership in the Texas Women's Press Association.

Although Laura Hamner was only in her twenties when she first became interested in writing for publication, family circumstances prevented her from actively pursuing this interest for almost thirty years. In addition to teaching school and helping her father with the Claude newspaper, Hamner supplemented the family's meager income by supervising girls' camps and giving public lectures wherever and whenever she got an opportunity. Then her sister Mary died, and Hamner gave up teaching and took a position as postmistress in Claude so that she could look after Mary's infant son and her invalid parents. When a change in government administration resulted in the termination of her job as postmistress, Hamner campaigned for and won an appointment as Potter County superintendent of schools. Only after the death of her young nephew as the result of a tragic accident and the deaths of both her elderly parents did the fifty-year-old Hamner turn her attention to writing.

In the forty years that followed, Laura Hamner would write daily and weekly newspaper columns and enough radio scripts to fill a book. She would author nine books of poetry and non-fiction and receive literary honors from the Texas Senate, the Texas Institute of Letters, and the Texas Press Association. She would be named Texas Woman of the Year by both *Progressive Farmer* magazine and the Texas Press Association, and she would serve as poet laureate of Texas. On her ninety-second birthday, Hamner would receive the Texas Heritage Foundation National Medal in recognition of her outstanding contributions to Texas literature. But on April 20, 1919, when she and Phebe Warner waited in the lobby of the Amarillo Hotel for other women writers to join them, Laura Hamner was a middle-aged, want-to-be writer.

Phebe K. Warner, cofounder of the Panhandle Pen Women, was equally as optimistic and energetic as Hamner. Warner had been writing feature articles about country life for Texas newspapers for approximately three years when she and Hamner decided to organize a club for women writers. She had come to Texas in 1897 from her home state of Illinois to marry a young doctor, a Panhandle resident whom she had met when they were both students at Wesleyan College. In the twenty-plus years that she had lived in the Panhandle, Warner had devoted much of her time to the promotion of social causes. She helped to organize rural women's clubs, to secure home demonstration agents, and to promote adult education classes throughout the Panhandle. She would later lead a successful campaign to have the Palo Duro Canyon declared a state and national park, but on April 20, 1919, Phebe Warner, like her friend Laura Hamner, was a relatively unknown writer.[8]

After so much planning and anticipation, the two women must have experienced disappointment when only four women showed up at the Amarillo Hotel for the meeting. Three of the four, like Hamner and Warner, were working as journalists. Mildred Jester Cheney, a former schoolteacher, wrote articles for

Louisiana and West Texas newspapers and helped her husband edit the *Southwest Plainsman,* a country weekly specializing in agricultural development of the Panhandle. Mabel Timmons, a former schoolteacher listed in some articles as Mrs. Jerome B. Hooker and in others as Mrs. Mabel Law Fish, wrote a Sunday editorial for the *Amarillo Globe.* She had moved to the Panhandle from Abilene, Texas, in 1913. Sophia Meyer, a native of Savannah, Georgia, who moved to Amarillo from Topeka, Kansas, in the early 1900s, was society editor of the *Amarillo Daily News.* Coco Thompson, a member of the newly organized Poetry Society of Texas, was the only attendee who was not working as a journalist.[9]

Although few in number, the six women quickly set to work to establish a club that could serve the needs of a large number of Panhandle writers for many years to come. Displaying a preference for organization that set the future course of the club, the women established a format for club meetings, formulated plans to increase the membership, and elected a full slate of officers. Each woman who attended the meeting was elected or appointed to an office. Laura Hamner was chosen to serve as president, a position she would hold four times over the next thirty years. The women also drafted the following objective for the new club: "To learn by the experiences of others, to grow by association of those who are growing, to know those who are working to the same ends that we are working, to aid ourselves personally and to forward the Panhandle section as a whole by exploiting its history and its advantages."[10]

The women decided to ask for affiliation with the Panhandle Press Association and to submit an application for membership to the First District of the Texas Federation of Women's Clubs. Both requests were granted within the week. The women also discussed the possibility of affiliation with the Texas Women's Press Association and voted to submit an application for membership to that organization. However, evidence that the application process took place could not be located.[11]

Within a few days of the organizational meeting, the names Johanna Nicholl, Mary Miller Beard, and Annie Dyer Nunn were added to the list of charter members. Like the six women who attended the first meeting, none of these individuals were natives of the region. They had come to the Panhandle plains from somewhere else — from the South, the Midwest, or other regions of Texas. At least two had come alone. The rest accompanied husbands or fathers who were attracted to the region by the promise of cheap land and economic opportunity.[12]

The reluctance of other Panhandle women to move from the private into the public sphere is indicative of the extent to which values and ideas of a Victorian age dominated the Texas agrarian society and dictated proper roles for women. But in reality, a number of charter members of PPW engaged in business ventures and exhibited independent and courageous attitudes generally associated with males of the period. Laura Hamner traveled with a train full of men from Amarillo to the Panhandle of Oklahoma to homestead a tract of land and lived alone in a log cabin long enough to fulfill homestead requirements. Sophia Meyer invested in oil exploration and gold mining and helped form the San Juan Basin Oil Stock Pool. And Phebe Warner exhibited the independent and courageous spirit that was common to many women of the Panhandle in her following admonition to newcomer Loula Grace Erdman: "'Don't fuss about the wind,' she told me. 'It's what has made it possible for our kind of people to stay here.' . . . she went on to explain . . . the role of the wind in this new land. It had powered the windmills which in turn, were necessary if the homesteader . . . were to remain. . . .'"[13]

With each meeting of the new club, more members were added to the roll as Panhandle women overcame their reluctance to join the group. Before long, the membership encompassed married and unmarried women of a variety of ages, origins, educational backgrounds, and socioeconomic levels. Teachers, journalists, homemakers, and ranch wives all joined the association and became Panhandle Pen Women.[14]

Newspaper reports of early meetings link the club's organization to the ideals of "the cult of true womanhood." One reporter referred to the group as the Panhandle's manifestation of an evolution taking place across the nation as American women engaged in activities that broadened their horizons, aided society, and elevated the home to a higher status. In an article that appeared on May 2, 1920, Sophie Meyer indicated that club members were aware of the potential for power that resided in their ability to wield a pen. When Mrs. S. H. Madden, an officer of the Texas Federation of Women's Clubs, addressed the club on May 13, 1921, she reminded PPW members that as writers they had an opportunity to mold readers to their liking. And in one of Phebe Warner's addresses to the group, she spoke about the service that club members could perform if they would submit informative stories to supplant crime articles in local newspapers. Warner encouraged the women to specialize in writing "good and moral things" that would counteract the effects of "'trashy' literature."[15]

In one of Laura Hamner's early addresses to the club, she expressed her hope that the Panhandle Pen Women would encourage the literary, musical, and artistic ambitions of Panhandle women. She warned that literary fame was seldom quick or spectacular and told the women that good writing would require years of persistent effort on their part. Hamner encouraged the women to adopt the following resolve: "I am going to endeavor to develop myself and help my town and community by a persistent and well directed use of my pen." This early emphasis on the use of their pens to influence society may account, in part, for the fact that club members demonstrated more interest in producing popular literature and less in producing what they called "highbrow" literature that would appeal only to a limited audience of intellectuals. PPW members' preference for popular literature is reflected in the 1938 list of publications where their work had appeared in the last year: *American True Detectives, Outdoor Recreation, Popular Mechanics,* the *Cattleman, American Home, Western Stories, Home and Garden, Rangeland Love, Popular Mechanics,* the *Ladies Home Journal,* farm periodicals, poetry magazines, anthologies, and other women's magazines.[16]

PPW members also placed strong emphasis on writing for financial gain. Two years after the club was organized, the officers conducted a blind poll to determine how much money the Pen Women had earned from their writing during the past two years. The total came to $8,259.25, an impressive sum of money in the 1920s. By 1925, all forty-eight active members were receiving remuneration for their work, and in 1955, when Laura Hamner commented about the club's accomplishments, she said, "Few women have joined Pen Women without eventually selling some of their writings."[17]

Meeting times and meeting places varied during the first year, but in the second year, the club adopted a quarterly meeting schedule. The founding members' plan to hold at least one meeting each year in conjunction with the Panhandle Press Association's annual convention was abandoned. Male members of the Press Association were not happy when their wives insisted on accompanying them to conventions, and women journalists, who often needed to attend sessions in both organizations, experienced conflicts. In addition, the membership of PPW soon included painters, playwrights, and musicians who had no connection with the Texas Press Association.[18]

As the club grew, it became even more highly organized with written by-laws, a board of directors, and standing committees to handle specialized tasks such as the newsletter, membership, press releases, and the planning of a yearly program. Roll call at meetings was a formal affair in which members answered the call with predesignated responses that fit the occasion. On Texas Day, members responded by giving the name of a Texas author, and when Karle Wilson Baker spoke to the group in 1923, each member recited an incident particular to the history of the Panhandle region.[19]

Quarterly meetings soon became eagerly anticipated events composed of morning, afternoon, and evening sessions. The program format included the club president's address, a business meeting, lectures on various aspects of writing delivered by members and invited guests, readings of original compositions and critique sessions called "Roundtable Discussions," musical performances by members and/or their daughters, a covered-dish luncheon, and an evening banquet. Occasionally, exhibits of members' artwork were staged in conjunction with the weekend's activities. Morning sessions were restricted to PPW members, but guests were welcome to attend afternoon sessions, and many residents of the community did. Men were not eligible for club membership, but they participated as speakers or as guests at afternoon sessions.[20]

Each new applicant for membership had to be sponsored by two current members. The applicant was required to submit a formal application along with samples of published work. More samples were required if the applicant had not been paid for her writing. Applications were approved or disapproved by a majority vote of the entire membership in the club's early years. Later in the organization's history, a board of directors, made up of five past presidents, approved or rejected these applications.[21]

As the membership list continued to grow, so did PPW members' determination to improve. In a 1922 article in *Pen-Points,* Laura Hamner writes: "We are growing in numbers. As to our growth in ability, we are too young yet to judge. A little more confidence, a little stronger determination, more definite direction of effort—these are all that thus far we can recognize. But we know each other and like each other, and we are trying to get others to share our good times, and so our work thus far has been productive of good."[22]

PPW members' ability to give and receive criticism also improved to the point that critique sessions became a highlight of club meetings. Most members were eager to read their work and to receive comments from the group. Members who wished to present their compositions for critique placed their names in a random drawing that took place on the day of the meeting. Those members whose names were drawn read their work before the group. The critique sessions that followed the readings were conducted in a courteous and orderly manner with great care taken by participants to avoid displaying jealousy or hurting the presenter's feelings. In the words of Laura Hamner, "We do not wait until our fellow-member collapses from discouragement, but we pat each other on the back and urge that we try on, regardless of apparent failure. . . ."[23]

As the club continued to grow, the number of individuals who wished to present work for critique finally increased to the point that the club had to adopt a new method of selection that would be fair to everyone. Reading times began to be assigned on a rotating schedule that proceeded through the membership list in alphabetical order according to last names. If, for some reason, a member missed her turn to read, she had to wait until the entire rotation was completed before she got another opportunity. Because the membership was constantly increasing and meetings were limited to four per year, a member's turn to present work for critique might not come around but once each year.[24]

The club's growth brought about other changes as well. Meetings were shifted from location to location to accommodate the ever increasing membership. Over the years, PPW meetings were held in hotels, churches, schools, the library, private homes, local businesses, the country club, the municipal auditorium, and the Potter County courthouse.[25]

PPW meetings became popular social events, and at times, descriptions of luncheon arrangements and decorations took up more space in the club minutes and in newspaper reports than news about the club's programs. Members who lived outside of Amarillo traveled by train to attend meetings that were sometimes called "conventions." These members took great pride in attending, even when adverse weather conditions made travel hazardous. A greeting committee of local members was waiting at the railroad station to transport out-of-town visitors to the Amarillo Hotel or to homes of members to spend the night. Out-of-town guests returned to their homes by train at the conclusion of the proceedings.[26]

Laura Hamner, Phebe Warner, and other charter members had organized PPW primarily to fill the needs of professional writers. In an effort to encourage PPW members to focus more attention on their writing and less on social aspects of these meetings, a yearly writing contest was instituted in 1922 that imposed stringent rules regarding PPW members' participation in these contests. In a newspaper article that appeared in the *Amarillo Globe* in the 1940s, Sophia Meyer writes, "The rules of the organization have always been enforced. A member must write or pay a fine. There is no alternative. And rather than pay a fine (which is big enough to hurt) they write." The fine accessed for nonparticipation was equal to the member's yearly dues.[27]

Club members served as judges for early contests that included competitions for a club emblem, a club song, and a club motto. The winning motto, "The elevator of success is not running; take the stairs," reveals the optimistic attitude and determination of club members. In later years the club sponsored contests in song, play, poetry, short story, feature article, greeting card verse, advertising jingle, and newspaper column writing; there were also contests judging members' artwork. Entries were then sent to established critics who were not members of the club for blind judging. Winners in the various divisions of the contests were announced at one of the quarterly meetings. Winners read their compositions before the group, prizes were awarded, and judges' comments were read aloud so that the entire membership could benefit. Additional prizes were awarded to the member who had sold work to the best magazine and to the member who had submitted the most work for publication during the past year. The presentation of awards became a much anticipated highlight of the yearly program.[28]

In 1938, in another effort to direct members away from so-cial activities and toward the production of writing, PPW offi-cers drafted bylaws that imposed more stringent membership requirements. To qualify as an active member of PPW, an indi-vidual must have sold a book, two articles, a poem, a short story, a scenario, or a play that had been produced by a theatrical com-pany. In addition to presenting proof of publication, active members had to demonstrate that they were writing a mini-mum of thirty thousand words a year. Manuscripts and word count reports were presented to the club's officers once each year, and individuals who failed to meet these requirements were moved to the associate member list. Associate members had to write only fifteen thousand words per year and prove that they had sold some work for publication. Complimentary memberships were made available to beginning writers, but these memberships expired at the end of one year and could not be renewed. The only requirement for complimentary member-ship was proof that the applicant was actively engaged in cre-ative writing.[29]

Even with new bylaws in place, the group's tendency to function as a social club was not eliminated entirely. Admoni-tions like the following one continued to appear in PPW publi-cations from time to time: "PPW is always on the lookout for members who will want to work and who will try to grow by as-sociation with the group. Mere membership is not the objec-tive. This is a professional group, not a social gathering." PPW member Rosemary Kollmar recalled attending meetings at the country club in the 1950s when members dressed in their finest attire, including hats and gloves, and made their way to the meeting room where representatives of the press and local tele-vision stations waited to take pictures and to report on club pro-ceedings. Kollmar was unwilling to call PPW meetings social affairs, but she acknowledged that membership in the organiza-tion had a certain "social status."[30]

News of club activities, announcements of members' accomplishments, and notices of arts-related activities in the Panhandle area were communicated to the PPW membership through a quarterly news bulletin. The organization also sponsored other publications that promoted the work of members. In 1924, PPW assumed full responsibility for an entire issue of the *Amarillo Globe-News* and filled the forty-four-page edition with creative work by PPW members. PPW historians have claimed that this was the first special edition of any newspaper in the United States to be produced entirely by female writers. In 1941, PPW celebrated the club's twenty-first anniversary with the publication of a coming-of-age anthology entitled *Pen Points,* which featured work by some of the club's most notable authors.[31]

As news of the success of PPW writers spread, the club attracted members from towns throughout the Panhandle. Some of these women wanted to meet more frequently than four times a year and to engage in more intensive study than the quarterly PPW meetings provided. Smaller groups of writers spun off from the parent organization and began to meet in other locations with the full approval of the PPW directors. Spin-off groups in Borger, Miami, Pampa, and Shamrock remained affiliated with the parent organization, and males who were not eligible for membership in the large group sometimes joined these smaller gatherings.[32]

In 1927 and again in 1928, PPW brought the first out-of-area speakers to the Panhandle to give a series of lectures. Willard E. Hawkins spoke in 1927 and Blanche Y. McNeil, in 1928. In June, 1931, and February, 1933, the club sponsored six-day writing courses that were open to all residents of the Panhandle. Forty-seven would-be writers registered for the first of these events. In the words of one reporter, the event "reawakened the old ambitions and brought forgetfulness of the discouragements of depression days." Despite the success of these events, the club did not sponsor another week-long workshop until 1947, when

PPW member Loula Grace Erdman agreed to direct a yearly workshop called Writer's Roundup.[33]

Erdman moved from Missouri to the Panhandle in 1927 to teach elementary school. After earning a B. S. degree from Missouri State College, she took graduate courses at the University of Wisconsin, and it was there that she became acquainted with the daughter of PPW founder Phebe Warner. Erdman began to write for her own enjoyment after Warner urged the young teacher to become involved in PPW activities. Erdman was still a novice writer when she won the yearly PPW short story contest. This was the first of many prizes that Erdman would receive for her writing. In 1946, her first novel, *The Years of the Locust,* won the coveted ten-thousand-dollar award sponsored by *Redbook* and Dodd, Mead. She went on to win many national awards for her writing and became one of the most successful writers ever to be associated with PPW. As the following statement by Hamner in a "Light and Hitch" radio script indicates, the entire PPW membership benefited from Erdman's success: "The reason that Loula Grace was able to bring us news hot off the New York publisher's griddle so that we could know what was being printed and what was needed, is that she went up there to finish her new book. . . ."[34]

Erdman left the Panhandle to complete her M.A. at Columbia University, but she later returned to teach creative writing at Amarillo College. West Texas State College recruited Erdman to fill a vacancy in its Creative Writing Department, but college administrators assured her that the position was for a period of only one year. They told Erdman that the position ultimately would be filled by a male professor with a Ph.D. Erdman took the temporary position and became a great favorite with students, who enjoyed her classes, and with professors, who admired her work ethic. With each additional publication and each additional award, her reputation as a writer increased. She was in great demand as a public speaker and as a writing teacher throughout the state and the nation. Each year when Erdman's contract at West Texas State came up for renewal, it was extended. No male professor with a Ph.D. ever replaced her. Eventually, the university offered Erdman a permanent position as artist in residence, a position she held until her retirement.[35]

In 1947, with West Texas State College's approval, Erdman assumed the directorship of PPW's annual workshop, Writer's Roundup. She recruited two nationally known personalities in the field of writing to serve as workshop leaders — Stanley Vestal of the University of Oklahoma and Fred N. Litten, dean of the Medill School of Journalism at Northwestern University. These workshops were successful events cosponsored by the Panhandle Pen Women and West Texas State College and supported by financial donations from Panhandle businesses.[36]

In the 1950s, when the Writer's Roundup outgrew PPW resources, West Texas State College assumed full financial sponsorship of the workshops, and Erdman continued as director until 1959. Speakers and teachers whom Erdman recruited to appear on Writer's Roundup programs include S. Omar Barker, Al Dewlin, J. Frank Dobie, Charles Ferguson, John Fischer, Fred Gipson, Bill Hosokawa, Wes Izzard, Siddie Joe Johnson, Mabel Major, Lewis Nordyke, James Street, Lon Tinkle, Eleanor Graham Vance, and George Williams.[37]

Loula Grace Erdman retired at the end of the 1950s, and in the early 1960s the Writer's Roundups were discontinued when a group of PPW members from Borger and another group from Pampa became embroiled in a dispute that threatened the very existence of the club. This disagreement centered on the need to define standards of "good literature" to be employed whenever a new writer applied for membership. In the view of some current PPW members who granted interviews, this argument was precipitated by the financial success of a member who wrote true-confession stories that offended the sensibilities of a majority of PPW members.[38]

PPW members, who do not wish to be named, identified

the member whose work was at the center of this dispute as Evelyn Louise Nace, one of the most prolific writers in the history of the club. She wrote a weekly newspaper column, "Mending Mature Marriages," for the *Amarillo Daily News* for a period of fifteen years. She also wrote fifty novels, over three hundred fact-crime articles and/or detective stories, and countless true-confession stories under the pen name Louise Pierce. Nace was a member of the National League of American Pen Women and several other honorary writers' organizations.[39]

The dispute over Nace's writing is an interesting phenomenon, for in the nonfiction book *A Time to Write,* Loula Grace Erdman, one of the most respected writers in the history of the Panhandle Pen Women, confides that she also wrote true-confession stories under a pen name early in her writing career. Erdman, who even won a contest sponsored by a true-confession magazine, was very well paid. She stopped writing these stories when the editors of these types of magazines began rejecting her stories because they no longer conformed to the formulas imposed by the genre. Erdman's later writing reflects the moral and religious values upheld by the conservative agrarian society that settled the Texas Panhandle. Many members of the Panhandle Pen Women held these same values, and a number of the women composed poems, stories, and essays that appeared in religious publications.[40]

One of the PPW members who achieved the greatest publication success in religious markets was Laurene Chinn, the daughter of a Methodist minister. Born in Iowa in 1902, Chinn earned a degree from Hastings College and moved to Borger in the 1930s when her husband took a job as a petroleum engineer with Phillips Petroleum Company. Chinn was a thirty-six-year-old schoolteacher when she first began to write short stories and submit them for publication. She achieved instant success when forty of her short stories were accepted for publication within an eighteen-month period. She retired from teaching to meet the demand for her work and produced more than a hundred short stories that appeared in popular magazines and religious publications. One of Chinn's stories, "Spelling Bee," was reprinted more than forty times in various anthologies, but she was best known for her historical romances. Chinn produced five popular novels: *The Unanointed,* a Literary Guild and Doubleday Book Club selection in 1959, *Voice of the Lord, Believe My Love, Marcus,* and *The Soothsayer.* Four of these novels were based on the lives of well-known Bible characters. The fifth, a romance that has a preacher's daughter as the main character, is set in the modern period. Chinn's novels were well received by the national literary establishment, and in 1945 the International Mark Twain Society awarded her an honorary membership for her contribution to literature.[41]

With so many members of the club holding conservative views and with members like Chinn achieving success in religious markets, it is possible that the dispute that took place among PPW members in the 1960s had more to do with religious beliefs and moral standards than with literary values. Whatever was at the base of the disagreement, it had an adverse effect on the organization. Membership declined from over one hundred members to a total of twenty. Writer's Roundups were discontinued, no celebration was staged to mark the club's fiftieth anniversary, and the remaining members discussed disbanding the organization altogether.[42]

Interest in the club revived in the 1970s, and the organization underwent a major reorganization. Officers raised membership dues, increased the number of meetings from four to six per year, and reinstated the annual writer's conference. The Frontiers in Writing conference took the form of one-day workshops with various groups organized according to genre. Guest speakers who have appeared on programs at these conferences include Texas writers Paul Christensen, Charles Ferguson, Robert Flynn, Shelby Hearon, Elmer Kelton, William Owens, Clay Reynolds, and Joyce Gibson Roach.[43]

From the time PPW was organized until the present, the

club has been the recipient of respect and support from the local community. In the early 1920s, the Board of City Development paid the entire cost of the evening banquet at one quarterly meeting. When the club celebrated its seventy-fifth anniversary in 1995, a number of Amarillo businesses, along with West Texas A&M University, Amarillo College, the Amarillo Chamber of Commerce, and the Texas Commission on the Arts, helped finance the year-long celebration. Throughout the club's long history, articles and feature stories about the club and various PPW members have appeared in area newspapers.[44]

In return, the club has initiated, promoted, and encouraged artistic endeavors in the Panhandle of Texas for more than eighty years. In 1935, PPW began subscribing to various writers' magazines and placing these magazines in the Amarillo Public Library for the use of Panhandle citizens. The club contributed an ongoing collection of books authored by PPW members and guest speakers that is housed in the Amarillo Public Library for the use of Panhandle plains residents. The club has sponsored student contests, given student scholarships to Frontiers in Writing and Writer's Roundup conferences, and awarded cash prizes to promising young writers. PPW officers and noted writers in the group have appeared at assemblies in public and private schools throughout the Panhandle region. The club has enjoyed close and reciprocal associations with West Texas A&M University (formerly West Texas State Teachers College) and with Amarillo College. Professors on the staffs of these schools have become influential PPW members, and PPW members have, in turn, provided service as teachers of creative writing at both schools. From time to time PPW has also promoted projects in the Panhandle that have not been associated directly with writing. Under the leadership of club founder Phebe Warner, members promoted Palo Duro Canyon as the site of a state and national park, and the club supported Amarillo's Little Theater by becoming a shareholder in that venture.[45]

One of the most significant contributions that the Panhandle Pen Women have made to the people of the Panhandle is the preservation of the region's history. In fiction, poetry, history, biography, plays, and essays, many PPW members have recorded the stories of the Panhandle and its people, and current members who were interviewed for this project agreed that the most important historian in the group was PPW founder Laura Hamner. For years before she began to write for publication, Hamner scribbled notes about happenings in the region as told to her by original pioneers. Later, she used these notes to compose newspaper columns, radio scripts, short stories, and five volumes of Panhandle history. Hamner's first book, *The No-Gun Man of Texas: A Century of Achievement 1835–1929,* is a biography of legendary rancher Charles Goodnight. Goodnight himself served as a consultant for the book, sharing his memories with Hamner and correcting later drafts of the manuscript. The book begins with Goodnight's entry into Texas at the age of ten and ends with news of the ninety-four-year-old rancher's death going out by telegraph to Panhandle residents. In the intervening pages, Hamner relates Goodnight's experiences as trailblazer, Texas Ranger, Indian negotiator, founder of a ranching empire, visionary cattle breeder, political activist, and philanthropist. Hamner's account of Goodnight and his partner Oliver Loving's trailblazing cattle drives is refreshingly realistic compared to more romanticized versions of this western experience. She provides a view of frontier life that is missing from most accounts of the pioneer experience — frontier life as the females in Goodnight's family experienced it. Hamner also includes Goodnight's firsthand account of the recapture of Indian captive Cynthia Ann Parker by Lawrence Sullivan Ross and the Texas Rangers. Many of the incidents in this book have, by now, been recorded by other historians and fictionalized in numerous western novels and movies, but Goodnight's participation in the project lends the authenticity of an eyewitness account to these events.[46]

Hamner's goal, when she undertook the writing of Goodnight's biography, was to preserve a portion of Panhandle history for future generations. When she could not find a publisher, she printed the book at her own expense and traveled about the state, distributing copies from the trunk of her car. In a successful attempt to get this self-published book adopted as a textbook in public schools, Hamner embarked on a thirteen-thousand-mile trip across Texas to visit state officials.[47]

Hamner's second book, *Short Grass & Longhorns,* tells the stories of the men and women who came to the Panhandle in the 1870s and 1880s to establish large ranches. *Light 'n Hitch: A Collection of Historical Writing Depicting Life on the High Plains* is a collection of vignettes that Hamner composed originally for her weekly radio program. In these short nonfiction essays, Hamner once again writes the history of the region. In the essay "Pioneer Women," she tells about the hardships that isolation imposed on women of refinement and culture who were accustomed to beautiful clothes, fine furnishings, and the companionship of other women. Hamner writes of the bravery of widows who shared their husbands' dreams, stayed on in the Panhandle to become successful businesswomen after their husbands died, and made lasting contributions to the developing culture.[48]

In *Prairie Vagabonds,* Hamner's only collection of poems, she once again focuses on West Texas landscapes and Panhandle people. A recurring theme in Hamner's poetry is the positive effects on the human character that result from living in a harsh land. Laura Hamner's efforts to preserve the history of the region won for her the title Mother of the Panhandle. In one "Light 'n Hitch" radio script, the announcer says of Hamner, "Of her work, it might be said that she has made a whole section of the country conscious of itself."[49]

PPW member Loula Grace Erdman explored many of the same themes in her popular novels that Laura Hamner explored in poetry and nonfiction. Erdman wrote twenty novels that feature strong females as central characters. In the historical novel

The Edge of Time, she portrays in the fictional characters Wade and Bethany Cameron the courage and endurance of early homesteaders who traveled by covered wagons to make their homes in dugouts. In the dedication of this novel, Erdman acknowledges that the homesteader and the rancher were both dominant figures in the taming of the Texas Panhandle: "Much has been written about the romance of the range. . . . It is the homesteader that I choose to write [about]. . . . the story of his stubborn courage has been overlooked in the greater glamour that is the ranch legend."

In her research for this historical novel, Erdman gathered more material about the courageous settlers of the Panhandle than she could include in one book. Because the book was so well received by readers and critics alike, she utilized the leftover materials to write another historical novel. *The Far Journey* features a young woman named Catherine Delaney who migrates to the Panhandle from Missouri in a covered wagon, traveling most of the way with her four-year-old son as her only companion. In both *The Edge of Time* and *The Far Journey,* Erdman presents figures of the female pioneer that match their male counterparts in both determination and courage. Through the fictional characters and invented plots of these popular novels, Erdman brought the story of early Panhandle settlers to the attention of people all over the United States.[50]

In a period when many writers of the modern period were experimenting with new styles of writing, Erdman employed traditional methods of composition. Her strengths were her ability to portray strong characters and to develop believable plots. Her style was simple, elegant, and transparent, and her themes were easily deciphered. She employed few metaphors and refrained from engaging in literary games with her readers. As a result, her novels were popular with a wide range of readers and achieved commercial success. Erdman's first novel, *The Years of the Locust,* made the best-seller list, became a book club

Loula Grace Erdman was an elementary school teacher when she penned her first short story to enter in the Panhandle Pen Women's yearly competition. Ms. Erdman won first place and went on to become a best-selling novelist whose work won a number of national awards. She was artist in residence at West Texas State Teachers College where she taught creative writing classes for many years. *Photograph courtesy of the* Amarillo Globe-News

choice, was translated into a number of foreign languages and Braille, and remained in print for more than twenty-one years. Numerous other novels by Erdman received Literary Guild and Junior Guild recommendations and were book club selections.

Like Erdman's literary fame, the influence of the Panhandle Pen Women was not confined to the Panhandle of Texas. When members celebrated the club's golden anniversary, former members were located in sixteen Texas towns, eight states, and several foreign countries. Articles in the *Amarillo Globe-News* and in PPW scrapbooks indicate that PPW members resided in New Mexico, Oklahoma, Kansas, Louisiana, Colorado, Utah, California, and New Hampshire. Some of these women began writers' groups in these new locations. Important clubs modeled after the Panhandle Pen Women were established in Norman, Oklahoma, and in Dillon, Montana. The group in Norman, begun by former PPW member Joanna Hoskinson, convinced

Stanley Vestal to start a creative writing class at the University of Oklahoma. This class eventually became a university creative writing department.[51]

In 1987, PPW members voted to change the club's name from Panhandle Pen Women to Panhandle Professional Writers, retaining the initials PPW. Since that time membership has been open to male as well as female writers. Many male writers have joined the club since that time, but women writers still compose a majority of the membership. Approximately two-thirds of the current members reside in Amarillo. They are involved in a variety of occupations that include college professor, lawyer, physician, veterinarian, teacher, cowboy, and homemaker. The membership is composed of writers of varying ages, but most leadership positions are filled by individuals in their thirties and forties.[52]

The club was reorganized at the same time it was renamed. Meetings, now one-day affairs, occur on the third Saturday of every other month. The format of meetings includes a business meeting, an address by a special speaker, critique sessions, a catered luncheon, and an evening social hour. Membership requirements are not as strict as in former years. All that active members must do to attain membership in the group now is to prove they are actively writing and have sold a minimum of two articles, poems, or other literary works. Associate members must prove only that they are actively writing.[53]

The membership includes approximately two hundred writers of varying abilities and experiences. Approximately one-half of these members are actively seeking publication. Some are nationally recognized novelists; others are novices. Club members produce work in a wide variety of forms and genres, including poetry, mystery, romance, brochure, limerick, song lyric, short story, nostalgia, cowboy poetry, video script, inspirational material, newspaper column, and investigative article. Current members' achievements are numerous and ongoing.

Novels by PPW members consistently appear on best-seller lists and receive high achievement awards in genres such as romance, history, western, mystery, and children's literature. Any attempt to list current members' achievements would be outdated before the list appeared in print. Nevertheless, members of Panhandle Professional Writers who were interviewed for this project expressed their belief that neither this club nor the writers associated with the club have received the acclaim that their achievements deserve. When longtime PPW member Nova Bair was informed that research on this club's history was being conducted, she exclaimed, "It's about time."[54]

Evidence exists that PPW members' impressions that this group's accomplishments have been overlooked have some validity. Of the five hundred writers who have been members of the club during its eighty-plus-year history, only a few have been listed in publications such as *Contemporary Authors*. But for the purposes of this study, the success of this club lies less in the accomplishments of individual writers than in the organization's influence on cultural development of the surrounding region.

PPW member Loula Grace Erdman indicates the extent of this club's influence in a statement she made in the 1960s: "There is a greater percentage of writers per capita in this area than anywhere. And I believe it is due in large part to the activities of the Pen Women. Not only because of the women themselves, but also because of the creative atmosphere they have helped bring about."[55]

For more than eighty years PPW, one of the oldest continuously operating writers' groups in the United States, has brought Panhandle writers together in a venue where they can exchange encouragement, inspiration, writing tips, and marketing knowledge. Largely through the efforts of this group, the history of the Texas Panhandle has been preserved in writing, and what was once a backward frontier town has become a center of literary activity. As one current member said, because of the efforts of the Panhandle Pen Women, the Texas Panhandle has developed into "a writers' neighborhood."[56]

Individuals Who Are Known to Have Been Members of Panhandle Professional Writers

So many individuals have been members of this club during the organization's eighty-year history that the presentation of a complete list is impossible. The following list of women who were members between 1920 and 1970 appears in Panhandle Pen Women Golden Anniversary Plus Two: 1920–1972. *Charter members are marked with an asterisk.*

Margaret McKenzie Abrams
Mrs. Margaret Rose Aikin
Ethel Allen
Mrs. R. L. Allen
Winifred Almond
Odette Ruth Anderson
Martha Arnold
Adele Barnes
Nellie Bartlett
Mrs. H. G. Baucom
Mary Miller Beard*
Bernice Pyle Beck
Mrs. Carol Bigley
Mary Boyd
Coco Brashear
Mrs. W. M. Breining
Mrs. Daisy Brewer
Mrs. T. L. Brown
Beatrice Brummet

Anne Dodson Buck
Mrs. Dollie Buckley
Abbie Burch
Ann Burney
Mrs. James A. Bush
Mrs. James Bush
Mary Brown Bussey
Roberta Campbell
Wanda Campbell
Edith Raynor Canant
Helen Reithman Carter
Dr. Maud Chambers
Nellie N. Chandler
Mildred J. Cheney*
Laura Enna Clark
Elizabeth Clarke
Mrs. Lucy Ann Clawson
Pat Cleveland
Mrs. Frank Clowe

Mrs. Clyde Cockrell
May Cohea
C. May Cohen
Mrs. I. D. Cole
Magye Cullwell Collingsworth
Lillian Rice Corse
Mrs. J. M. Crain
Mrs. Jim Curtis
Mrs. J. O. Curtis
Pauline Daughenbaugh
Elise Davis
Mrs. W. E. Davis
Mrs. J. M. Delzell
Mrs. May Despar
Annette Barrett Dewey
Katherine Roberts Dial
Theanna Dickey
Olive King Dixon
Helen Doyal
Cordie Duke
Estelle Duncan
Ida Tyler Dye
Helen Dykes
Mrs. J. H. Eaton
Winifred Ruth Eaton
Jean Ehly
Augusta Erwin
Mrs. C. B. Eubanks
Mary Lou Watts Fairbain
Christie Fish
Mrs. Margie Fleener
Mrs. Loyd Fletcher
Mary Fulton
Roberta Underwood L. Gear

Chris Gelin
Leona Gelin
Mrs. R. H. Gentry
Violet George
Capitola Gerlach
Daffin Gilstrap
Aida Munford Gilvin
Lucille Graham
Vida Gray
Ina Gregg
Bernice Gregory
Ruth Griffin
Mrs. J. E. Griggs
Gladys Grooms
Mrs. B. F. Guthrie
Grace T. Guthrie
Katheryn Hagerman
Stacy Tutner Hasner Hall
Dorothy Hamilton
Laura V. Hamner*
Mrs. Dana T. Harmon
Minnie Tims Harper
Helen Harrell
Eva K. Harris
Mrs. E. A. Harvey
Dorothy O. Hastings
Barbara Hayes
Beth C. Henwood
Mrs. F. H. Hill
Lucille Hill
Kean Hilton
Vera Holding
Alma Holmes
Ethel Holt

Mrs. B. R. Hook
Naomi Hopson
Maycella Ann Hudson
Mrs. Floy Harlan Hugg
Mrs. C. F. Hunkapillar
May Stevens Isaacs
Mattie Bell Jack
Lucille Jago
Adele Kalman
Mrs. J. I. Kendrick
Margaret Kirk
Mary Elizabeth Kisner
Helen Kochan
Louella Lacefield
Mrs. C. G. Laing
Fran Lewis
Mrs. Horace Lindsey
Mrs. Lorene Locke
Mrs. Julia Lockett
Mary Lutz
Rosa Lee Marquis
Mrs. N. Finley Martin
Mrs. R. B. Masterson
Venita Maston
Helen Mayne
Inez McCluskey
Helene Huff McCormick
Lois Tyson McCormick
Mrs. C. M. McDaniel
Mrs. G. C. McDaniel
Flora McGee
Delia McKenzie
Hope Bussey McKenzie
Carolyn McLean

Mary Mamie McLean
Elizabeth Merchant
Grace Meredith
Alvah Meyer
Elizabeth Meyer*
Ruth Meyer
Sophia Meyer
Genevee Mikesell
Mrs. Adelyn Mitchell
Mrs. H. E. Mitchell
Genivee Monroe
Shriley Morgan
Mary Natho
Bess Griffith Naugle
Lillian Neely
Mrs. L. B. Newby*
A. Lincoln Newell
Verda Belle Nichols
Rose Jasper Nickell
Johanna Nicolai*
Ramona Noel
Dorothy Nordyke
Lorna Novak
Annie Dyer Nunn
Zula Nunn
Peggy Ormson
Mrs. David A. Park
Deolece Miller Parmalee
Lee Patrick
Margaret H. Patterson
Mattie Patterson
Macie L. Pickett
Laura Kirkwood Plumb
Daphne Porter

Millie Alice Jones Porter
Thelma Porter
Myrtle M. Powell
Francis Prall
Peggy Pratt
Mary Moore Prideaux
Edna Sherwood Ramsey
Ida Ellen Rath
Mrs. J. Ray
Mrs. T. V. Reeves
M. Moss Richardson
Creola Richbourg
Helen Risenhoover
Lena Rittenhouse
Kay Robbins
Trudy Roddy
Sella Rodman
Virginia Rogers
Maude Smith Rorex
Minnie Alice Ross
Fannie May Rucker
Mrs. Anna Saigling
Mrs. Gene Sanders
Grace Sanford
Tuth C. Scurlock
Blythe Gwyn Sears
Ina Gregg Seed
Mrs. Mollie Shaw
Mrs. W. R. Silvey
Mrs. B. F. Smith
Mrs. H. E. Smith
Mrs. Joe H. Smith
Faith Sone
Geneva Stevens

Mary Carolyn Stiteler
Mrs. John Swafford
Cleo Tom Terry
Alma McGowan Thompson
Carolyn Deason Timmons*
Mabel Timmons
Mrs. Bertha Tinsley
Mrs. S. C. Toullous
Mary Kay Tripp
Helen Truax
Carlile Umphres
Edith Buell Underwood
Hazel Cook Upshaw
Pauline Virnelson
Eleanor Waggoner
Norma Waits
Phebe K. Warner*
Alvah Myer Warren
Mrs. C. R. Warren
Mrs. Forest Warren
Wilda Warren
Florence Kingsland Watkins
Louise Hopper Watten
Dolla Cox Weaver
Bess Weilenman Webb
Gladys Heyser Webb
Mrs. J. M. Webb
Edith Wells
Mrs. Joe Wells
Elisie Montgomery Wilbanks
Eliza Jane Myers Williams
Doris Wilson
Mrs. Maude Wilson
Osie Backwell Wilson

Alice Wright   Mrs. Paul Zehringer
Jessica Morehand Young

In this same publication PPW lists the following "out-standing" writers.

Mildred Jester Cheney   Sophia Meyer
Laurene Chinn   Evelyn Pierce Nace
Loula Grace Erdman   Carolyn Deason Timmons
Mabel Christia Fish   Phebe K. Warner
Minnie Timms Harper

CHAPTER FOUR

The Border Poets of Kingsville

We grow out of what we are within our own landscape,
amidst our own people, and our own interpreters can present
to the world something not found anywhere else.

Robert Adger Law, *Southwest Review*

Temperatures still registered in the high eighties at midday, but by early December South Texas residents had turned their calendars to pictures of frozen ponds, evergreen forests, and snow-laden landscapes that bore little resemblance to the scenery they viewed when they looked out their windows. Arid country stretched out like a tabletop in every direction. Cacti, thistles, mesquite trees, and other native plants grew in abundance in the sandy soil and varied only slightly with the change of seasons. There was a monotonous sameness about this part of South Texas — no pine forests, grassy plains, undulating hills, or scenic mountain vistas to inspire a poet's imagination. The land once known as Wild Horse Desert was not the kind of place where a visitor to the area would expect to encounter a poet, certainly not a whole group of poets.

But on the evening of December 2, 1932, poets from the South Texas towns of Bishop, Robstown, Refugio, and Corpus Christi converged on the campus of Texas A&I College in Kingsville to attend the organizational meeting of the South Texas Federation of Poetry Societies. Once a month for eleven months, between twenty and thirty poets and would-be poets made the long, often hot and dusty drive to attend meetings of

Border Poets provided leadership for campus organizations like the Dora K. Cousins English Club at Texas A&I College. Members of the club in the order they are pictured are: (back row) Dr. W. A. Francis, Dr. Robert Rhode, William Hall, Frank Goodwyn, Orlan Sawey, Offutt Francis; (second row) Miss Martinez, Anita Gonzales, Betty Jo Fry, Julia Kriegel, Nina Ewing, Eddie Nell McDonald; (first row) Virginia Kemp, Sarah Marie Kullin, Lorena Henry, Maryon Waldman, Marie Nelson Hall, and Dixie Allen. *Photograph courtesy of South Texas History and Archives, Texas A&M University at Kingsville*

a club they named the Southwest Poetry Society. To accommodate members who had to drive the greatest distances, the group met alternately in Kingsville and Corpus Christi.[1]

Little information about those early meetings exists, but when the new club had been holding meetings for five months, the A&I College newspaper, the *South Texan,* gave the following positive report of club proceedings: "The Southwest Poetry Society is making noteworthy progress in its work to foster the development of Texas, particularly this region of the state, into a literary center." However, on November 10, 1933, just six months after this report appeared, the Southwest Poetry Society split into two factions. One group retained the original name and henceforth held meetings exclusively in Corpus Christi. The second faction, composed primarily of Kingsville residents, organized a new club and adopted a new name — the Border Poets. Individuals who attended the organizational meeting of the Border Poets and continued to meet on the Texas A&I College campus included Loyce Adams, Frances Alexander, Frank Goodwyn, Henriola Gregg, Margaret House, Siddie Joe Johnson, Ann Kirven, Gertrude Ray Plummer, Clyde T. Reed, Mrs. J. S. Scarborough, Ann Sullivan, and Ninon Yeager.[2]

No reason for the separation of these two groups could be found, and none appears in newspaper accounts of the two clubs' later activities. Former Border Poets who granted interviews for this study did not know or could not recall why the division in the original club occurred. The distances that some members had to travel to attend meetings may have been a factor, but some Corpus Christi residents continued to drive to Kingsville to meet with the Border Poets after the split occurred. It is also possible that members of the original group did not share the same goals and objectives. The stated objective of the Border Poets — to stimulate creative writing and to create a venue for the exchange of criticism — was far less grandiose than the stated objective of the Southwest Poetry Society — to foster the development of Texas and especially the region of South Texas into a literary center.[3]

The South Texas region was far from becoming a literary center in the year 1932. The fact that the organization of these two poetry clubs took place a full twelve years later than other clubs in this study is significant, for it indicates the extent to which cultural development in South Texas lagged behind that in other regions of the state. This delay was due, in large part, to the inhospitable physical environment, to racial tensions, and to slow economic development in the area situated geographically between the Nueces River and the Rio Grande. As former Border Poet Elizabeth Goodwyn stated in an interview with this author, "South Texas in the 1930s was in many ways still a frontier."[4]

Progress in the area was delayed initially by a territorial dispute between the United States and Mexico in the 1800s. This dispute began when the United States annexed Texas and culminated in the Mexican-American War by midcentury. In Daniel Webster's address to the U.S. Senate in 1848, he gave the following description of the area when he opposed the appropriation of additional funds for the war effort: "The whole country may be truly called a perfect waste, uninhabited and uninhabitable . . . poor, rocky and sandy; covered with prickly pear, thistles and almost every sticking thing. . . . For any useful or agricultural purpose the country is not worth a sou."[5]

Almost one hundred years later, Border Poet Frank Goodwyn gave a more poetic but equally stark description of the landscape in *The Magic of Limping John:* "Modern innovations are scarce in the South Texas brush country. Things of eternity prevail. Dry winds and cottony clouds move out of a southeast that never empties into a northwest that never fills. Trees, weeds, prickly pear seem to grow without getting larger. Only the sun is generous. Only the heat is plentiful."[6]

In the years that intervened between Webster's speech and Goodwyn's book of folklore, riverboat captain Richard King and his associates turned this barren countryside into one of the largest and most productive ranches in the United States. The visionary King realized, as he traveled across the countryside by horseback in 1852, that land that supported large herds of wild cattle and mustangs could be used for cattle ranching. He and his partners began purchasing tracts of land that were originally granted by three governments—Spain, Mexico, and the Republic of Texas—and established the now-legendary King Ranch. For most of a century, the history of the King Ranch and the history of this South Texas region were identical.[7]

Mexican American ranch hands and their families made up the majority of the sparse population. Only a few Anglos inhabited the area, and they were imported by King Ranch management because they possessed skills necessary to ranch operations. Values represented by the self-reliant, self-made Captain King and by the romantic, mythical figures of the vaquero and the cowboy took precedence in day-to-day operation of the ranch over the spiritual and intellectual concerns of King's strong-willed wife, Henrietta Chamberlain King. Unlike her husband, Henrietta King was a devout Presbyterian who was college educated. She was working as a schoolteacher in South Texas when she met Richard King and later agreed to marry him. She insisted that the King children and grandchildren attend the finest boarding schools in Corpus Christi and that schooling be provided on the ranch for the children of ranch employees. These early educational facilities were one-room schoolhouses situated at various locations on the King Ranch. The buildings and the teachers who served as instructors were secured and financed by the King Ranch management.[8]

Additional settlement of the area occurred after Richard King died and his son-in-law Robert Kleberg took over management of the King Ranch. Kleberg was a descendant of German immigrants who came to Texas in 1834. The Kleberg family's presence in South Texas confirms claims of early Texas historians that cultured European immigrants resided on the Texas frontier. Robert Kleberg's father was a hero of the battle of San Jacinto, but he was also a graduate of the University of Goettingen, read classical Greek and Latin, and spoke three modern languages. His wife, Rosa von Roeder Kleberg, was a descendent of minor Prussian nobility.[9]

Robert Kleberg discovered an aquifer beneath the arid surface of the land and initiated the drilling of deep water wells that made it possible to irrigate food crops. Further improvements in the economy of the region occurred in 1904, when Kleberg established the town of Kingsville to serve as headquarters for a new railroad company that was to operate a rail line that connected the seaports of Houston and Galveston to the area, ter-

minating in Brownsville. This rail line made possible the trans-
portation of food crops and cattle from South Texas to northern
markets.[10]

Richard King's widow made land available for the new town
site, but she also imposed her moral and religious values on future residents. Henrietta Chamberlain King donated generous
amounts of land and money for the construction of a school and
a Presbyterian college devoted to the education of Mexican
American boys, but she inserted a clause into land-buying contracts that permanently barred the sale of alcoholic beverages in
the town of Kingsville. This clause had a great effect on the character of the new town. Unlike more established towns in South
Texas, Kingsville became a community with schools and
churches but without saloons and gambling houses.[11]

In 1909, just five years after the township of Kingsville was
established, the Woman's Literary Club was organized for the
primary purpose of establishing a library, but for the most part,
life in Kingsville remained primitive. Only one main highway
through the area was paved. Entertainment of any kind was
scarce, and as a result, any event that took place in the way of culture or entertainment was well attended. In addition to these
limitations, life in South Texas encompassed certain elements of
danger. Prolonged periods of drought increased the risk of fires,
and hurricanes that blew in from the nearby Gulf of Mexico
sometimes destroyed both lives and property. Raids by Mexican
bandits were such a threat that the U.S. government stationed
soldiers in Kingsville to ensure that the railroad was safe from attack.[12]

Although the King family contributed generous amounts of
land and money to establish educational facilities in the region,
primitive conditions, the risks involved in living in the area, and
the language barrier that existed between Hispanics and Anglos
made the recruitment of teachers to serve in these educational
facilities difficult. A majority of the students spoke mostly Spanish, but the absence of a teachers' college in the region made it

impossible to train Spanish-speaking teachers who could not afford to attend colleges located outside the local area.

Eventually, South Texas State Teachers College, whose name later became Texas Arts and Industrial College (Texas A&I College), was established in Kingsville in 1925. The new school initially experienced slow growth, but the influx of educated individuals to serve on the faculty was a stimulus to cultural life in the region. Frances Alexander, who by all accounts became the leader of the Border Poets, was one of the teachers recruited to serve on the first faculty.[13]

Alexander was a native of Blanco, Texas, where she was valedictorian of the 1905 graduating class. She earned an undergraduate degree in mathematics from Baylor College in 1911 and taught mathematics for a time at schools in San Marcos, Dallas, Port Arthur, and Houston before she entered Columbia University to earn an M. A. in English. Shortly after her graduation and return to Texas, Alexander was offered her first full-time teaching position in higher education—a full professorship in English at the new South Texas Teachers College in Kingsville. Frances Alexander had grown up on a ranch in the Hill Country and was accustomed to small-town life and rural people. She was bright and eager and not afraid to embark on new adventures. Even so, the young schoolteacher must have experienced some reservation when she arrived in Kingsville to discover that unmarried female faculty members were to be housed in a Catholic-operated dorm for nuns who closely monitored the residents' activities.[14]

The following passage from Frances Alexander's unpublished memoir, "My Sun-Dial Report," indicates the feelings of alienation that she and other faculty members experienced when they first began their tenure at the new college: "Kingsville was a ranch town on the edge of King Ranch, and much more interested in cattle than it was in learning. . . . Gradually the reluctant Kingsville accepted us in their churches and social affairs. . . ."[15]

Such feelings were not uncommon among Anglo residents who moved into this region of Texas for the first time. Fifty years after moving to Kingsville, Mrs. H. T. Collins recorded her bitter memories of the experience in her diary. She tells how promoters and developers lured skilled workers like her husband to the area with promises of employment. She writes, "To say that I was a misfit is putting it mildly."[16]

When Robert Rhode brought his new bride to the area in 1938, she surveyed the countryside through the car window and asked, "Did you say there was a college down here somewhere?" Dr. Rhode, a new recruit to the college faculty after the school underwent its name change, described the town of Kingsville when he and his wife first arrived: "Few streets were paved. The college consisted of a few buildings surrounded by cotton fields and mesquite trees. The air base was here when we came and the Celenese Corporation and the College, but not much else except the King Ranch. The population was a mixture of educated people and hicks."[17]

To Charlotte Baker (Montgomery) the area appeared "almost like a foreign country" when she arrived to teach at the college in the 1940s. Even Siddie Joe Johnson, a Border Poet who had grown up in nearby Corpus Christi, was distressed by the social instability she encountered when she returned to the area to teach school at Refugio after attending college in Fort Worth.[18]

Whatever Frances Alexander's reservations when she arrived in Kingsville, she soon set to work with other faculty members and administrators to establish the new college. By all accounts, Alexander was a lively woman with an inquiring mind and an engaging personality. She was also a talented organizer whose willingness to promote a variety of social and educational activities proved to be a valuable asset to the school. In "My Sun-Dial Report," Alexander tells that the administration of the new school encouraged such activities: "Since we were in a region that had never known a college, Dr. Cousins urged us to help schools and clubs of nearby communities."[19]

Frances Alexander, key figure in the success of the Border Poets Club, served on the faculty at South Texas Teachers College/Texas A&I College and the University of Texas at Austin. She won several TIL awards for her writing. *Photograph courtesy of South Texas History and Archives, Texas A&M University at Kingsville*

In 1931, after serving six years on the English faculty, Frances Alexander took a much needed leave of absence and traveled to China with her sister on vacation. Instead of keeping a travel journal of her experiences, Alexander elected to record her impressions of the Orient in poetic forms that she had learned while teaching English classes. Alexander explained in an interview some years later, "It was the first time I'd had time to write."[20]

When she returned to Kingsville, Alexander submitted some of her compositions for publication. The first poem she sent out was accepted on receipt by *Survey Graphic* and reprinted in *Literary Digest*. A second poem won a prize offered by a major poetry magazine. With each notification that one of her poems had been accepted for publication, Alexander's interest in composing verses increased. She continued to write, both poetry and prose, and to submit her work for publication. She eventually produced three volumes of poetry: *Seven White Birds, Time at the Window,* and *Conversation with a Lamb.* She also wrote the following books for children: *Chac, the Chachalaca,* a book of fiction, *The Diamond Tree,* a book of verses for children; *Mother Goose on the Rio Grande,* an English translation of Spanish nursery rhymes; *Pebbles from a Broken Jar,* a book of Chinese folktales; and *Orphans on the Guadalupe,* a historical novel for juveniles. With her sister Mary, Alexander also coauthored *Handbook on Chinese Art Symbols,* and her individual poems appeared in numerous poetry magazines and anthologies. Alexander won a number of prizes for her work, including TIL awards in 1938, 1969, and 1970. She was selected for membership in the Texas Institute of Letters and was an active member of the Poetry Society of America for many years.[21]

Former Border Poet Robert Rhode described Frances Alexander as the "ramrod and leader of the Border Poets." Other former members confirmed that she was the key figure in the success of the organization, but when poets from South Texas first gathered on the Texas A&I College campus to form the Southwest Poetry Society, Frances Alexander had been writing poetry for less than a year. Newspaper accounts of early meetings of the society indicate that Mrs. Cleveland Wright, a member of the Federated Women's Clubs who had an international reputation as a poet, was elected president of the club. Dr. Clyde Reed, a biology professor at Texas A&I College, was elected vice president. Frances Alexander's name does not even appear on the list of officers until after the Southwest Poetry Society split into two factions. When the split occurred and the group that became the Border Poets held its first organizational meeting, Alexander was elected president of the club she would lead for the next twelve years.[22]

Newspaper reports indicate that the Border Poets' meetings were initially conducted with a moderate amount of structure and formality. At the very first meeting, the group elected a full slate of officers, formulated a formal objective, and appointed a committee to draw up a constitution and a second committee to plan a program. Later, after the new poetry club was more firmly established, such formalities were relaxed, and the number of officers was reduced to a minimum — a president, a secretary, and an editorial committee.[23]

Membership in the Border Poets was limited to twenty-five active writers. In the beginning, anyone who wished to join the group was required to submit one poem and pay a membership fee of one dollar. Current members were constantly on the lookout for likely candidates, and once located, these individuals were encouraged to submit applications for membership in the club. New members were admitted by a majority vote of existing members, but anyone who wished to join the group could usually do so in those early years. Later on, when members of the club became more proficient in giving and receiving criticism, the waiting list for membership grew longer and requirements for membership became more stringent. Applicants were then required to submit poems in four different forms — a sonnet, a triolet, a lyric poem, and one poem in a form of the poet's choice — to a membership committee for evaluation. The purpose of this requirement was to discourage individuals who did not have an adequate knowledge of poetic forms and therefore could not contribute to profitable discussions from becoming members. But the Border Poets was never an exclusive group, and anyone who went to the trouble to compose poetry in the four required forms and to submit these compositions to the membership committee was generally accepted into the club when a vacancy occurred.[24]

The membership of the Border Poets encompassed diversity in age, gender, education, occupation, and writing ability. One-third to one-half of the members were college students, but retired citizens from the community became some of the most active members. Females consistently outnumbered males, but both genders participated in the club's activities and shared leadership responsibilities. Married couples comprised a large proportion of the membership. Socioeconomically the membership ranged from lower to upper middle class. Border Poets engaged in a variety of occupations. They worked as teachers, musicians, dentists, ranchers, farmers, homemakers, journalists, librarians, small-business owners, and naval air base employees. The majority had received some college training, and several members held doctorates, but some of the most accomplished poets in the group had not attended college. The group was equally diverse in personality. Recognized community leaders and individuals who were considered "queer ducks" and "recluses" by a majority of South Texas citizens were drawn together by their love of poetry and their ability to communicate through poetic language.[25]

In a region where Mexican Americans comprised a majority of the population, the Border Poets' membership was composed almost entirely of Anglos. This lack of racial diversity within the membership reflects the social separation that had long existed between the two predominant races of people in the South Texas region. Only three Spanish names appear on any published lists of members of the Border Poets, but the presence of these three names indicates that Mexican Americans were not barred from membership in the group. Former Border Poets Frank and Elizabeth Goodwyn explained that at the time the club was holding meetings, only a few Mexican Americans in the region had received formal educations that would have enabled them to enter into group discussions about poetry. These individuals, therefore, had little interest in becoming members of a poetry club.[26]

To maintain membership in the Border Poets, an active member was required to submit at least one poem for critique at the monthly meeting. Members who did not submit poems regularly were encouraged to discontinue their affiliation with the group. Because the abilities of club members varied so greatly, a wide range of work, from shabby and amateurish to polished and professional, was produced and presented for group critique. These poetic offerings were submitted anonymously to the club secretary on the first of each month. The secretary then mimeographed the poems, assembled them into a bulletin, and placed copies of this bulletin into portfolios to be distributed to members of the club at the monthly meeting. This process required much time and effort on the part of the secretary, but the Border Poets felt that the objective criticism that resulted from anonymous submissions was worth the extra effort required to produce these bulletins.[27]

A primary goal of the Border Poets throughout the club's history was the encouragement of younger members of the community, particularly A&I students, to develop poetic skills and literary interests. College students were actively recruited by professors who were members of the Border Poets. Many of these student members were shy and felt intimidated in the presence of college professors. As a result, student members maintained a degree of formality and never called professors by their first names, but these same students had little reluctance to participate openly and honestly in criticism of a professor's poetry if the selections were read anonymously.[28]

A critic who was not a Border Poet was engaged to read monthly poetry submissions, to rank the poems, and to produce written criticisms of each poem before the meeting took place. Most of the individuals who served as critics were natives of the South Texas area who had some knowledge of poetry, such as English professors at Texas A&I College, professors from other branches of liberal arts, and local journalists. On occasion, poems were sent to more renowned judges who resided outside the region. Each of these critics and judges was invited to attend the monthly meeting to give a lecture to the group if the judge so desired.[29]

At the monthly meeting, an outside reader who had some experience in dramatic art read each poem in the portfolio aloud two times. After all the submitted poems were read, each member ranked the poems according to the five the member liked best and the five liked least. Scores were collected and while they were being tabulated, the merits of each poem were discussed in an open forum. Former members used the following words to describe what took place in these critique sessions: "lively," "invaluable," "invigorating," "rewarding," and "a godsend to our writing." In the process of defending their work in these lively sessions, authors sometimes revealed their identity before the results of the voting were announced. Elizabeth Goodwyn said, "We all attacked the poems earnestly and gravely. . . . I don't think there was ever any reluctance to criticize or any reluctance to accept the criticism given."[30]

When all discussions were completed, Border Poets and their guests enjoyed a period of socializing. At times, the number of visitors in attendance almost equaled the number of members, and during the time set aside for socializing, all visitors were introduced and made to feel welcome. This period of fellowship was an important part of the meeting, because in South Texas, where forms of recreation were limited, these meetings served an important social as well as literary function for club members and their friends. The Border Poets rotated the responsibility of preparing refreshments and serving as hosts for the meetings, and newspaper reports of the club activities rarely failed to make mention of the "delicious refreshments." In the community of Kingsville, where the sale of alcoholic beverages was prohibited, tea was the drink of choice at Border Poets' affairs.[31]

In addition to a business meeting, poetry readings, critique session, and a period of socializing, Border Poets' meetings included reports of various members' achievements and any acceptances for publication that had occurred since the last gathering. Occasionally a reading of some famous poet's work or a discussion of some author's work took place, and sometimes a lecture on a topical subject related to poetry writing was added to the program. More than a few meetings included discussions of "modern poetry."[32]

The highlight of the monthly meeting came at the end of the social hour when the identities of the authors of the anonymous poems were revealed. Two winning poems were selected, one that was determined by a popular vote of the membership and one that was determined by the guest critic for the month. Prizes in the form of cash, books, or watercolor paintings were awarded for a variety of "best"—best triolet, best sonnet, best free verse, best ballad, and so on. These contests were extremely popular, and members who lived too far from Kingsville to attend meetings on a regular basis sent their entries in by mail to be judged.[33]

As the club's reputation increased, more and more writers came from communities as far away as San Antonio, McAllen, Beeville, and Laredo to take part in Border Poets events. In order to accommodate individuals who drove extended distances, the club continued to hold meetings only once a month. To accommodate college students and faculty members, who were often out of town in the summer, the Border Poets met only during the nine months of the academic year. At various times and for a variety of reasons, meetings were held on Monday, on Friday, and on Saturday evenings, but the second Saturday evening of the month was the preferred time throughout the club's history. The group generally met on the Texas A&I College campus, but from time to time members gathered at the homes of Border Poets who lived within the Kingsville city limits. Meetings convened around seven-thirty or eight o'clock in the evening, and members generally departed some time between ten and eleven o'clock. Border Poets who came from out of town often didn't get back to their homes until the early hours of the following morning.[34]

One Border Poet who routinely made this late-night trip was Siddie Joe Johnson. Johnson, who was a founding member of the Southwest Poetry Society and later of the Border Poets, drove first from Refugio, where she taught school, and later from Corpus Christi, where she worked as a librarian, to attend monthly meetings. Just why Johnson chose to drive to Kingsville and meet with the Border Poets instead of meeting with the Southwest Poetry Society in Corpus Christi after the split in the original group occurred is not clear. She was one of the youngest members of the original group and, at that time, a recent graduate of Texas Christian University. It is possible that she felt more comfortable and had more in common with university students and professors than with the middle-aged matrons who comprised the majority of the membership of the Southwest Poetry Society. Although Johnson was among the youngest poets in the group, she had a firmly established reputation as a writer. Her poems and stories had been published in children's magazines since her childhood, and she established her reputation as a writer of adult poetry by winning the Texan Prize offered by the Texas Poetry Society when she was still in high school. As a student at Texas Christian University, she published a number of poems in respected regional and national poetry magazines. No doubt Siddie Joe Johnson's association with the Border Poets accounts, in part, for the high esteem accorded this entire group by acknowledged leaders of the Texas literary establishment, such as J. Frank Dobie.[35]

Siddie Joe Johnson's sister, Lena Agnes, was also a charter member of the Southwest Poetry Society and the Border Poets, but Lena Agnes had been a Border Poet for less than a year when she died suddenly of pneumonia. Siddie Joe, who had no library training at that time, gave up her teaching position in Refugio to become children's librarian at La Retama Public Library in Corpus Christi, the position Lena Agnes had held at the time of her death.[36]

If Siddie Joe Johnson had been the only member of the Border Poets who achieved success, the organization's contribution to Texas letters still would have been immeasurable. As children's librarian at public libraries in Corpus Christi and later in Dallas, Johnson initiated programs that served as models for libraries throughout the United States, and as a result, she was in-

Siddie Joe Johnson, second from the left, performs her duties as children's librarian at the Dallas Public Library. The names of the other people in the photograph are not known, but one Dallas child who attended Ms. Johnson's creative writing classes for children became the novelist Elizabeth Forsythe Hailey. *Photograph courtesy of the Texas/Dallas History and Archives Division, Dallas Public Library*

strumental in improving education for thousands of American children. The most famous of these programs and the one most widely adopted by other libraries was Story Hour. The second most popular was the Creative Writing Club. In 1954, Johnson received the first Grolier Society award ever given in recognition of her outstanding contributions to young people, and in 1964 the Texas Library Association honored her as Librarian of the Year. She eventually became more famous for her contributions to the field of library science than for her writing, but she never ceased to write and to think of herself primarily as "a literary person."[37]

Johnson published two collections of poetry, *Agarita Berry* and *Gallant the Hour,* and her individual poems appeared in many poetry and popular magazines and newspapers, including the *New York Times* and *Poetry, A Magazine of Verse.* Some of these poems won awards from the Texas Poetry Society and Kaleidograph. She wrote book reviews, newspaper columns, radio scripts, countless articles for library journals, and five books of fiction for juveniles. When the Texas Institute of Letters formed in 1936, Siddie Joe Johnson was the youngest writer invited to become a charter member. In 1952, she won the TIL Cokesbury Book Award for the Best Juvenile Book of the Year, *A Month of Christmases.* In addition to working as librarian and writing poetry and fiction, Johnson taught creative writing classes at Texas Women's University, Southern Methodist University, the University of Texas, the University of Arizona, and North Texas State Teacher's College. Johnson resigned her membership in the Border Poets in 1938 when she moved to Dallas to become children's librarian at the Dallas Public Library, where she worked until her retirement in 1965.[38]

Such departures from the Border Poets club were not unusual. The club's membership was constantly in flux, as individuals who worked at the air base, in the oil industry, or at Texas A&I College transferred in and then out of the region. Some of these individuals stayed in South Texas for only a few months. Others, like Siddie Joe Johnson, lived in the area for many years before transferring to a new location. This mobility within the membership prevented stagnation within the club, as writers with varied experiences moved in and introduced new methods and ideas into the core group.[39]

One young writer whose stay in Kingsville was brief was Charlotte Baker, a native of Nacogdoches and the unmarried daughter of the well-known Texas poet Karle Wilson Baker.

Charlotte Baker (later known as Charlotte Baker Montgomery) was working as an artist and illustrator when she accepted an offer to head up the Arts Department at Texas A&I College. She filled this position for only one academic year before she resigned to become director of the Portland Art Museum. Her stay in Kingsville was so brief that after the passage of so many years, she could remember only a few details about the club's meetings; however, she did remember that through her association with the Border Poets, she formed a close and lasting personal friendship with the club's leader, Frances Alexander.[40]

Soon after Baker left Kingsville, she published two mystery novels for adults, *A Sombrero for Miss Brown* and *House of the Roses,* but she is best known as an author of books for children. These books include *Hope Hacienda,* a Pro Parvula Book Club selection; *Necessary Nellie* and *Nellie and the Mayor's Hat,* both Junior Guild selections; *Magic for Mary M* and *The Best of Friends,* Texas Institute of Letters Cokesbury Award winners; and *Thomas the Ship's Cat,* a Parents Magazine Book Club selection. In addition to her novels and books, Baker produced one play, numerous short stories, and many short articles that appeared in regional and national publications. She was selected for membership in the Texas Institute of Letters.[41]

Everett Gillis was another writer whose tenure as a Border Poet was brief. Gillis was born in Cameron, Missouri, but he spent most of his life in Texas. He established a reputation as a notable poet when he was still a student at Texas Christian University. When he came to Kingsville to serve on the English faculty of Texas A&I College, he had already published two volumes of poetry and won several awards in Texas Poetry Society contests. He left Kingsville after a tenure of only two years to take a position in the English Department at Texas Tech College, where he taught for many years. Gillis became chair of the Texas Tech English Department and eventually retired from that university as professor emeritus. He published a number of collections of Southwestern poetry, including *Angels of the Wind,*

*Ballads from Texas Heroes, Heart Singly Vowed, Hello the House!,
South by West, Sunrise in Texas,* and *Who Can Retreat?* In addition to writing poetry, he coauthored an English textbook,
wrote many articles for publication in academic and literary
journals, and composed choral works. Everett Gillis founded
Pisces Press, primarily to publish his books of poetry. He was selected to membership in the Texas Institute of Letters and
served as president of both the Southwestern American Literature Association and the Texas Folklore Society. He was also a
life member of the Poetry Society of Texas and served a term as
vice president of that organization.[42]

Despite the high rate of mobility within the organization's
membership, the Border Poets' existence was never threatened.
The number of members remained consistently close to twenty-five. Even when key members of the group departed, a core of
long-term South Texas residents provided stability and continuity for the group.[43]

One Kingsville resident whose life changed direction as a result of his association with this club was Dr. J .V. Chandler, a native of Belton, Texas, who moved to Kingsville in the 1920s to
set up a dental practice. He and his wife, Helen, became respected community leaders who involved themselves in religious, civic, and cultural affairs in Kingsville. The Chandlers
were not charter members of the Border Poets, but they were
recruited to membership in the club early on. Writing had been
a hobby for Chandler while he was actively practicing dentistry,
but when a heart attack forced his retirement, he began to devote more and more of his time and energy to verse writing.
Former members of the Border Poets who granted interviews
for this study were of the opinion that although Chandler did
not produce the best poetry in the group, he was, by far, the
most prolific verse writer. He specialized in what one former
member described as "light verse that many magazines purchased as fillers." Poems written by Chandler appeared in many
popular magazines, periodicals, newspapers, and poetry jour-

nals, and he produced two collections of his work: *Night Alone* and *Petals Fall*. C. Vann Chandler served as president of the Border Poets, the Chaparral Writers, and the American Poetry League and as vice president of the Poetry Society of Texas. He became a professional poetry critic, judged poetry contests throughout the state, and served as editor, analyst, associate editor, and columnist for a number of poetry magazines. The high point of Chandler's writing career came in 1959 when he was named poet laureate for the state of Texas. In his seventies by then, Chandler drove over ten thousand miles to visit Texas schools, colleges, and universities, where he made speeches and gave readings.[44]

A few individuals who became Border Poets when they were students at Texas A&I College later became some of the most successful writers to come out of this organization. One of these individuals was Frank Goodwyn, the son of a King Ranch foreman, who was born on the King Ranch, attended the ranch school at Norias, and attended high school in Kingsville. Goodwyn worked at a variety of odd jobs, including ranch hand, truck driver, musician, funeral assistant, and justice of the peace. In the early 1930s, members of the King Ranch management encouraged him to enter Texas A&I College and earn a teacher's certificate so that he could teach at one of the ranch schools. Goodwyn taught school on the ranch during the school year and attended Texas A&I in the summers. It was at Texas A&I that he met Frances Alexander and became a student member of the Border Poets. As a result of his studies at Texas A&I and his association with the Border Poets, Frank Goodwyn developed a desire for scholarly pursuits that changed the direction of his life.[45]

In 1933, one year after he became associated with the Border Poets, Goodwyn self-published his first volume of verse. He was still a student at Texas A&I when Christopher Publishing of Boston published a second volume of verse, *Behind the Scenes*. In 1936, Goodwyn, who spent the early part of his life surrounded

Frank and Elizabeth Goodwyn as they appeared at their
granddaughter's wedding in 1990. They met one another at a
Border Poets meeting when they were students at Texas A&I.
Photograph courtesy of the Goodwyn family

by Mexican Americans who spoke Spanish, produced a collec-
tion of folk stories in Spanish, *The Devil in Texas*. In 1937, he met
Elizabeth Miller, another Texas A&I student and member of the
Border Poets, and they eventually married. At his wife's urging,
Goodwyn earned a second B.A. degree and an M.A. before he
left Texas A&I. On the recommendation of his cousin J. Frank

Dobie, Goodwyn received the first J. Frank Dobie Fellowship in Southwestern Literature at the University of Texas at Austin. A year later he received a Julius Rosenwald Fellowship. These awards enabled the young South Texan to earn a Ph.D. in Spanish folklore.[46]

During his tenure at the University of Texas at Austin, Goodwyn became an active member of the Texas Folklore Society. He served a term as president of that organization and was selected for membership in the Texas Institute of Letters. In 1944, he received the TIL Best Book Award for *The Magic of Limping John,* a novel based on a character from Hispanic folklore. Other books by Goodwyn include *Life on the King Ranch,* an excellent source of information on ranch life; *Lone Star Land,* a book in which Goodwyn portrays the state and its people as they appeared in the 1950s; *The Black Bull,* another novel based on a character from Hispanic folklore; and a collection of poems, *Poems about the West.* Goodwyn went on to teach courses at Texas A&I College, the University of Texas, the University of Colorado, and Northwestern University before accepting a position as head of the Modern Languages Department at the University of Maryland, where he worked until he retired as professor emeritus. Although Goodwyn lived outside Texas for many years, he returned to his home state to give lectures and readings at Texas universities and writers' groups.[47]

Another student member who went on to achieve a measure of academic and literary success was Orlan Sawey, a native of Grit, Texas. After graduating from Texas A&I College, he earned a Ph.D. in English from the University of Texas and taught at a number of colleges and universities, including Harding College, Lincoln Memorial University, University of Virginia, and Pan American College in Edinburg, Texas. At Pan American College, he served as head of the English Department and as director of Arts and Sciences. Sawey returned to Texas A&I to serve on the English faculty in 1969, where he eventually became chairman of the English Department. Sawey wrote two

Twayne biographies, *Bernard DeVoto* and *Charles A. Siringo,* and with his wife, Nina, he coedited *She Hath Done What She Could: The Reminiscences of Hettie Lee Ewing.* He wrote many book reviews and articles for newspapers, literary journals, religious publications, and folklore journals. Sawey served as president of the Texas Folklore Society during 1973–74.[48]

For writers such as J. V. Chandler, Frances Alexander, Frank Goodwyn, and Siddie Joe Johnson, the Border Poets provided an avenue for publication at a time and in a place where few opportunities existed. Other members of the club attended Border Poets' meetings for their own personal fulfillment and enjoyment. These individuals did not think of themselves as professional writers, and they had little interest in submitting their work for publication. In a 1971 interview, Frances Alexander relates that when she published her first book of poetry in 1938, she felt "like a fish in a bowl." She was the only person on the Texas A&I campus who was writing for publication, and she was so embarrassed that she shared her success with no one but her mother.[49]

Nevertheless, the group as a whole exerted a great deal of pressure on members of the club to submit work to literary magazines for publication. Robert Rhode used words like "bullied" and "intense" to describe the coercion that took place. He explained that some members who became published writers never would have submitted their work for publication if pressure to do so had not been applied by other Border Poets. Some of the members who expressed little interest in publication eventually engaged in enough creative or academic writing to merit a listing in *Contemporary Authors,* but as the following comments indicate, they continued to maintain a realistic view of their accomplishments.[50]

This quote by Orlan Sawey appears in *Contemporary Authors:* "I probably should not appear in a list of contemporary writers, because I have never thought of myself as a professional writer. . . . I have always written about things which interested me, with little concern about whether my readers were interested. . . ." In another volume of the same publication, Robert Rhode states, "To me writing has always been a collateral activity, not a proper means for earning a living. This is not to say that writing is not important. . . . A writer should never become a merchant fashioning his wares for the market. . . ." Even Frances Alexander said, in a 1949 interview, "I do not feel that I have arrived as a writer. . . . I don't feel that I have a maximum of talent, but I love to write."[51]

Even those Border Poets who claimed to write for their own enjoyment engaged in club-sponsored competitions that resulted in the publication of their work. At the end of each academic year, an editorial board made up of members of the Border Poets selected what they considered to be the best poems submitted during that year. These selections were then forwarded to a panel of well-known poets for judging. Jurors for these contests included some of the best-known poets in America, such as William Rose Benet, Louise Bogan, Witter Bynner, Robert P. Thristen Coffin, Richard Everhardt, Robert Frost, Marianne Moore, John Crowe Ransom, Carl Sandburg, Steven Spender, and Robert Penn Warren, and well-known regional poets, such as David Russell. These poet-judges commented on each of ten poems selected by the club's editorial committee, sometimes for fees as low as twenty-five dollars. They offered comments and made suggestions for revisions that were shared with the entire group at a club meeting. The contest judge(s) selected the best poem of the year to receive a Silver Spur award and ten additional poems for inclusion in the next volume in the Border Poets series. The club's editorial committee then selected additional poems by Border Poets to fill out the collection.[52]

The Border Poets published seven books of poetry in this series in approximately thirty years: *Serenata* in 1937, *Cantando* in 1939, *Silver Spur* in 1942, *Ceneso Spray* in 1947, *Silver Spur V: Yucca Trail* in 1951, *Silver Spur VI: Cactus Tongues* in 1955, and *Silver Spur VII: Buenos Dios* in 1962. The club's goal was to publish a volume every two years, but due to limitations of time and money, collections actually came out every four or five years.[53]

Enthusiasm for writing poetry was never higher than when the possibility of a new publication was being discussed. Robert Rhode explained that almost no market for poetry existed in South Texas during those years, so club members had to create their own market. The Texas Poetry Society published one book in the Border Poets series, but the club self-published the other six volumes. Only a few hundred issues of each of these editions were printed, and these sold out rapidly. In addition to publishing these seven volumes of verse, the Border Poets also put out a poetry journal, *The Border Poets' Magazine.* Individually and collectively, club members self-published individual collections, staged signing parties, bought one another's books, and recommended these books to friends and relatives.[54]

In the small Texas town of Kingsville, where entertainment was so scarce that reports of children's birthday parties were published in the society section of the newspaper, readings and book signings by Border Poets were major events. Some members of the club were respected community leaders, and many people turned out to hear them read poetry. The citizens of Kingsville, who had been so reluctant to accept Texas A&I faculty into its community in 1925, were impressed by what they heard and, by the early 1940s, had gained "a great deal of literary awareness" as a result of the Border Poets' activities.[55]

The positive attitude that flowed from the community to the Border Poets was reciprocal. Members of the club composed poems and gave readings for community events. They took time off from their jobs to deliver talks and readings at public schools and area colleges. In addition, the club sponsored Kingsville appearances by at least one well-known writer each year. Admission fees for these special literary events were sometimes as low as twenty-five cents, and most Kingsville residents who wished to attend could afford to do so. As a result, these guest writers spoke to large audiences, and after they read, they were entertained at social events staged by some of Kingsville's most prominent citizens. Authors who came to Kingsville during those years included writers of regional renown, such as Karle Wilson Baker, J. Frank Dobie, and Patrick Moreland, and writers with national reputations, such as Carl Sandburg.[56]

The Border Poets' influence was not confined to Kingsville. From time to time the Border Poets held joint meetings with other South Texas literary groups, such as La Ceniza Writing Club of Corpus Christi. Border Poet Hortense Ward directed an ongoing summer writing conference in Corpus Christi, sponsored by the Corpus Christi chapter of Penwomen of America. Several Border Poets were associated with the Byliners, a group in Corpus Christi that sponsored the Southwest Annual Writer's Conference, a conference that is still held in Corpus Christi annually. Border Poets, such as Robert Rhode, served as judges and critics for area writing contests. Others spoke about poetry and gave readings of their work to writing clubs throughout Texas.[57]

The Border Poets' influence was not limited to the South Texas region. Most members of this club were also members of the Poetry Society of Texas at some point in their careers. Some won Texas Poetry Society contests; others served in leadership capacities in that organization. A few even achieved membership in the more select American Poetry Society. Frances Alexander and Siddie Joe Johnson attended the 1936 meeting of Sigma Tau Delta in Belton, where they participated in a discussion that eventually resulted in the creation of the Texas Institute of Letters. Siddie Joe Johnson, Frank Goodwyn, Everett Gillis, Frances Alexander, and Charlotte Baker Montgomery were all selected for TIL membership.[58]

Frances Alexander, leader and sponsor of the Border Poets, left Texas A&I to take graduate classes several times during her tenure at the college. In 1946, on the recommendation of J. Frank Dobie, she was offered a scholarship in Southwestern literature at the University of Texas on the strength of a collection of Mexican folk rhymes for children entitled *Mother Goose on the Rio Grande,* a book that Alexander had self-published in 1944. At the time she accepted the scholarship, Alexander intended to return to her post at Texas A&I at the conclusion of her studies, but the illness of an elderly relative who lived in Blanco prevented her return. In 1951, after teaching classes at the University of Texas on a temporary basis for several semesters, she resigned from the faculty of Texas A&I and moved back to her family's ranch to care for her ailing aunt. After her aunt died, Alexander remained in the Austin area and devoted herself to writing full-time.[59]

The Border Poets continued to meet for at least ten years after Frances Alexander left Kingsville, first under the leadership of Dorothy Rhode, then Dr. J. V. Chandler, and finally Robert Rhode. But the departure of Frances Alexander and the loss of what one Border Poet called "her vibrant leadership" triggered the club's gradual decline, and in 1963, after thirty-one years of continuous operation, the Border Poets ceased meeting. Many individuals who were key figures in the success of the club in earlier years had moved from the area by this time. Others had either died or quit producing poetry. Those original Border Poets who remained were elderly and rarely came to meetings, and younger members did not have enough interest in the club to assume responsibility for the organization's activities. Dr. Rhode credits increased television ownership and the desire of the younger poets in the club to produce something that could somehow appear on the television screen as a factor in the club's decline. Another factor was a decrease in the number of English faculty employed by Texas A&I College in the early 1960s. Several unsuccessful attempts were made in the ensuing years to revive the club.[60]

The accomplishments and contributions of Frances Alexander, J. V. Chandler, Everett Gillis, Frank Goodwyn, Siddie Joe Johnson, Charlotte Baker Montgomery, and Orlan Sawey have

Both Robert and Dorothy Rhode served terms as president of the Border Poets after club founder Frances Alexander moved from Kingsville to Blanco. *Photograph courtesy of Dr. Robert Rhode*

been noted earlier in this chapter. Robert D. Rhode, who was a major source of information for this chapter, served as dean and eventually became vice president of Texas A&I University. He contributed articles, poems, and reviews to newspapers, literary magazines, academic journals, and college textbooks.[61]

The work of other Border Poets has been noted in a number

of anthologies. Biographical sketches of Loyce Adams, Frances Alexander, Medford Evans, Lena Agnes Johnson, Lena Williams Johnson, Siddie Joe Johnson, Gertrude Ray Plumber, and Clyde Reed appear in *A Century with Texas Poets and Poetry.* Loyce Adams, Frances Alexander, Frank Goodwyn, Sarah Lois Grimes, Lena Agnes Johnson, Viola Wheless McKinney, Isabel Scarborough, and Alice Sullivan are listed in *Texas Writers of Today.* Lillian Loyce Adams, Frances Alexander, Viola Wheless McKinney are featured in *Notable Women of the Southwest,* and listings for Frances Alexander, Everett A. Gillis, and Siddie Joe Johnson appear in *Southwestern American Literature.*[62]

In poetry, in fiction, and in nonfiction, writers who were Border Poets preserved in artistic forms a record of human life as it was lived in a region of the state where few stories had previously been written. In dramatic nature poems, both Siddie Joe Johnson and Frances Alexander utilized harsh elements of the South Texas landscape as metaphors for human existence. Although nature poems like theirs were not uncommon during the 1930s and 1940s, only a few poets have utilized the Texas landscape more effectively than Johnson does in "Cruel Beauty," a poem that incorporates elements from the Texas Gulf Coast to portray the difficulty of an artistic existence; or than Frances Alexander does in "Siesta," a poem in which the Spanish tradition of taking a period of rest in the afternoon is used as a metaphor for eternal rest.[63]

Folklore, especially the translation of Mexican American folklore into English, was of particular interest to Frances Alexander, Everett Gillis, Frank Goodwyn, and Orlan Sawey. In stories, poems, and nonfiction compositions, these writers preserved stories that previously had existed only in an oral storytelling tradition. As Goodwyn states in the introduction to *The Devil in Texas,* these stories had been handed down by "deep-voiced old fellows, who . . . have known nothing but the cool, soothing breath of wind against their tough faces and the warm, comforting light of the sun above their sweating backs."[64]

Frank Goodwyn and Frances Alexander preserved narratives of the Anglo culture in Texas that are historically significant as well. Goodwyn's *Life on the King Ranch* includes factual history, character sketches, personal remembrances, and myths and tales told by ranch hands. Alexander's *Orphans on the Guadalupe* dramatizes the story of a group of German orphans who migrated to Texas in 1844 and lived in an orphanage on the banks of the Guadalupe River in Central Texas after their parents died of bubonic plague.

Perhaps the best summary of the Border Poets' accomplishments appears in the organization's 1942 publication *Silver Spur:* "The Border Poets, an independent group of poets living in South Texas . . . have added new members until no more could be accommodated, they have carried out workshop projects, they have established annual awards, they have presented Texas poets in recital, they have encouraged in every way possible the writing and publication of verse in their native region. . . ."[65]

In "My Sundial Report" Frances Alexander makes a statement that was expressed, in one way or another, by all former members of the Border Poets who granted interviews for this study: "We had lots of fun but no major poets. . . ." As Alexander acknowledges, only a few members of this club produced work of national significance. Nevertheless, it is the consensus of former members and long-time Kingsville residents that the Border Poets club was a significant part of the cultural history of South Texas for many years.[66]

Individuals Who Are Known to Have Been Border Poets

Bertha Acevedo	Harriette Bludworth
Joel R. Acevedo	Louise Bogglan
Loyce Adams	Edna Bryant
Frances Alexander	J. Vann Chandler
Inez Elliott Andersen	Elizabeth Davis

J. DeWitt Davis

Chlo Dickenson

Bertha Dominguez

Katherine Eubanks

Katherine Evans

Medford Evans

Ellen Giles

Everett Gillis

Elsie Rose Givens

Elizabeth Miller (Goodwyn)

Frank Goodwyn

Sarah Lois Grimes

Grace Baer Hollowell

Lena Williams Johnson

Siddie Joe Johnson

Ann Kirven

Viola Wheeless McKinney

Charlotte Baker (Montgomery)

Gertrude Ray Plummer

Clair Medlin Puckett

Clyde T. Reed

Perry Reed

Dorothy K. Rhode

Robert Rhode

Katherine Rogers

Bernice Rolf

Maude Salyer

Orlan Sawey

Isabel Scarborough

Marion Blanchard Stoner

Alice M. Sullivan

Jake Trussell, Jr.

Hortence Ward

Mildred Herron Williams

Dee Wood

CONCLUSION

*The role of clubs and lodges in American life has been rich
and constant. They were a refuge from the loneliness
that beset the pioneer, and not less from the more acute
and tormenting loneliness that came with
swift urbanization.*

Charles W. Ferguson,
Fifty Million Brothers: A Panorama of American Lodges and Clubs

L iterary societies and writing clubs have been much
more important in the cultural development
of Texas than scholars have acknowledged. Individuals with intellectual abilities, academic training, and literary
talent have resided in the region since its frontier period, but for
many years thereafter, a career in literary arts was almost impossible to sustain. Few institutions of higher learning existed, employment for artists and academics was extremely limited, and
people who engaged in artistic activities had little contact with
one another. Texas writers were separated from major publishing centers in the northeast, and regional publishing houses
were almost nonexistent. Authorship under these conditions
was uncertain at best, and for most individuals who engaged in
literary arts during those early years, writing was, of necessity,
an avocation rather than a profession.[1]

By the early 1940s, conditions for Texas writers were greatly
improved. The Texas Institute of Letters and the Poetry Society
of Texas were bringing writers throughout the state into contact

133

with one another. One highly respected academic journal, several regional poetry journals, and a few small publishing houses were established, and Texas writers were achieving publication in some of the leading popular magazines and national literary journals of the period. As this study of four clubs that were operational during this period of time demonstrates, literary societies and writing clubs played an important role in effecting these changes.[2]

An examination of these four clubs has illuminated a number of similarities. Feelings of isolation played a role in the formation of all four groups. The organization of at least three of the four clubs, the Border Poets, the Makers, and the Panhandle Pen Women, was initiated by a key figure who was college educated and had limited experience in creative writing. After this individual moved to Texas and realized that institutional support for the arts was limited or lacking entirely, she or he set about organizing a club and recruiting as members people who shared an interest in the literary arts. And after the club was organized, this key figure remained in a position of leadership for several years.[3]

All four clubs examined in this study filled a social as well as an educational need in the lives of members. Monthly or bimonthly meetings provided opportunities for them to come together, form friendships, and exchange ideas with like-minded people. Even when university writing classes existed in close proximity to literary club activities, as they eventually did in all four communities, these clubs continued to hold meetings. Such gatherings appear to have fulfilled the social needs of members in a way that academic venues did not.

Two patterns of club development emerged from this admittedly limited study. In the first pattern the idea to form a writing club originated with an individual who was associated with an academic institution. Once the club was formed, its influence quickly spread to other members of the community who were not directly associated with a college or university, and in time, the club's activities enriched the larger community. This pattern is evident in the organization of the Makers of Dallas and in the Border Poets of Kingsville.

In the second pattern an individual within the community who had no association with an institution of higher learning initiated the organization of a club. Later on, after some members of the club had their works published and gained a measure of critical acclaim, the club's influence spread to and involved local academic institutions when these accomplished writers were recruited to teach college-level writing classes. This pattern is evident in the organization of the Manuscript Club of Wichita Falls and the Panhandle Pen Women of Amarillo.

All four clubs provided a forum whereby members and others within the local community were brought into contact with leading literary figures of the modern period. The Makers, the Border Poets, and the Panhandle Pen Women sponsored lectures and readings by nationally renowned writers. In so doing, each club brought well-known writers, publishers, and editors from outside the state into contact with aspiring Texas writers, enabling them to establish contacts in important literary markets.

These clubs also engaged Texas writers to appear on club programs and to give readings of their work at club-sponsored events. By staging such venues, the clubs increased contacts between Texas writers and provided additional opportunities for featured speakers to sell books and expand their readership, thereby augmenting their income from literary efforts.[4]

A primary goal of each of the four clubs in this study was the channeling of young people toward literary pursuits. In each club, one or more young members who were introduced to writing through literary club activities went on to achieve literary success.

Some members of each club became teachers of writing. These individuals taught in public schools, in universities, in community writing courses, and in seminars and short courses sponsored by libraries and other literary groups throughout the state of Texas. As teachers of writing, these writers traveled extensively, giving readings and speeches throughout the state and, in some cases, throughout the nation. Other club members went on to achieve positions of leadership in education as administrators in Texas colleges and universities, and in these positions, they influenced countless numbers of young Texans.

Some of the most talented writers in these clubs left the state to take jobs in literary centers in the Northeast, where they were then in positions to aid and promote the work of other Texas writers. Some writers who left the state later returned to Texas on a permanent or part-time basis, becoming purveyors of culture who transported news and ideas from major literary centers in the Northeast to Texas writers. Still other literary club members moved to locations outside the state and organized clubs that were patterned after Texas clubs. In this way, these individuals also extended the reputation of Texas clubs and Texas writers.[5]

A review of the literature in club-sponsored publications indicates that a majority of the members of these four clubs were not gifted writers. But a small number in each group were among the most accomplished writers in the state prior to 1950. Today, only a few Texans know of the existence of poems, stories, and novels written by Frances Alexander, Anne Pence Davis, Loula Grace Erdman, Charles Ferguson, Frank Goodwyn, Laura Hamner, Siddie Joe Johnson, Fania Kruger, Charlotte Baker Montgomery, David Russell, Winifred Sanford, and Laura Faye Yauger. Most books authored by these writers are out of print, although some have been reissued by Texas university presses in recent years. Other works by these individuals merit attention and an opportunity to be reintroduced to Texas readers.[6]

Males as well as females participated in the activities of these clubs, but females joined in greater numbers and usually took the lead in organizing the program. Although more females participated in these groups, more males achieved professional writing careers, and in situations where male and female members of the same club possessed equivalent intelligence, education, and vocational or academic training, the work of male members received greater public acclaim. One possible explanation is that many of the women attained professional status as writers of children's books, a field that has never received as much recognition as books written for adult audiences.

Facts that came to light as a result of this investigation into the activities of these four clubs seem to indicate that some inequities between male and female writers did exist in Texas in the time period covered by this study. However, the factors that contributed to these inequities are varied and complex. Certainly, the promotion of Southwestern literature and the mythic images of the cowboy, the Indian, and the outlaw as the regional ideals contributed to the exclusion of work by some female authors. But factors other than gender contributed to this oversight as well. Work by Texas writers of either gender that fell outside the romantic Southwestern tradition suffered a certain amount of exclusion in the 1930s and 1940s.

Some justification for the derogatory label "pink tea poets" that came to be applied to members of Texas writing clubs in the 1930s does exist. When refreshments were served in conjunction with club meetings, as they almost always were, the beverage of choice was tea. Female members did outnumber male members in each of these four groups, and a majority of these female members were not accomplished writers. In an article entitled "Leave the Ladies Alone," Vaida Montgomery, coeditor of the Dallas-based poetry journal *Kaleidoscope,* tells that in the 1930s more women were writing and submitting more poetry for publication in that journal than were men. More women were also subscribing to more poetry magazines, buying more books, and spending more money in literary causes than men. Montgomery reasons, quite logically, that because more women were writing verse, more poor verse was being written by women.

This article quotes Gamaliel Bradford as saying that little great verse was being written by either gender, but just as much good poetry was being written by women as by men.[7]

Members of both genders participated in the organization of statewide associations for the continuing support of the arts in Texas. Border Poets Siddie Joe Johnson and Frances Alexander were among the group of English teachers who initiated the idea for an organization for Texas writers that became the Texas Institute of Letters. When TIL was organized, Laura Faye Yauger, Winifred Sanford, Siddie Joe Johnson, and Laura Hamner were invited to become charter members. Other members of these four clubs were invited to join TIL at later dates. Still others became active members of the Texas Folklore Society and the Texas Poetry Society and provided leadership for these organizations for many years.

Perhaps the most significant contribution that these four clubs, and others like them, made to cultural and artistic development within the state of Texas was the creation of a local community of readers. The fact that most club members engaged in creative writing solely as a recreational activity and that members who engaged in writing on a professional level did not sustain their living solely from the proceeds of their writing should, in no way, denigrate the contributions of these groups. Only a few individuals who engage in creative writing ever become noted writers, but many people who make attempts at creative writing develop an appreciation for good literature and much respect for writers who accomplish it. By providing a venue whereby Texas citizens could engage in creative writing and share this interest with other people in the community, these clubs aided the development of a literary community that could eventually support and enable the work of ensuing generations of Texas writers.

In her 1924 book review of Ruth Cross's *Golden Cocoon,* Clara Edgar McClure predicts that great Texas literature, when it occurs, will be the product of a series of evolutionary stages.

There can be little doubt that literary societies and writing clubs like the four featured in this study played an important role in the evolutionary process to which McClure alludes.[8]

The years 1896 and 1941 mark but one stage in this process, and these dates are only arbitrary markers that have been imposed upon a vast subject in order to narrow the focus of one, very limited study. The story of literary societies and writing clubs does not begin with the frontier period of the state of Texas. Clubs like these have been a part of American life since the colonial period. More studies of the activities of literary clubs in other regions and in other time periods need to be conducted before the role of such clubs in the cultural development of societies can be fully determined.

Just as the story of literary societies and writing clubs does not begin with the frontier period of Texas, the story also does not end with the advent of World War II. Formally and informally, Texas writers and would-be writers continue, even now, to meet together in groups to study literature and to engage in the criticism of literary compositions. Groups such as Trinity Writers in Irving, Golden Triangle Writers Guild in Beaumont, Houston Writers League, San Angelo Night Writers, Almost Every Other Wednesday Club in Abilene, and the DFW Writers in Euless-Bedford are currently meeting in towns and cities across the state. The story of Texas writing clubs is ongoing, and many additional chapters remain to be written.

APPENDIX

Texas Literary Clubs

The following list of literary clubs that met in Texas before 1950 is by no means complete nor entirely accurate with regard to literary activities and/or writing. Determining the exact time period in which some of these clubs met was impossible in many cases. Many of these names also appear on lists of women's clubs and in club publications located in the Women's Collection at Texas Women's University in Denton. Certainly, not all the clubs associated with the Texas Federation of Women's Clubs and the Texas Association of Women's Clubs were dedicated solely to the study of literature or creative writing. Therefore, an attempt has been made to eliminate from this list those groups whose purpose was strictly social or civic or whose programs were dedicated to the study of music, history, drama, gardening, homemaking, or current events. Some large associations, such as women's clubs and women's forums, have been included because these organizations often were divided into departments according to special interests and included creative writing and literature groups. As this list of clubs demonstrates, literary club activity in Texas was widespread.

Abilene Penwomen
Abilene Study Club
Abilene Woman's Forum
Abilene Woman's Forum, Jr.
Acacia Study Club of Corpus
    Christi
Acacia Study Club of Snyder
Adelphian Club of Crowell

Adelphian Club of Denton
Afflatus Club of Cooper
Afflatus Club of Harlingen
Afflatus Club of Kaufman
Afflatus Club of the Rio Grande
    Valley
Afflatus Study Club of Commerce
Aglaian Study Club of Alvin

Aglaian Study Club of Galveston
Alamo Club of Greenville
Alethea Society of Laredo
Alethean Study Club of San Angelo
Alethian Study Club of Kenedy
Alethia Society at Mary Hardin
  Baylor of Independence
Aliceans of Alice
Alice Freeman Palmer Club of
  Denton
Aliyah Study Club of Lockney
Allen Bi-Weekly Club of Allen
Alpha Art Club of Fort Worth
Alpha Art Club of Port Arthur
Alpha Centuria Literary Club of
  Denison
Alpha Civic and Art Club of Tyler
Alpha Delphian Club, Junior of
  Crowell
Alpha Delphian Club of Baird
Alpha Delphian Club of Commerce
Alpha Delphian Club of Dennison
Alpha Delphian Club of Eastland
Alpha Delphian Club of Mt.
  Pleasant
Alpha Delphian Club of Phillips
Alpha Delphian Club of San Angelo
Alpha Delphian Club of Teague
Alpha Delphian Society of Archer
  City
Alpha Delphian Study Club of
  Eldorado
Alpha Literary Club of Robstown
Alpha Study Club of Aqua Dulce
Alpha Study Club of Eagle Pass
Alpha Study Club of Snyder
Alpha Study Club of Truscott
Alpha Sub Junior Adelphian Club of
  Crowell
Alpha Tau Study Club of Fort
  Hancock

Alphin Charity and Art Club of Fort
  Worth
Altruesa Study Club of Roscoe
Altrui Junior Study Club of Earth
Altruisa Study Club of Vernon
Alvin Art League of Alvin
Amasavourien of Salado
American Literature Club of Paris
Amherst Study Club, Junior
Amherst Study Club of Amherst
Amherst Sub-Junior Study Club
Amitié Junior Study Club of Snyder
Amitié Study Club of Snyder
Amity Club of Moran
Amity Club of Olney
Amity Junior Study Club of Post
Amity Study Club of Atlanta
Amity Study Club of Batesville
Amity Study Club of Garza
Amity Study Club of Iowa Park
Amity Study Club of Lubbock
Amity Study Club of Post
Amity Study Club of Ralls
Anabel Bluntzer Study Club of
  Corpus Christi
Andrews Study Club of Andrews
Arden Club of Dallas
Ariel Club of Denton
Ariel Study Club of Paris Junior
  College in Paris
Arlington's Federated Woman's
  Club
Arlington Forum
Armo Art Club of Pampa
Art and Civic Club of Leakey
Art Appreciation Club of Childress
Artcele Study Club of Electra
Art Club of Coolidge
Art Club of McKinney
Art Guild of Bay City
Art Guild Study Club of Snyder

Artist and Writer's Vespers of Houston
Arts and Civic Club of Goldthwaite
Arts and Civic Club of Lefors
Arts and Crafts Club of Ft. Worth
Art Study Club of Port Arthur
Art Unit: Women's Forum of Abilene
Ascarte Woman's Club of Ascarte
Association of Friends of Minerva of Houston
As You Like It Club of Belton
As You Like It Club of Plainview
Atalantean Club of Memphis
Athena Club of Dallas
Athena Club of Palacios
Athenaeum Club of Alvin
Athenaeum Club of Amarillo
Athenaeum Club of Atlanta
Athenaeum Club of Balmorhea
Athenaeum Club of Corpus Christi
Athenaeum Club of Denton
Athenaeum Club of Ft.Worth
Athenaeum Club of Lubbock
Athenaeum Club of Plainview
Athenaeum Club of San Benito
Athenaeum Club of Shamrock
Athenaeum Club of Sweetwater
Athenaeum Literary Club of Texas State College for Women in Denton
Athenaeum Study Club of Colorado City
Athenaeum Study Club of Loraine
Athenaeum Study Club of Snyder
Athena Junior Study Club of Lockney
Athene Study Club of Bloomington
Athenian Club of Abilene
Athenian Club of Commerce
Athenian Club of Corpus Christi

Athenian Club of Grand Saline
Athenian Club of San Benito
Athenian Club of Whitsboro
Athenian Study Club of Daingerfield
Athenian Study Club of Slaton
Aurora Literary Club of San Benito
Aurora Study Club of Lott
Authors and Composers Club of San Antonio
Ava Moran Delphian Club of Crane
Avolonchettes Federation Fine Arts Club of Fort Worth
Axson Club of Houston
Barrington Fiction Club of Dallas
Bay View Century Club of Dallas
Bay View Club of Hedley
Bay View Club of Hereford
Bay View Reading Club of Cooper
Bay View Study Club of Hereford
Bear Creek Study Club of Junction
Bear Creek Study Club of Menard
Beaux Arts Club of Wichita Falls
Belle Arts Club of Dallas
Bellerophon Quill Club of Goliad
Bertram Literary Club
Beta Literary Club of Robstown
Big Bend Study Club of Presidio
Big Lake Study Club
Blanket Study Club
Bluebonnet Book Club of Bedias
Bluebonnet Club of Albany
Blue Bonnet Club of Byers
Bluebonnet Club of Kingsville
Bluebonnet Club of Richardson
Blue Bonnet Club of Texarkana
Blue Bonnet Delphian Club of Corpus Christi
Bluebonnet Junior Club of Houston
Blue Bonnet Literary Club of Gilmer

Bluebonnet Study Club of Albany
Blue Bonnet Study Club of Alpine
Blue Bonnet Study Club of Baytown
Bluebonnet Study Club of
  Chillicothe
Bluebonnet Study Club of Pontotoc
Blue Bonnet Study Club of Saint Jo
Blue Bonnet Three Arts Club
Blue Springs Study Club of
  Canton
Bogata Book Club
Bohemian Scribblers
Book Club of Clarendon
Book Club of Texas
Book Lovers Club, Junior of Alice
Book Lovers Club of Alice
Booklovers Club of Austin
Book Lovers Club of Morton
Book Lovers Club of Royse City
Book Lovers Study Club of Alice
Book Lovers, YMCA of Austin
Book Trailers Club of Austin
Border Poets of Kingsville
Breckenridge Club of San Antonio
Breckenridge Club of San Marcos
Briargrove Woman's Club of
  Houston
Bronte Club of Victoria
Browning Club of Dallas
Browning Club of Waco
Browning Club of Wichita Falls
Brownsville Study Club
Burkburnett Study Club of
  Burkburnett
Byliners of Corpus Christi
Cactus Study Club of Junction
Cadmean Club of Ft. Worth
Cadmean Literary Club of Houston
Calliopean Society at Baylor in
  Waco
Calvert Woman's Club

Cambridge Study Club of Queen
  City
Cameron Delphian Club
Campus Study Club of College
  Station
Canyon Study Club
Capital Study Club of Austin
Caria Study Club of Paris
Carleton Study Club of Fort Worth
Carnegie Club of Terrell
Carrizo Springs Literary Club
Carrollton's Woman's Club
Carthage Book Club
Castanette Social, Civic and Art
  Club of Sweetwater
Catholic Poetry Society
Centennial Study Club of Austin
Centennial Study Club of Leonard
Centennial Study Club of White
  Deer
Centennial Study Club of Wichita
  Falls
Century Club of Brownwood
Century Club of Cisco
Century Culture Club of Marfa
Century-Ette Study Club of Dumas
Century Study Club of Grand
  Prairie
Century Study Club of Quanah
Cenzio Study Club of Tilden
Chaparral Club of Denton
Chautaugua Literary and Scientific
  Club of Graham
Cheerio Study Club of Canyon
Chico Women's Club of Chico
Child Culture Study Club of El Paso
Christian Home Talent Club of Paris
Civic and Culture Club of Idalou
Civic and Study Club of Hull-
  Daisetta
Classic Literary Group of Dallas

Clematis Circle of Fort Worth
Clement Sorosis Study Club of
   Lubbock
Cleopatra of Seguin
Clio Club of Alvarado
Clover Club of Kaufman
Clyde Study Club
Colfax Study Club of Canton
College Club of Dallas
College Hill Literary Club of
   Sherman
College Women's Club of Houston
Collegiate Club of Tyler
Collinsville Woman's Club
Colonial Study Club of Hamilton
Colored Woman's Progressive Club
   of Galveston
Columbian Club of Crowell
Columbus Study Club
Comanche Study Club
Comstock Study Club of Conroe
Conservative Arts Club of Houston
Contemporary Study Club of
   Burkburnett
Contemporary Study Club of
   Dalhart
Contemporary Study Club of
   Odessa
Coolidge Study Club
Coolidge Woman's Club
Cora M. Crittenden Literary & Art
   Club of Fort Worth
Cordie Whitfield Study Club of
   Edna
Coterie Club of Paris
Coterie Culture Club of Commerce
Country Woman's Club of Bluff
   Dale
Covington Study Club of
   Covington
Crane Study Club of Crane

Creative Arts Club of Witesboro
Creative Study Club of Big Lake
Creative Writing Group of the
   AAUW in Abilene
Critic Club of Dallas
Critics of Dallas
Crockett Culture Club of Crockett
Crosby Sorosis Club of Crosby
Cosmorama Study Club of Snyder
Cultu Mea Club of Mount Pleasant
Cultu Mea Club of Tyler
Cultura Club of La Feria
Culture and Art Club of
   Throckmorton
Culture Club Junior of Commerce
Culture Club of Booker
Culture Club of Crockett
Culture Club of Farmersville
Culture Club of Jayton
Culture Club of La Feria
Culture Club of Mathis
Culture Club of Mount Pleasant
Culture Club of Odessa
Culture Club of Pampa
Culture Club of Roscoe
Culture Club of Sanderson
Culture Club of Sour Lake
Culture Club of Tom Bean
Culture Club of Van Alstyne
Culture Club of Wolfe City
Culture Study Club of Paducah
Cum Concilio Club of Nacogdoches
Cumtux Study Club of Cleburne
Current Culture Club of Athens
Current Literature Club Junior of
   Denton
Current Literature Club of Bonham
Current Literature Club of
   Burkburnett
Current Literature Club of
   Daingerfield

Current Literature Club of Houston
Current Literature Club of
LaGrange
Current Literature Club of
Megargel
Currer Bell Study Club of Victoria
Curtain Club of Austin
Daedalian Study Club of Junction
Dale Book Review Club of Dallas
Daleth Study Club of Gladewater
Dalhart Contemporary Study Club
Dalhart Junior Sorosis Club
Dalhart Junior Women's Club
Dallas Delphian Federation
Dallas Junior Fine Arts Club
Dallas Pan-American Round Table
Number One
Dallas Pen Women
Dallas Press Club
Dallas Story League
Dallas Wednesday Study Club
Dallas Women's Club
Dallas Women's Forum
Dallas Women's Press Club
Dallas Writers' Club
Daughters of 1933 Study Club of
Spur
De Algodon Study Club of
Goodland
Decatur Junior Woman's Club
Decatur Woman's Club
Delian Club of Denton
Delian Club of Olney
Delphian Club of Abilene
Delphian Club of Archer City
Delphian Club of Baird
Delphian Club of Big Spring
Delphian Club of Chillicothe
Delphian Club of Cisco
Delphian Club of Commerce
Delphian Club of Hunt

Delphian Club of Kermit
Delphian Club of Memphis
Delphian Club of Mineola
Delphian Club of Mount Pleasant
Delphian Club of Port Arthur
Delphian Club of San Marcos
Delphian Club of Vernon
Delphian Daughters of Lamesa
Delphian Study Club of Cisco
Delphian Study Club of Paducah
Delta Delphin Study Club of
Plainview
Delwin Study Club
Distaff Study Club of San Saba
Docilis Club of Higgins
Donna Civic and Study Club
Donna Woman's Club
Douglas Club of Austin
Dramatic Art Club of Marshall
Dramatic Readers Club of Dallas
Dundee Study Club of Dundee
Dundee Study Club of Holiday
Eagle Lake Study Club
Eclecta Club of Forney
Edelweiss Club of McKinney
Edelweiss Club of Winnsboro
Eden Study Club
Edgewood Study Club
El Concho Study Club of Christoval
Eldorado Study Club
Eleanor Breckenridge Literary Club
of Edna
Eleanor H. Jones Cultural &
Literary Club of Fort Worth
Eleanor Roosevelt Study Club of
Skellytown
Elizabethean Club of Tyler
El Paso Women's Club
El Progreso Club of Uvalde
El Progreso Study Club of Alpine
Elsa Civic and Study Club of Elsa

Emanon Study Club of Corpus
  Christi
Emanthian Club of Burleson
Emerald Study Club of Shamrock
Emerson Club of Waco
Emlea Smith Junior Study Club of
  Morton
En Avant Club of Jayton
En A'Vant Club of Justin
En Avant Club of McKinney
Entre Nous Club of Hillsboro
Entre Nous Club of McKinney
Entre Nous Study Club of
  Brownwood
Eola Study Club
Erisophian Literary Society of
  Baylor at Independence
Etaerio Club of LaGrange
Ethel Green Study Club of Rosebud
Ethel Ransom Art and Literary Club
  of Houston
Ethel Ransom Art and Literary Club
  of Fort Worth
Ethel Ransom Cultural Club of Fort
  Worth
Ethical Culture Society of Houston
Eumathian Club of Burleson
Eureka Club of Marshall
Eureka Progressive Art and Civic
  Club of Orange
Evening Study Club of Bryan
Evening Study Club of Sanderson
Excelsior Civic and Art Club of Fort
  Worth
Excelsior Club of Beaumont
Excelsior Club of Gorman
Excelsior Study Club of Menard
Fannie M. Heath Junior Women
  Club of Fort Worth
Fannie Stephens Study Club of
  Ballinger

Farwell Study Club of Farwell
Fine Arts and Service Club of
  Burnet
Fine Arts Club of Atlanta
Fine Arts Club of Commerce
Fine Arts Club of Del Rio
Fine Arts Club of Eden
Fine Arts Club of Harlingen
Fine Arts Club of Lefors
Fine Arts Club of Menard
Fine Arts Club of Midland
Fine Arts Club of Mount Pleasant
Fine Arts Club of Odessa
Fine Arts Club of Orange
Fine Arts Club of Robstown
Fine Arts Club of Talco
Fine Arts Club of the Panhandle
Fine Arts Club of Tyler
Fine Arts Club of Weslaco
Fine Arts Club of Winnsboro
Fine Arts Society of Oak Cliff
First Literary Club of Tyler
Forsan Study Club of Forsan
Fort Davis Study Club of Fort Davis
Fort Stockton Literary Club
Fort Worth Poetry Society
Fort Worth Woman's Club
Forum Study Club of Burkburnett
Franklin Study Club of Franklin
Friday Afternoon Club of Dallas
Friday Club of Mexia
Friday Literary Club of Whitewright
Friday Literary Club of Wichita Falls
Friday Study Club of Stephenville
Friendship Study Club of Wichita
  Falls
Futuristic Study Club of Sunray
Gamma Mu Sigma Study Club of
  Levelland
Ganado Study and Serve Club of
  Ganado

Georgetown Study Club of
  Georgetown
Giddings Study Club of Giddings
Golden Gate Club of Houston
Goliad Reading Club
Gordon Woman's Club
Granbury Woman's Club
Grand Prairie Study Club
Grand Prairie Study Club, Junior
Grand Prairie Twentieth
Groesbeck Junior Study Club
Groesbeck Shakespeare Club
Groesbeck Study Club
Hallsville Study Club of Groesbeck
Happy Study Club
Harden Study Club of Bishop
Hardin Simmons Round Table of
  Abilene
Hardon Study Club of Big Springs
Hartley Study Club
Hawkins Study Club
Hawthorne Club of Cuero
Hawthorne Club of Eastland
Hearne Study Club
Heritage Study Club of Levelland
Heritage Study Club of Lubbock
Heritage Study Club of Midland
Heritage Women's Club of Canyon
Hesperian Club of Colorado
Hesperian Daughters Study Club of
  Colorado City
Hesperian Study Club of Colorado
  City
Highland Park Society of Arts
Highland Study Club of Junction
Highland Study Club of Roscoe
Hinchman Study Club of Houston
Historical Literary Society at
  Independence
Historic and Literary Club of
  Lufkin

Horizon Junior Study Club of Iowa
  Park
House Literary Club of Corpus
  Christi
Houston Expression Club
Houston Junior Forum
Houston Lyceum
Houston Pen Women
Houston Press Women
Houston Scribblers
Houston Story Tellers
Houston Writers' Workshop
Huaco Study Club of Waco
Huntsville Study Club
Hurst Study Club
Hyde Park Reading Club of Austin
Hy Lands Study Club of Silverton
Hyperion Club of Big Spring
Il Penseroso Junior Study Club of
  Lockney
Ingleside Sorosis Club of Lubbock
Ingleside Study Club of Snyder
Inquirer Study Club of Wichita Falls
Irving Club of Galveston
Irving Club of Lockhart
Isleta Junior Woman's Club of Isleta
James H. Lowery Club of Denton
Jayton Culture Club
Jeffersonian Club of Houston
Jewish Literary Society of Houston
J. O. A. Conner Study Club of Waco
Junior Afflatus Club of Cooper
Junior Amity Club of Wichita Falls
Junior Aurora Club of San Benito
Junior Bay View Club of Cooper
Junior Bayview Study Club of
  Deport
Junior Bluebonnet Club of
  Kingsville
Junior Bluebonnet Study Club of
  Chillicothe

Junior Bronte Club of Victoria
Junior Cherio Club of Canyon
Junior Club of Coolidge
Junior Culture Club of McLean
Junior Culture Club of Miami
Junior Culture Club of Post
Junior Culture Club of Roscoe
Junior Culture Club of Winters
Junior Culture Club of Wolfe City
Junior Current Literature Club of
  Houston
Junior Delphian Club of Baird
Junior Delphian Club of Lamesa
Junior Delphian Club of Mount
  Pleasant
Junior Eumathian Club of Burleson
Junior Fine Arts Club of Midland
Junior Forum of Denton
Junior Forum Study Club of
  Burkburnett
Junior Hesperian Club of Colorado
Junior Hesperian Study Club of
  Colorado City
Junior Hyperion Club of Big Spring
Junior Ladies Reading Club of
  Houston
Junior Les Arts Club of Clarendon
Junior Literary Club of Bertram
Junior Literary Club of Dalhart
Junior Literary Club of Denison
Junior Literary Club of Hamlin
Junior Mayflower Club of
  Greenville
Junior Oak Cliff Society of Fine Arts
Junior Pallas Club of Greenville
Junior Pioneer Study Club of
  Hereford
Junior Progressive Study Club of
  Burkburnett
Junior Progressive Study Club of
  McLean

Junior Quid Prope Club of San
  Angelo
Junior Review Club of Killeen
Junior Self-Culture Club of
  Colorado City
Junior-Senior Culture Club of
  Quitaque
Junior-Senior Shakespeare Forum of
  Denton
Junior Sesame Club of Hillsboro
Junior Shakespeare Club of Abilene
Junior Shakespeare Club of
  Arlington
Junior Shakespeare Club of Denton
Junior Shakespeare Club of Mt.
  Vernon
Junior Shakespeare Club of
  Sherman
Junior Sorosis Club of Paducah
Junior Sorosis of Benjamin
Junior Sorosis Study Club of
  Lubbock
Junior Southern Literary Club of
  Ladonia
Junior Standard Club of Greenville
Junior Standard Club of Sulphur
  Springs
Junior Standard Club of Wichita
  Falls
Junior Study Club of Alpine
Junior Study Club of Big Lake
Junior Study Club of Bronte
Junior Study Club of Crane
Junior Study Club of Cross Plains
Junior Study Club of Crystal City
Junior Study Club of Dimmitt
Junior Study Club of Happy
Junior Study Club of Harlingen
Junior Study Club of Joshua
Junior Study Club of Littlefield
Junior Study Club of Lufkin

Junior Study Club of Monahans
Junior Study Club of Perryton
Junior Study Club of Rusk
Junior Study Club of Sudan
Junior Study Club of Wink
Junior '32 Club of San Angelo
Junior Thursday Afternoon Club of
  Eastland
Junior Thursday Club of Celeste
Junior Twentieth Century Club of
  Brownwood
Junior Twentieth Century Club of
  Cumby
Junior Twentieth Century Club of
  Lubbock
Junior Twentieth Century Club of
  Nocona
Junior Twentieth Century Club of
  Odessa
Junior Twentieth Century Club of
  Pecos
Junior Twentieth Century Club of
  Stephenville
Junior University Club of
  Burkburnett
Junior Wednesday Club of Baird
Junior Wednesday Club of
  Galveston
Junior Wednesday Club of Midland
Junior Woman's Association of
  Midland
Junior Woman's Book Club of
  Canyon
Junior Woman's Club of Canadian
Junior Woman's Club of Cleveland
Junior Woman's Club of Commerce
Junior Woman's Club of Corpus
  Christi
Junior Woman's Club of El Campo
Junior Woman's Club of Eldorado
Junior Woman's Club of Floydada

Junior Woman's Club of Friona
Junior Woman's Club of Jacksboro
Junior Woman's Club of Marshall
Junior Woman's Club of Megargel
Junior Woman's Club of Ozona
Junior Woman's Club of Pecos
Junior Woman's Club of
  Raymondville
Junior Woman's Club of Refugio
Junior Woman's Club of Sanderson
Junior Woman's Club of Taft
Junior Woman's Club of
  Throckmorton
Junior Woman's Culture Club of
  Commerce
Junior Woman's Culture Club of
  Llano
Junior Woman's Forum of Big
  Spring
Junior Woman's Literary Club of
  Dalhart
Junior Woman's Literary Club of
  Rochester
Junior Woman's Study Club of
  Dumas
Junior Woman's Study Club of Fort
  Worth
Junior Woman's Study Club of
  Littlefield
Junior Woman's Study Club of
  Lorenzo
Junior Woman's Study Club of
  Putnam
Junior Woman's Study Club of San
  Angelo
Junior Woman's Wednesday
  Association of Midland
Junior Women's Club of San
  Antonio
Junior XX Century Club of
  Brownwood

Kaffeekraenzchen of Fredericksburg
Kalier Club of Commerce
Kalir Klub of Commerce
Kaufman Study Club of Kaufman
Kermit Study Club
Key Poetry Class of Eastland
Kilgore Woman's Club
Kimberly Junior Woman's Club
Kimichi Study Club of Olton
The King's Daughters' Club of
    Austin
Knox City Study Club of Knox City
Koinonia Study Club of
    Nacogdoches
Kolonial Club of Fort Worth
Koshare Club Junior of Levelland
Kwill Club of Austin
La Afflatus Estudio Club of
    Hereford
La Candela Jr. Study Club of
    Plainview
La Ceniza Writing Club of Corpus
    Christi
La Cultura Study Club of Pampa
Ladies and Lassies Study Club of
    Valley View
Ladies Art and Social Club of
    Hillsboro
Ladies Friday Club of Houston
Ladies Progressive Club of Paris
Ladies Reading Circle of Dallas
Ladies Reading Circle of Paris
Ladies Reading Club of Bastrop
Ladies Reading Club of Houston
Ladies Reading Club of La Porte
Ladies Reading Club of Paris
La Douzaine of Houston
La Junta Study Club of Junction
La Kee Kon Club of Sweetwater
L'Allegro Junior Study Club of
    Morton

Lamar Study Club of Paris
Lamesa Woman's Study Club
La Mode Club of Fort Worth
Lane Study Club of Edgewood
LaPetite Jr. of Beaumont
La Plata Study Club of Hereford
La Porte Literary Club
La Pryor Study Club
La Retama Club of Corpus Christi
La Rosetta Civic and Cultural Club
    of Tyler
Las Amigas Club of Mexia
Las Amigas Junior Study Club of
    El Paso
Las Amigas Study Club of Littlefield
La Senisa of Corpus Christi
Las Fidelis Study Club of Levelland
Las Leales Club of Corpus Christi
Las Madres Study Club of Coleman
La Societe de Beaux Arts Club of
    Waco
Las Viajeras Study Club of Dalhart
Laura Clark Reading Club of
    Houston
Learners Club of Brownsville
Learners Club of Marlin
Lefors Art and Civic Club of Lefors
Lefors Fine Arts Club of Lefors
Les Beaux Arts Club of Clarendon
Les Beaux Arts Junior Club of
    Clarendon
Les Premiers Club of Commerce
Les Progrès Study Club of Plainview
Les Temps Club of Amarillo
Leti Study Club of Junction
Levelland Junior Study Club of
    Levelland
Levelland Junior Woman's Club of
    Levelland
Liberty Woman's Club of Liberty
Linden Study Club of Linden

Library Study Club of Rusk
Litera Club of Higgins
Literai Club of Nacogdoches
Literary and Civic Club of Haskell
Literary and Civic Club of New
   Boston
Literary and Fine Arts Club of
   Harlingen
Literary and Review Club of San
   Angelo
Literary and Service Club of Winters
Literary Club of Fort Stockton
Literary Club of Lufkin
Literary Club of San Angelo
Literary Club of Schulenburg
Literary Club of Waco
Literary Club of Yoakum
Literary Review Club of San Angelo
Literary Review Club of Weslaco
Literary Study Club of Rusk
Literary Study Club of Toyah
Little Acorn Study Club of Three
   Rivers
Live Oak Study Club of Three
   Rivers
L. M. Study and Civic Club of
   Lometa
Lone Star Club of Celeste
Lone Star Junior Club of Celeste
Lone Star Study Club Junior of
   Hereford
Lone Star Study Club of Hereford
Lone Star Study Club of Putnam
Longview Fine Arts Club
Longview Woman's Forum
Los Ebanos Study Club of Mercedes
Lotus Club of Paris
Lotus Club of San Antonio
Louise Woman's Club of Louise
Love One Another Junior Study
   Club of Silverton

Lovers of Good Literature of
   Granger
Lowell Literary Club of Thomaston
Lower Valley Woman's Club of
   El Paso
Lucy Bridges Reading Club of
   Center
Lufkin Historical and Literary Club
   of Lufkin
Lufkin Literary Club of Lufkin
Lula Johnson of Crittenden
Literary and Art Junior Club of Fort
   Worth
Magno Usui Study Club of Fort
   Stockton
Maia Study Club of Daingerfield
Maids and Matrons Club of Nocona
Maids and Matrons Culture Club of
   Levelland
Maids and Matrons of Aransas Pass
Maids and Matrons of Brownfield
Maids and Matrons Social Art and
   Literary Club of Marlin
Makers of SMU of Dallas
Malakoff Woman's Club of Malakoff
Mamie Willet Book Review Club
Manuscript Club of Wichita Falls
Marantha Study Club of Colorado
   City
Marathon Study Club of Marathon
March of Time Club of Silverton
Marfa Junior Study Club of Marfa
Marfa Study Club
Mariam Lutcher Stark Arno Art
   Group of Austin
Mariann Pierian Club of Lampasas
Marion G. White Study Club of
   Odessa
Mark Twain Study Club of Nixon
Marpessa Club, Junior of
   Commerce

Marpessa Club of Commerce
Marshall Study Club
Martin's Mill Study Club of Canton
Mathis Book Lover's Club
Mathis Culture Club
Mathis Literary Club
Mathis Study Club
Matron's Junior Book Review Club of Abilene
Matrons Study Club of Levelland
Mayflower Club of Greenville
M. B. Kavanaugh Cultural Club of Fort Worth
McAllen Study Club
McCamey Social, Civic & Art Club
Meadow Study Club
Medina Valley Woman's Club
Megregor Woman's Club
M. Eleanor Brackenridge Club of Denton
Menard Reading Club
Men's Library Club of Dallas
Merrie Maids of Refugio
Merry Wives of Pecos
Midkiff Study Club
Midland's Woman's Club
Miguel de Cervantes Study Club of Corpus Christi
Millie L. Allen Cultural Club of Fort Worth
Mineola Junior Literary Club
Minerva Study Club of Bay City
Minerva Study Club of Baytown
Mission Study Club
Mockingbird Chapter of the Poetry Society of Texas of McKinney
Modern American Study Club of White Deer
Modern Century Study Club of Wichita Falls

Modern Matron Art & Civic Club of Port Arthur
Modern Study Club Junior of Pecos
Modern Study Club of Amarillo
Modern Study Club of Burkburnett
Modern Study Club of Henderson
Modern Study Club of Hughes Springs
Modern Study Club of Killeen
Modern Study Club of Midland
Modern Study Club of Odessa
Modern Study Club of Paris
Modern Study Club of Pecos
Modern Study Club of Wolfe City
Modern Woman's Forum of Big Spring
Modern Writers of Waco
Monday Club of Corpus Christi
Monday Club of Hillsboro
Monday Club of Houston
Monday Literary Club of Houston
Monday Review Club of Dallas
Monday Review Club of Greenville
Monday Review Club of Hillsboro
Monthly Book Review Club of Brownsville
Moran Delphian Club
Moran Study Club
Morning Study Club of Victoria
Mothers Self Culture Club of Hale Center
Mothers Self Culture Club of Lamesa
Mothers' Self-Culture Club of Midland
Mothers' Self Culture Club of the Panhandle
Mother's Self Culture Club of Wellington
Mothers' Study Club of Winters
Muleshoe Study Club of Muleshoe

Munday Study Club of Munday
Mutual Improvement Club of Blum
National Association of American
  Pen Women[I]
National Society of Arts and Letters
  of San Antonio
Nautilus Club of Prairie View
Nautilus Study Club of Corpus
  Christi
New Century Club of Elgin
New Century Club of Taylor
New Century Study Club of Olton
New Culture Club of Del Rio
New Era Club of Brownsville
New Era Club of Lufkin
New Era Club of Ranger
New Era Club of Tyler
New Era Junior Study Club of
  Longview
New Era Study Club of Longview
New Era Study Club of Lufkin
Nineteenth Century Club of Pilot
  Point
Ninety-nine Club of Mount Pleasant
Noino Study Club of Princeton
Nuc Futura Study Club of Sexton
  City
Nuevo Study Club of Turkey
Nu Gamma Study Club of
  Monahans
Oak Cliff Browning Club
Oak Leaf Study Club of Three
  Rivers
Odessa Social, Civic and Art Club
Odessa Study Club
Odessa Woman's Forum
O Ki Hi Study Club of Stratford
Olton Study Club
Omicron Study Club of Tulia
O'Moore Literary Club of Deport
Order of the Bookfellows

Orgatron Study Club of Houston
Our Reading Club of San Antonio
Owl Club of Decatur
Owl Club of McKinney
Owlettes of Dallas
Owl Forum of McKinney
Ozona Junior Woman's Club
Ozona Woman's Club
Ozona Woman's Forum
Ozona Woman's League
Paint Rock Study Club of Paint
  Rock
Pallas Club of Commerce
Pallas Club of Greenville
Pandora Study Club of Daingerfield
Panhandle Pen Women
Panhandle Poets
Panhandle Speech & Arts
  Association
Paris Council of Study Clubs
Paris Noon Study Club
Paris Women's Study Club
Park Place Junior Literary Club of
  Houston
Park Place Literary Club of Houston
Park Place Woman's Club of
  Houston
Pass of the North Study Club of El
  Paso
Pathfinders Club of Austin
Pathfinders Club of Clarendon
Pathfinders Club of Memphis
Pathfinders Study Club of Littlefield
Pearl Chappell Study Club of Dallas
Pegasus Study Club of Vanderbilt
Pen Chat Club of Burnet
Penelope Club of Fort Worth
Pennybacker Club of Forney
Perennial Cultural Club of Fort
  Worth
Permian Study Club

Perryton Sorosis Club of Perryton
Phalba Study Club of Mabank
Philomathesian of Independence
Philomathian Literary Club of
　Houston
Philomathian Study Club of San
　Angelo
Philomath Study Club of Corpus
　Christi
Phi Los Study Club of Lubbock
Phoebe K. Warner Club of Tahoka
Phoenix Club of Aspermont
Phoenix Club of San Antonio
Phoenix Study Club of Corpus
　Christi
Phyllis Wheatley Art Club of
　Oakwood
Phyllis Wheatley Club of Bonham
Phyllis Wheatley Club of El Paso
Phyllis Wheatley Club of Marshall
Pierian Club Junior of Menard
Pierian Club of Abilene
Pierian Club of Amarillo
Pierian Club of Corpus Christi
Pierian Club of Dallas
Pierian Club of Lampasas
Pierian Club of Oak Cliff
Pierian Club of San Antonio
Pierian Club of Seymour
Pierian Club of Stamford
Pierian Club of Waco
Pierian Sorosis Club of Lubbock
Pierian Study Club of Dumas
Pierian Study Club of San Antonio
Pierian Study Club of San Saba
Pierian Study Club of Tyler
Pierian Study Club of Wichita Falls
Pioneer Literary Club Junior of
　Kerns
Pioneer Literary Club of Kerns
Pioneer Study Club of Bailey

Pioneer Study Club of Hale Center
Pioneer Study Club of Hereford
Pioneer Study Club of Odessa
Pittsburg Study Club
Plainview Delphin Club
Plainview Delphin Club Junior
Plano Study Club of Plano
Pleasanton Junior Woman's Club
Pleasanton Woman's Club
Ploma Collins Study Club of Waco
Poetry Club of Abilene
Poetry Club of Fort Worth
Poetry Study Club of Wichita Falls
Portfolio Club of Deport
Port Lavaca Junior Woman's Club
Poteet Study Club
Poteet Women's Club
Prairie Blume
Prairie Girl's Club of Spearman
Predicta Study Club of Roaring
　Springs
Presidio Valley Woman's Club of
　Presidio
Press Club of Waco
Primero Study Club of Amarillo
Priscilla Arts Club of Dallas
Progress Club of Pharr
Progressive Alliance of Cultural
　Women of Fort Worth
Progressive Club Junior of McLean
Progressive Club of Wichita Falls
Progressive Culture Club of
　Greenville
Progressive Literary and Art Club of
　Fort Worth
Progressive Study Club of Amarillo
Progressive Study Club of Andrews
Progressive Study Club of Atlanta
Progressive Study Club of
　Beaumont
Progressive Study Club of Big Lake

Progressive Study Club of Corpus Christi
Progressive Study Club of Dallas
Progressive Study Club of Friona
Progressive Study Club of Gorman
Progressive Study Club of Haskell
Progressive Study Club of Kenedy
Progressive Study Club of Lubbock
Progressive Study Club of McLean
Progressive Study Club of Midland
Progressive Study Club of Normangee
Progressive Study Club of Odessa
Progressive Study Club of Pittsburg
Progressive Study Club of Quanah
Progressive Study Club of Snyder
Progressive Study Club of Sweetwater
Progressive Study Club of Tulia
Progressive Study Club of Valley Mills
Progressive Study Club of Wheeler
Progressive Study Club of Wichita Falls
Progressive Study Club of Wink
Prospectus Study Club of Stratford
Provarsu Study Club of Fort Worth
Quaero Literary Club of Tyler
Quanah Study Club of Quanah
Quest Club of Tyler
Questers Club of Plainview
Quid Nunc Club of Tyler
Quill Club of Austin
Ralls Junior Study Club
Ralls Senior Study Club
Ralls Study Club
Rankin Study Club of Rankin
Raymondville Woman's Club
Readers and Reviewers of Austin
Reader's Club of Dallas
Readers Guild of Austin

Reading Club of Abilene
Reading Club of Bryan
Reading Club of Hallettsville
Reading Club of Menard
Rhome Women's Club
Rio Grande Art League
Rittenhouse Poetry Society of Houston
Rochelle Study Club
Rocksprings Woman's Club
Rosebud Study Club of Rosebud
Rosetta Club of Beeville
Rosary Reading and Art Club of San Angelo
Round Rock Woman's Club
Round Table of Corpus Christi
Round Table of Dallas
Round Table of Denton
Round Table of Kingsville
Round Table of SMU in Dallas
Roxton Book Club of Roxton
Royall Academia of Mary Hardin Baylor at Independence
Rufus C. Burleson Society at Baylor College in Waco
Sadler Study Club of Corpus Christi
Salado Ladies Reading Society
San Angelo Delphian Club
San Angelo Poetry Society
San Antonio Pen Women
San Antonio Self Culture Club
San Antonio Writers' Club
San Augustine Junior Study Club
San Augustine Study Club
Sandhill Study Club of Wink
San Jacinto Woman's Club of Houston
Santa Anna Self-Culture Club
Sapphonian Study Club of Fort Stockton
Saturday Club of Rising Star

Scarab of Dallas
Schulenburg Literary Society
Scott Study Club of Corpus Christi
Scribblers of Austin
Searchlight and Junior Club of
   Deport
Seguin Woman's Club
Self Culture Club of Brownsville
Self Culture Club of Caddo Mills
Self Culture Club of Colorado
Self Culture Club of Colorado City
Self-Culture Club of Corpus Christi
Self Culture Club of Falfurrias
Self Culture Club of Hebbronville
Self-Culture Club of Palestine
Self-Culture Club of San Antonio
Self-Culture Club of Santa Anna
Self Culture Club of Sweetwater
Self Culture Club of Waco
Seminole Junior Study Club
Seminole Study Club
Service and Study Club of Deport
Sesame Club of Hillsboro
Sesame Club of Houston
Sesame Club of Hughes Springs
Sesame Club of Marshall
Sesame Club of Sterling City
Sesame Literary Club of Hughes
   Springs
Sesame Study Club of Gonzales
Sesame Study Club of Waco
Seward Woman's Club
Shakespeare Club of Abilene
Shakespeare Club of Arlington
Shakespeare Club of Ballinger
Shakespeare Club of Coleman
Shakespeare Club of Dallas
Shakespeare Club of DeLeon
Shakespeare Club of Denton
Shakespeare Club of Flatonia
Shakespeare Club of Ft. Worth

Shakespeare Club of Groesbeck
Shakespeare Club of Hearne
Shakespeare Club of Lancaster
Shakespeare Club of Longview
Shakespeare Club of Lubbock
Shakespeare Club of Mount Vernon
Shakespeare Club of Nixon
Shakespeare Club of North Zulch
Shakespeare Club of Oak Cliff
Shakespeare Club of Seguin
Shakespeare Club of Sherman
Shakespeare Club of Smithville
Shakespeare Club of Vernon
Shakespeare Club of Waco
Shakespeare Club of Waxahachie
Shakespeare Club of Wichita Falls
Shakespeare Followers of Dallas
Shakespeare Followers of Oak Cliff
Sigma Lambda Kappa Study Club,
   Junior of Abilene
Sigma Lambda Kappa Study Club
   of Abilene
Sigma Tau Delta[2]
Silsbee Woman's Club
Silver Leaf Art Club of Austin
Simmons Round Table of Abilene
Social Book Club of Lott
Social Science Club of Terrell
Socratic Study Club of Rule
Sodalitas Club of Hedley
Sonora Woman's Club
Sorosis Club Junior of Perryton
Sorosis Club of Benjamin
Sorosis Club of Brady
Sorosis Club of Center
Sorosis Club of Coleman
Sorosis Club of Ft. Worth
Sorosis Club of Houston
Sorosis Club of Humble
Sorosis Club of Kerns
Sorosis Club of Knox City

Sorosis Club of Livingston
Sorosis Club of Lubbock
Sorosis Club of Matador
Sorosis Club of Olney
Sorosis Club of Paducah
Sorosis Club of Perryton
Sorosis Club of San Antonio
Sorosis Club of San Marcos
Sorosis Club of Sweetwater
Sorosis Club of Vernon
Sorosis Study Club of Abilene
Sorosis Study Club of Amarillo
Sorosis Study Club of Granfalls
Sorosis Study Club of Turkey
Southern Literary Club of Ladonia
South Side Literary Club of
  Denison
Southwestern Poetry League of
  Amarillo
Southwestern Poetry League of
  Corpus Christi
Southwestern Writers Guild of
  Houston
Southwest Poetry Society of Corpus
  Christi
Spearman Study Club
Sphinx Club of Alvarado
Stafford Club of Galveston
Standard Club of Austin
Standard Club of Dallas[3]
Standard Club of Greenville
Standard Club of Oak Cliff
Standard Club of Sulfur Springs
Standard Club of Tyler
Standard Club of Wichita Falls
Standard Club of Winnsboro
Standard Literary Club of Austin
Standard Reading Club of Ennis
Stanton Study Club
Stellona Study Club of Lone Star
Stephenville Study Club

Stratford Contemporary Study Club
Stratford Club of Dallas
Stratford Club of Oak Cliff
Story League of Dallas
Study Club Junior of Sour Lake
Study Club Junior of Wortham
Study Club of Abernathy
Study Club of Albany
Study Club of Amarillo
Study Club of Alpine
Study Club of Baytown
Study Club of Big Spring
Study Club of Bronte
Study Club of Caddo Mills
Study Club of Clyde
Study Club of Colorado
Study Club of Colorado City
Study Club of Comanche
Study Club of Coolidge
Study Club of Dimmitt
Study Club of Dumas
Study Club of Earth
Study Club of Edna
Study Club of Estelline
Study Club of Fort Davis
Study Club of Fort Stockton
Study Club of Hallsville
Study Club of Harlingen
Study Club of Hart
Study Club of Hempstead
Study Club of Hull-Daisetta
Study Club of Leila Lake
Study Club of Lewisville
Study Club of Livingston
Study Club of Lufkin
Study Club of Luling
Study Club of Marathon
Study Club of Meridian
Study Club of Odem
Study Club of Penwell
Study Club of Pittsburg

Study Club of Riggold
Study Club of Rochelle
Study Club of Royse City
Study Club of Seymour
Study Club of Silverton
Study Club of Wortham
Sudan Culture Club
Sudan Study Club
Summerfield Study Club
Sundown Junior Study Club
Sundown Study Club
Sylvan Literary Club of La Porte
Talpa Study Club
Tarleton Campus Club of
    Stephenville
Tau Lambda Study Club of
    Monahans
TAWC of Fort Worth
Teague Delphian Club
Teague Study Club
Tejas Study Club of Denver City
Tejas Study Club of Harper
Temple Study Club
Terra Study Club
Texarkana Story League
Texarkana Woman's Club
Texas Study Club of Wichita Falls
Texas Writers Club
Texoma Woman's Club of
    Witesboro
Texon Study
Thalian Club of Rusk
Thalian Culture Club of Commerce
Three Arts Club of Gladewater
Three Arts Club of Mount Vernon
Thursday Afternoon Club of
    Eastland
Thursday Club of Atlanta
Thursday Club Bowie
Thursday Club of Celeste
Thursday Club of Claude

Thursday Club of Dublin
Thursday Club of Oakwood
Thursday Club of Plano
Thursday Club of Rockdale
Thursday Educational Club of
    Albany
Thursday Fine Arts Club of
    Shamrock
Thursday Forum of Abilene
Thursday Forum of Baytown
Thursday Literary Club of Nocona
Thursday Literary Club of
    Shamrock
Thursday Reading Club of Rockdale
Thursday Review Club of Wheeler
Thursday Study Club of Atlanta
Thursday Study Club of Bertram
Thursday Study Club of Corpus
    Christi
Thursday Study Club of Jacksboro
Thursday Study Club of Odessa
Thursday Study Club of Plano
Thursday Study Club of Plano #3
Thursday Study Club of Rhome
Thursday Study Club of Wichita
    Falls
Town and Country Study Club of
    Lampasas
Town and Country Study Club of
    Morton
Trivium Club of Liberty
Troup Study Club
Tuesday Club of Brady
Tuesday Club of Granger
Tuesday Club of Manor
Tuesday Club of Milford
Tuesday Club of Mission
Tuesday Club of Temple
Tuesday Club of Tyler
Tuesday Evening Study Club of
    Houston

Tuesday Literary Club of Groesbeck
Tuesday Literary Club of Sherman
Tuesday Music and Literature Club
of Laredo
Tuesday Reading Club of Tyler
Tuesday Review Club of Big Lake
Tuesday Study Club of Amarillo
Tuesday Study Club of Andrews
Tuesday Study Club of Anson
Tuesday Study Club of Brady
Tuesday Study Club of Fort Worth
Tuesday Study Club of Grange
Tuesday Study Club of Orange
Grove
Tuesday Study Club of Sudan
Tuesday Study Club of Teague
Tuesday Study Club of Wink
Tulia Literary Arts Club of Tulia
Twentieth Century Club of Ailmer
Twentieth Century Club of Alice
Twentieth Century Club of Amarillo
Twentieth Century Club of Big Lake
Twentieth Century Club of Borger
Twentieth Century Club of
Brownwood
Twentieth Century Club of Cisco
Twentieth Century Club of Conroe
Twentieth Century Club of
Corsicana
Twentieth Century Club of Cumby
Twentieth Century Club of
Daingerfield
Twentieth Century Club of Dumas
Twentieth Century Club of Ennis
Twentieth Century Club of Farris
Twentieth Century Club of Gilmer
Twentieth Century Club of George
West
Twentieth Century Club of
Hamilton
Twentieth Century Club of Hondo
Twentieth Century Club of La Feria
Twentieth Century Club of
Longview
Twentieth Century Club of Lubbock
Twentieth Century Club of Melvin
Twentieth Century Club of Mineola
Twentieth Century Club of Mount
Pleasant
Twentieth Century Club of Nocona
Twentieth Century Club of
Normangee
Twentieth Century Club of Odessa
Twentieth Century Club of Pampa
Twentieth Century Club of Paris
Twentieth Century Club of Pecos
Twentieth Century Club of Pittsburg
Twentieth Century Club of Rice
Twenticth Century Club of Saint Jo
Twentieth Century Club of
Seymour
Twentieth Century Club of
Shamrock
Twentieth Century Club of Snyder
Twentieth Century Club of
Spearman
Twentieth Century Club of
Stephenville
Twentieth Century Club of
Timpson
Twentieth Century Club of Van
Horn
Twentieth Century Club of
Weatherford
Twentieth Century Culture Club of
Amarillo
Twentieth Century Culture Club of
Canadian
Twentieth Century Culture Club of
Normangee
Twentieth Century Culture Club of
Pampa

Twentieth Century Culture Club of Perryton

Twentieth Century Daughter's Club of Snyder

Twentieth Century Reading Club of Lufkin

Twentieth Century Round Table of Devine

Twentieth Century Study Club of Abilene

Twentieth Century Study Club of Burkburnett

Twentieth Century Study Club of Corpus Christi

Twentieth Century Study Club of Garland

Twentieth Century Study Club of Justin

Twentieth Century Study Club of Kenedy

Twentieth Century Study Club of Midland

Twentieth Century Study Club of Seagraves

Twentieth Century Study Club of Spur

Twentieth Century Study Club of Sunray

Twenty-Four Club of Crystal City

Twenty-One Study Club of Desdemona

Twenty-Six Literary Club of Houston

Twilight Civic and Cultural Club of Fort Worth

Two Arts Club of Corsicana

Tyler Girl's Forum

Tyler Woman's Forum

Ultie Dulcie Club of Seymour

Ultie Dulcie Club of Jacksonville

United Woman's Study Club of Gainesville

Unity Study Club of Claude

Unity Study Club of Tulia

Universal Writers Society

University Club of Austin

University Study Club of Burkburnett

University Study Club of Canyon

University Women's Club of Dallas

Up to the Minute Readers of Hempstead

Uterpean Club of Fort Worth

Valley "J" Study Club of Junction

Van Fine Arts Club

Van Horn Junior Woman's Club

Van Horn Woman's Club

Varietas Study Club of Pampa

Verdia C. Gratts Arts & Cultural Club of Fort Worth

Versecrafters' Guild

Verse-Makers Club of Austin

Victoria Junior Woman's Club

Victoria Women's Club

Victory Study Club of San Angelo

Waco Junior Woman's Club

Waco Literary Club

Waco Press Club

Walker's Art Club of El Paso

Wallis Tax Study Club of Canton

Walton Study Club of Athens

Waskom Study Club

Wasson Study Club of Denver City

Waverly Club of Sulphur Springs

Wednesday Afternoon Club of Claude

Wednesday Book Club of Wills Point

Wednesday Club of Abilene

Wednesday Club of Arp

Wednesday Club of Baird

Wednesday Club of Bartlett

Wednesday Club of Canton

Wednesday Club of Fort Worth
Wednesday Club of Galveston
Wednesday Club of Granbury
Wednesday Club of Hearne
Wednesday Club of Hempstead
Wednesday Club of Jacksonville
Wednesday Club of Kemp
Wednesday Club of Rosebud
Wednesday Club of Waco
Wednesday Club of West
Wednesday Club of Wills Point
Wednesday Junior Club of
    Galveston
Wednesday Morning Club of Dallas
Wednesday Review Club of Killeen
Wednesday Study Club of Arp
Wednesday Study Club of Bryson
Wednesday Study Club of Canton
Wednesday Study Club of Corpus
    Christi
Wednesday Study Club of Cross
    Plains
Wednesday Study Club of
    Frankston
Wednesday Study Club of Frisco
Wednesday Study Club of
    Henderson
Wednesday Study Club of
    Jacksonville
Wednesday Study Club of
    Joinerville
Wednesday Study Club of
    Monahans
Wednesday Study Club of Paducah
Wednesday Study Club of Roanoke
Wednesday Study Club of Rosebud
Wednesday Study Club of Roscoe
Wednesday Study Club of Sanger
Wednesday Study Club of Slaton
Wednesday Study Club of West
Wednesday Study Club of Wheeler

Weinert Study Club of Weinert
West Park Woman's Club of San
    Angelo
West Texas Press Association
Wharton Woman's Club
What to Read Club of San Benito
Whiteface Study Club
Wichita Falls Poetry Society
Wichita Falls Poetry Study Club
Wichita Falls Woman's Forum
Wimodaughsis Club of Sterling City
Wink Study Club of Wink
Wink Wednesday Study Club
Winodausis Club of Sterling City
Wise Community Study Club of
    Mabank
Woman's Book Club of Canyon
Woman's City Club of Houston
Woman's Club Junior of Atlanta
Woman's Club of Alpine
Woman's Club of Amarillo
Woman's Club of Anson
Woman's Club of Aransas Pass
Woman's Club of Arlington
Woman's Club of Atlanta
Woman's Club of Austin
Woman's Club of Ballinger
Woman's Club of Barnhart
Woman's Club of Baytown
Woman's Club of Beaumont
Woman's Club of Big Spring
Woman's Club of Brownwood
Woman's Club of Bryan
Woman's Club of Caldwell
Woman's Club of Canadian
Woman's Club of Carrizo Springs
Woman's Club of Cleveland
Woman's Club of Corpus Christi
Woman's Club of Cotulla
Woman's Club of Crane
Woman's Club of Dayton

Woman's Club of El Campo
Woman's Club of El Paso
Woman's Club of Galveston
Woman's Club of Georgetown
Woman's Club of Henderson
Woman's Club of Houston
Woman's Club of Jacksboro
Woman's Club of Kingsville
Woman's Club of Kountze
Woman's Club of La Grange
Woman's Club of Laredo
Woman's Club of Littlefield
Woman's Club of Marshall
Woman's Club of Miles
Woman's Club of Nixon
Woman's Club of Orange
Woman's Club of Ozona
Woman's Club of Palestine
Woman's Club of Plainview
Woman's Club of Pleasanton
Woman's Club of Putnam
Woman's Club of Raymondville
Woman's Club of Refugio
Woman's Club of Rio Grande City
Woman's Club of Rocksprings
Woman's Club of Rosenberg
Woman's Club of San Angelo
Woman's Club of San Antonio
Woman's Club of Smithville
Woman's Club of Sour Lake
Woman's Club of Taft
Woman's Club of Teague
Woman's Club of Temple
Woman's Club of Texarkana
Woman's Club of Valentine
Woman's Club of Van Horn
Woman's Club of Waco
Woman's Club of Wharton
Woman's Club of Ysleta
Woman's Culture Club of
   Commerce

Woman's Culture Club of Hedley
Woman's Culture Club of Llano
Woman's Culture Club of Memphis
Woman's Culture Club of Midland
Woman's Culture Club of Port
   Author
Woman's Culture Club of Post
Woman's Culture Club of Quitaque
Woman's Culture Club of San
   Benito
Woman's Culture Club of Snyder
Woman's Culture Club of Teague
Woman's Culture Club of Trenton
Woman's Exchange of Houston
Woman's Fine Arts Club of Anahuac
Woman's Friday Club of Mexia
Woman's Forum of Amarillo
Woman's Forum of Big Springs
Woman's Forum of Commerce
Woman's Forum of Dallas, Literary
   Branch
Woman's Forum of Gatesville
Woman's Forum of Plainview
Woman's Forum of San Angelo
Woman's Junior Club of Carrizo
   Springs
Woman's Literary Club of Dalhart
Woman's Literary Club of Hamlin
Woman's Literary Club of Hico
Woman's Literary Club of Morgan
Woman's Literary Club of Rochester
Woman's Monday Club of Corpus
   Christi
Woman's Reading Club of
   Beaumont
Woman's Reading Club of Center
Woman's Reading Club of Fort
   Worth
Woman's Reading Club of Franklin
Woman's Reading Club of Navasota
Woman's Reading Society of Salado

Woman's Reading Club of
   Woodville
Woman's Review Club of Greenville
Woman's Ruskin Club of Itasca
Woman's Shakespeare Club of
   Denton
Woman's Shakespeare Club of Fort
   Worth
Woman's Study Club of Angleton
Woman's Study Club of Anson
Woman's Study Club of Austin
Woman's Study Club of Belton
Woman's Study Club of Carrollton
Woman's Study Club of Dawson
Woman's Study Club of El Campo
Woman's Study Club of El Dorado
Woman's Study Club of Elysian
   Fields
Woman's Study Club of Garland
Woman's Study Club of Goose
   Creek
Woman's Study Club of Goree
Woman's Study Club of Gorman
Woman's Study Club of Happy
Woman's Study Club of Holland
Woman's Study Club of Krum
Woman's Study Club of Lamesa
Woman's Study Club of Littlefield
Woman's Study Club of Lorenzo
Woman's Study Club of
   Madisonville
Woman's Study Club of Marble
   Falls
Woman's Study Club of May
Woman's Study Club of Maypearl
Woman's Study Club of McCamey
Woman's Study Club of Menard
Woman's Study Club of Midland
Woman's Study Club of Miles
Woman's Study Club of Navasota
Woman's Study Club of Odem

Woman's Study Club of Palmer
Woman's Study Club of Pampa
Woman's Study Club of Pettus
Woman's Study Club of Port Lavaca
Woman's Study Club of Putnam
Woman's Study Club of Runge
Woman's Study Club of San Angelo
Woman's Study Club of Sheffield
Woman's Study Club of Sinton
Woman's Study Club of Smiley
Woman's Study Club of Stanton
Woman's Study Club of Temple
Woman's Study Club of Tulia
Woman's Study Club of Weimer
Woman's Study Club of Weslaco
Woman's Study Club of Whitney
Woman's Study Club of Woodville
Woman's Tuesday Club of Mission
Woman's Wednesday Club of Fort
   Worth
Woman's Wednesday Club of
   Granbury
Woman's Wednesday Club of
   Midland
Woman's Wednesday Study Club of
   Bartlett
Woman's Wednesday Study Club of
   Belton
Woman's Wednesday Study Club of
   Roscoe
Women's Club of Fort Worth
Women's Club of Menard
Women's Culture Club of Post
Women's Culture Club of Quitaque
Women's Self Culture Club of Waco
Women's Study Club of Alvin
Women's Study Club of Angleton
Women's Study Club of Chico
Women's Study Club of Holland
Women's Study Club of Houston
Women's Thursday Club of Dublin

Women's Wednesday Club of Kemp
Wortham Study Club of Wortham
Writers Club of Port Arthur
Writers' Department of the
    Woman's Forum of Wichita Falls
Writer's Round Table of Corpus
    Christi
XIT Study Club of Springlake
XIX Century Club of Pilot Point
XLI Club of Gainesville
XX Century Club of Alice
XX Century Club of Brady
XX Century Club of Brownwood
XX Century Club of Cisco
XX Century Club of Corsicana
XX Century Club of Corpus Christi
XX Century Club of Cumby
XX Century Club of Daingerfield
XX Century Club of Kenedy
XX Century Club of La Feria
XX Century Club of Lubbock
XX Century Club of Mineola
XX Century Club of Paris
XX Century Club of Pecos
XX Century Round Table of Devine
XXI Club of Abilene
XXI Club of Denison
XXXIII Club of Abilene
XXXVI Club of Ballinger
Yamparika Club of Vernon
Yoakum Literary Club
Yoakum Study Club
Young Ladies Literary Club of La
    Porte
Young Matrons Inc. Aux. El Paso
Young Matrons Junior Study Club
    of Morton
Young Men's Literary Society of
    Dallas
Young Woman's Club of Cleveland
Young Woman's Club of Decatur

Young Woman's Dramatic Club of
    El Paso
Ysleta Junior Woman's Club
Ysleta Woman's Club
Yucca Study Club of Penwell
Zend Avesta of Timpson
Zend Avesta of West
Zeta Delta Study Club of Colorado
    City
Zetagatian Study Club of Colorado
Zetagathian Study Club of Justin
Zetagathian Study Club of
    Colorado City
Zonta Study Club of Junction
1881 Club of Jefferson
'93 Club of Fort Worth
'99 Club of Mt. Pleasant
1904 Art Club of Conroe
1904 Club Juniorettes of Quanah
1904 Club of Quanah
1905 Hyperion Club of Big Spring
1906 Art Club of Houston
1906 Art Club of Paris
1913 Study Club of Memphis
1916 Ever Ready Club of Galveston
'17 Club of Newcastle
1917 Study Club of Spur
1919 Study Club of Hedley
1920 Club of Ranger
1920 Study Club of Lone Oak
'21 Club of Abilene
'21 Club of Desdemona
1921 Literary Club of Leonard
1921 Study Club of Colorado
1921 Study Club of Colorado City
1921 Study Club of Corpus Christi
1921 Study Club of Rotan
1922 Study Club of Wichita Falls
1923 Junior Study Club of Iowa Park
1923 Study Club of Crosbyton
1923 Study Club of Iowa Park

1923 Study Club of Paducah
1923–51 Study Club of Paducah
1924 Study Club of Wellington
1925 Study Club of Silverton
1926 Book Club of Clarendon
1926 Literary Club of Houston
1926 Study Club of Levelland
1927 Study Club of Wichita Falls
1928 Study Club of Dalhart
1929 Study Club of Floydada
1929 Study Club of Turkey
1930 Hyperion Club of Big Spring
1930 Study Club of Wichita Falls
1931 Study Club of Spur
'32 Club of San Angelo
1932 Study Club of Dumas
1932 Study Club of Estelline
'32 Wednesday Club of Abilene
1933 Culture Club of Wichita Falls
1933 Self Culture Club of Wichita
  Falls
1933 Study Club of Jefferson
1933 Study Club of Lubbock
1933 Study Club of Megargel
1934 Culture Club of McLean

1934 Study Club of Floydada
1934 Study Club of Wichita Falls
1935 Club of Shamrock
1935 Little Women Study of Sudan
1935 Sorosis Club of Paducah
1935 Study Club of Abernathy
1935 Study Club of Sudan
1935 Study Club of Wichita Falls
1936 Study Club of Austin
1936 Study Club of Avinger
1936 Study Club of Lampasas
1936 Study Club of Morton
1937 Study Club of Ladonia
1938 Study Club of Carbon
1938 Study Club of Vega
1938 Study Club of Vernon
'39 Club of Baytown
1939 Review Club of Sterling City
'39 Study Club of Goose Creek
1939 Study Club of Memphis
1939 Study Club of Muleshoe
'39 Study Club of Throckmorton
1940 Study Club of Brownwood
1940 Study Club of Burkett
1940 Study Club of Iowa Park

NOTES

Introduction

1. T. J. Pilgrim's quote appears in Davis Foute Eagleton, "Survey of the Field," in *Writers and Writings of Texas,* 8. Eagleton's claims that men of intelligence resided on the frontier are supported by Vaida Stewart Montgomery, *A Century with Texas Poets and Poetry;* Esse Forrester-O'Brien, *Art and Artists of Texas;* Hilton Greer, *Voices of the Southwest;* Cadwell Walton Raines, *Bibliography of Texas: . . . since 1536.* Even Olmsted documents encounters with a few cultured residents on his journey through Texas.

2. C. E. Evans portrays the leaders of the Republic of Texas as educated men in *The Story of Texas Schools.* D. W. Meinig pictures early Texas as a place of cultural diversity in *Imperial Texas,* notes that the Austin and Peters colonies were made up of cultured individuals, and suggests that Dallas's position as a cultural center began with the establishment of the utopian community La Reunion. In *Texas Prose Writings,* Sister M. Agatha laments the fact that the figure of the unruly adventurer has obscured other, equally valid, frontier figures.

3. For more information about Prairie Blume, see Annie Romberg, "A Texas Literary Society of Pioneer Days," *Southwestern Historical Quarterly* 60 (1947–48): 61–65. For information on the club at Four Mile Prairie, see Elise Waerenskjold, *The Lady with the Pen,* 3, 46–47.

4. See Paddy Dion Westergard Amyett, "A History of Literary Societies at Baylor University" (master's thesis, Baylor University, 1963), 125–26. For information about Amasavourien, see "Woman's Reading Society Formed at Salado College Believed First in State," *Dallas Morning News,* May 7, 1928.

5. In a telephone interview by the author, May 10, 1995, Dr. Paul Christensen told of his discovery that more than one hundred poetry societies were meeting in Texas at the turn of the century. He speculated that Texas had more literary societies per capita than any other state at that time. For information about the national club movement, see Joseph E. Gould, *The Chautauqua Movement,* 3–12. See T. R. Fehrenbach, *Lone Star,* 323, 595, on the state of cultural development on the frontier. For the contribution of clubs to developing culture, see Amyett, "History of Literary Societies," 125–26. Between 1867 and 1890, literary societies at Baylor University presented the first plays, endowed the first scholarships, published the first publications, and organized the first choral groups, orchestras, and debate teams of the colleges. See also "Texas Federation of Women's Clubs: Contributions to the Humanities — Library and Literacy," Texas Federation of Women's Clubs Inventory, MSS20. Texas women's clubs influenced the formation of the Texas Library Commission in 1897, established 85 percent of the state's libraries, influenced the formation of the Texas Arts and Humanities Commission, urged that art and music be taught in schools, established art scholarships, and arranged for a traveling art gallery. Information in the Texas Federation of Women's Club's repository also indicates that the establishment of a women's college in Denton in 1901 was a direct result of an 1897 call by Texas club women for an institution of higher learning for women.

6. In "The New Southwest," *Southwest Review* 1 (Oct., 1924): 91–99, Jay Hubbell refers to the increased interest in cultural activities as "a literary awakening." David Russell makes similar comments in "From the Incoming President," in *A Book of the Year — 1941*, 3–4. Lon Tinkle talks in terms of a "Southwestern renaissance" that took place in the twenties and thirties in *An American Original*, 116–220, and names J. Frank Dobie and John McGinnis as major voices of this movement. Tinkle recounts the antics of the "Texas Institute of the Unlettered," a group that included Dobie, Lea, Webb, and Dallas millionaires DeGolyer and McDermott. This group staged a stag event the morning after the annual Texas Institute of Letters (TIL) meeting "to blow off steam and to have at breakfast the culled genuine talent separated from the hitchhikers, the hangers-on and, above all, the, 'lady poets.'" In Grider and Rodenberger, *Texas Women Writers*, 26, Rodenberger attributes the term "pink tea poets" to Dobie, but the original source of this quote could not be located.

7. David D. Medina, "Reading in the Margins," *Sallyport* (spring, 1995): 27–31. Elizabeth Long, researcher of current reading clubs in Texas, states that literary clubs historically have been part of middle-class experience at least since the Reformation, but these clubs are difficult to track because so many participants have conducted meetings informally and have kept few written records.

8. See Fannie C. Potter, *History of the Texas Federation of Women's Clubs, 1918–1938*, 343; see also Theodora Penny Martin, *The Sound of Our Own Voices*, 3–4; Karen Blair, *The Clubwoman as Feminist*, 96.

9. In Medina, "Reading in the Margins," Long attributes the neglect of literary clubs to the fact that male scholars have not considered groups made up primarily of females to be important subjects for cultural studies. In Michael L. Gillette, *Texas in Transition*, 16–17, Diane Hobby notes that bibliographies of Texas writing edited by males have not given women writers ad-

equate attention. For proof of the validity of Hobby's statement, see J. Frank Dobie, *A Guide to Life and Literature of the Southwest;* A. C. Greene, *The Fifty Best Books on Texas;* Don Graham, James Ward Lee, and William T. Pilkington, *The Texas Literary Tradition;* James Ward Lee, *Classics of Texas Fiction;* C. L. Sonnichsen, *The Southwest in Life and Literature;* and Martin Shockley, *Southwest Writers Anthology.* See also Larry McMurtry, "Afterword," *My First Thirty Years,* by Edna Gertrude Beasley, 339–40. McMurtry writes that Beasley's account of her life in West Texas is an "embarrassing corrective to critics" like him who have claimed that writing in Texas began with Dobie.

10. A strong argument could be made that literary standards set as the ideal for Southwestern literature by males resulted in the exclusion of female writers. Such an argument would support claims by feminist scholars Elaine Showalter, Nina Baym, Margaret Ezell, and Tillie Olsen that writings by women do not meet male-instituted standards in regard to genre and subject matter. Another argument could be made that by joining together in writing clubs and participating in activities they considered to be play instead of work, Texas women developed "emancipatory strategies," as the term is described by Patricia Yaeger in *Honey-Mad Women.* Such "strategies" enabled these women to discover new avenues of expression, to alter their self-images, and to form new expectations about their writing. This reconstruction of their desires brought about changes in their lives and, eventually, in the society at large. A third argument could be made that the process wherein educated citizens moved into an unsettled region, formed literary clubs that operated on the margins of a primitive and materialistic society, and in turn enriched the entire community is proof of the theory of liminality presented by Victor Turner in *From Ritual to Theatre.*

11. See Lenore Hoffmann and Deborah Rosenfelt, *Teaching Women's Literature,* 7. See also Natalie Zemon Davis, *Fiction in the Archives,* 3; Dominick LaCapra, *Rethinking Intellectual History,* 60; Margaret Ezell, *Writing Women's Literary History,* 11–13.

12. Determining the quality of a work of literature is a complicated endeavor that involves value judgments that vary from individual to individual and from one time period to another. See Wayne C. Booth, "Who Is Responsible in Ethical Criticism, and for What?" *The Company We Keep: An Ethics of Fiction,* 125–55. To complicate matters even more, feminist literary scholars argue that the imposition of male-dominated standards of criticism upon literature by women has resulted in the exclusion of a whole body of literature from British and American canons. See Nina Baym, "Melodramas of Beset Manhood"; Margaret Ezell, *Writing a Woman's Literary History;* Caroll Smith-Rosenberg, *Disorderly Conduct;* Elaine Showalter, *A Literature of Their Own;* Sandra M. Gilbert and Susan Gubar, *No Man's Land.*

Chapter 1. The Manuscript Club of Wichita Falls

An earlier version of this material appeared in the April, 1994, issue of the *Southwest Historical Quarterly.* Reprinted here courtesy of Texas State Historical Association, Austin. All rights reserved.

1. Much information that appears in this chapter was taken from interviews and correspondence with former Manuscript Club members and daughters and friends of former members: Peggy Schachter, Bert Kruger Smith, Margaret Dvorken, Jenny Louise Hindman, Emerett Sanford Miles, Helen Sanford, Mary Sanford Gordon, and Laura Faye Yauger.

2. Quote from Jenny Louise Hindman, interview by author, Wichita Falls, Feb. 6, 1991.

3. "Manuscript Club Proves Methods by Successes," *Wichita Falls Daily Times,* n.d. Many details about the Manuscript Club's early history were taken from this undated and unattributed newspaper clipping in the scrapbook of former club member Peggy Schachter.

4. Quote from Peggy Schachter, interview by author, Dallas, Feb. 11, 1991.

5. "Manuscript Club Proves Methods."

6. Winifred Sanford, letter to Margaret Cousins, Oct. 5, 1945.

7. "Manuscript Club Proves Methods."

8. Mencken wrote seventeen letters of praise and encouragement to Sanford that reside with the Sanford family. Reviews of Kruger's work are located in Fania Kruger Papers, Harry Ransom Humanities Research Center, University of Texas at Austin. Auslander's praises of Yauger's poem are enumerated in "Manuscript Club Proves Methods." Bert Kruger Smith told of Engle's praise for her mother's work in a telephone interview by the author, July 6, 1993. For Anne Pence Davis's accomplishments, see Anne Lee Williams, "Distinguished Writer to Teach Creative Writing Courses at SMU," *Wichita Falls Times,* Jan. 11, 1970, C15. For proof of Sanford's and Yauger's TIL membership, see Rebecca Smith, "Minutes of the 1936 Meeting"; for proof of Kruger's and Davis's membership, see Rebecca Smith, "Minutes of the 1937 Meeting." William Vann, in *The Texas Institute of Letters 1936–1966,* 10–11, tells that Sanford assisted Karle Wilson Baker in teaching a fiction symposium at a TIL meeting. For Sanford's activities as a teacher of writing, see Winifred Sanford, "Writing the Short Story," *Southwester* 1 (Oct., 1935): 26–27.

9. In separate interviews, the daughters of Sanford and Kruger stated that Manuscript Club members in general and their mothers in particular placed family duties ahead of their writing. In a series of articles on Texas writers that appeared in the *Dallas Journal* and featured Yauger on March 20, 1935,

Kruger on June 5, 1935, and Sanford on July 8, 1936, Hilton Greer also indicates that these women did not think of themselves as professional writers.

10. "Manuscript Club Proves Methods."

11. In Helen Sanford's letter to Betty Wiesepape, July 3, 1993, she tells that scholars' interest in Winifred Sanford's fiction was stimulated when Suzanne Comer of Southern Methodist University Press discovered the Sanford family's edition of *Windfall and Other Stories*. SMU Press published a new edition in 1988 as part of the Southwest Life and Letters series.

See Don Graham, "Second Reader's Report," Mar. 31, 1987. Graham writes: "Next to Katherine Anne Porter, she seems to be the best woman short story writer of that era, but more than that, she seems the best short story writer next to Porter, gender aside. I can think of no one in Texas letters at that time who was doing work to match hers or Porter's. Certainly not G. S. Perry or J. Frank Dobie. . . . Sanford is a strong regionalist from the Thirties . . . she is a real writer, not a hack."

See also William T. Pilkington, "First Reader's Report," n.d. Pilkington writes: "The strong point of this little book is that it recovers a truly gifted "Texas Writer" that very few people have even heard of. . . . It seems a real loss not only to Texas literature, but to American literature . . . that Mrs. Sanford chose to give up her literary career so early in life."

In addition, see Dan Baldwin, review of *Windfall and Other Stories*, by Winifred Sanford, *Legacies I* 1 (1989): 39; S. S. Moorty, "Stories Reveal the Twenties as More Than Gin and Flappers," *Texas Books in Review* 9, no. 2 (1989): 14–15; Clay Reynolds, review of *Windfall and Other Stories*, by Winifred Sanford, *Western American Literature* 25, no. 2 (1989): 177–78; Don Graham, "The Short Story in Texas," p. xiv.

12. See Daniel Yergan, *The Prize*, 167–73; see also Walter Rundell, Jr., *Early Texas Oil*, 94–96.

13. Rundell, *Early Texas Oil*, 95–96, 110.

14. Ibid., 96.

15. Quote from Margaret Dvorken, interview by author, Wichita Falls, Feb. 6, 1991.

16. These quotes were taken from Dvorken interview and Hindman interview, respectively.

17. Quote from Hindman interview.

18. See Hilton Greer, "Poets of Texas: XXXVII Fania Kruger Different and Effective," *Dallas Journal*, June 5, 1935, 2.2; Myra Lindenberg, "Fania Kruger Returns to School," *The Justice*, 4.

19. One notable exception is Kruger's poem "Overnight Oil Town," in *Cossack's Laughter*, 76.

20. This information was taken from unattributed material in Kruger Papers.

21. Quote from Dvorken interview.

22. Ibid.

23. Ibid. Dvorken stated that characters and events in Davis's novel were so closely modeled after the Wichita Falls store that citizens became upset when the novel was published. For information about Davis, see the following newspaper articles in the Anne Pence Davis Collection, Manuscripts, Library of Special Collections, Western Kentucky University, Bowling Green; Bill Warren, "Mrs. Anne Pence Davis Is Inspired to Write Her First Book after Conversing with Young Bookworm," *Park City Daily News,* Feb. 16, 1936, n.p.; "Anne Pence Davis Again Honored," unattributed article, n.p.; Mabel L. Rossbach, "Department Store," review of *The Customer Is Always Right,* by Anne Pence Davis, *New York Times,* Mar. 24, 1940, n.p.; "Scores Another Hit," unattributed article, n.p.; see also Williams, "Distinguished Writer," n.p.

24. See "Scores Another Hit," n.p.; see also "Anne Pence Davis Again Honored," n.p.

25. See Williams, "Distinguished Writer," n.p.

26. See Greer, "Poets of Texas: XXXVII."

27. See Winifred Sanford, letter to Margaret Cousins.

28. See Greer, "Poets of Texas XXVI Fay M. Yauger Distinguished Ballad-Maker," *Dallas Journal,* Mar. 20, 1935, 1.6.

29. Additional information about Yauger's writing was taken from an untitled, unattributed article in the Laura Faye Yauger file, Texas/Dallas History and Archives, Dallas Public Library.

30. Greer, "Poets of Texas XXVI."

31. J. Frank Dobie, letter to William H. Vann, Sept. 28, 1936. See also "Texas Poet Will Be Guest Artist," n.p. This unattributed article indicates that Yauger's poetry received high praise from critics Joseph Auslander, Charles Hanson Towne, and William Rose Benet.

32. See Greer, "Poets of Texas XXVI."

33. Laura Faye Yauger, letter to William Vann, July 7, 1936, Texas Institute of Letters Records, Southwestern Writers Collection, Southwest Texas State University, San Marcos.

34. Quote from Hindman interview. Former Manuscript Club members could not remember exactly when the club disbanded, and no record of this information could be located.

35. Anne Pence Davis was the only member of the club whose name was on file in the archives of the *Wichita Falls Times,* and only one article resides in the file. Librarians at the Kemp Public Library where the Manuscript Club met were surprised to learn of the club's existence when informed by the author.

36. Quote from Hindman interview.

37. In 1935–36, Greer wrote a weekly series of articles for the *Dallas Journal* that featured various Texas poets and writers. In these articles Greer mentions the names of a number of clubs to which the featured writers belonged. In "Prose Writers of Texas: XXXX Winifred Sanford Distinguished Realist," *Dallas Journal,* July 8, 1936, 2.1, Greer refers to the Manuscript Club as "one of the most fruitful literary organizations" in the state. See also Crystal Ragsdale, *Women of Texas,* 248. Ragsdale tells that Texas author Dorothy Scarborough founded a writer's group called the Modern Writer's Group at Baylor University in Waco.

38. A perusal of newspapers published in Dallas, Fort Worth, Amarillo, and Houston in the 1930s revealed that groups of Penwomen met regularly in these Texas cities. See Karen Blair's introduction to *The Woman's Club of El Paso,* by Mary Cunningham, vii–viii.

39. See Mrs. J. C. Croly, *The History of the Woman's Club Movement in America,* 1094–1107; Mrs. P. W. Romain, Mrs. Leon Simpson, Mrs. Jack Akin, and Mrs. C. A. Bickley, *History of the Texas Federation of Women's Clubs 1938–1988.* These books, compiled by members of women's clubs, contain general historical information about the women's club movement in Texas.

40. See Blair, *The Clubwoman as Feminist,* 57–71; Martin, *Sound of Our Own Voices,* 48–59; Sheila M. Rothman, *Woman's Proper Place,* 64–66. See also Blair, introduction to *The Woman's Club of El Paso,* vii–xii.

Chapter 2. The Makers of Dallas

1. Dr. Edyth Renshaw, *SMU Video Oral History Interview,* with Judy Mohraz, June 20, 1983, Dallas. Renshaw relates that no creative writing classes were offered at SMU in the early 1920s, but creative projects were encouraged by professors in the English Department.

2. For information about the club's name, see Jay B. Hubbell, "The Makers," *Prairie Pegasus,* n.p.; see also "Poetry Society Elects Members," *Semi-Weekly Campus,* Apr. 29, 1925, 3. For information about the first meeting, see "Poetry Club Organized on Last Friday," *Campus,* Apr. 6, 1922, 1.

3. Information about the Makers' backgrounds came from Mildred Bond, telephone interview by author, July 2, 1996. See also Hilton Greer, "Poets of Texas XXVII William Russell Clark," *Dallas Journal,* Mar. 27, 1935, 10; Margaret Royalty Edwards, "David Russell," *Poets Laureate of Texas,* by Margaret Royalty Edwards, 37; "Rites Monday for Ottys E. Sanders," *Dallas Morning News,* Mar. 14, 1993, A:43; "Services Set for Ruth Sanders," *Dallas Morning News,* Sept. 25, 1985, A:26; "Winsett, Marvin Davis," in *Contemporary Authors,* ed. James Ethridge and Barbara Kapala, 1015–16. Hubbell's opinion of the Makers appears in Hubbell, "The Makers," n.p.

4. The quote by Crane is from Vaida Stewart Montgomery, "Texas Poets of the Past," in *A Century with Texas Poets,* ed. Vaida Stewart Montgomery, 16–17. For information about the history of Dallas, see Willie Newberry Lewis, "1886–1896," in *History of the Dallas Shakespeare Club: 1886–1970,* 2–3.

5. Quote from Mildred Bond interview. See also Don B. Graham, "Literature," in *The New Texas Handbook in Six Volumes,* 225–26. Graham describes poetry written in Texas during those early years: "Texas poetry flourished, but without distinction. Poets . . . were often influenced by minor poets of the past . . . poems are cloyed with phony archaic diction. . . . Few actually drew upon the Texas landscape or culture or people."

6. See Hilton Greer, "The Poetry Society of Texas," in *A Century with Texas Poets,* ed. Vaida Stewart Montgomery, 23–24.

7. See Hubbell, "The New Southwest," 93. Hubbell's statement comparing students' interest in poetry to their interest in football is almost certainly hyperbole, for in "Forty Girls Are Practicing for New Football Squad," *Semi-Weekly Campus,* Nov. 4, 1925, 1, forty girls tried out for the SMU girls' football squad. Evidence indicates that total membership in the Makers never exceeded twenty. For information on cultural activity in Dallas in the 1920s, see Rick Stewart, *Lone Star Regionalism: The Dallas Nine and Their Circle, 1928–1945,* 17– 40.

8. For information about Hubbell's importance to the Makers, see George Bond and Ottys Sanders, "Jay Broadus Hubbell, 1885–1979," Jay Broadus Hubbell Papers, Rare Book, Manuscript, and Special Collections, Duke University, Durham, 4. For evidence of Hubbell's desire to become a poet, see Jay B. Hubbell, *Lucinda, a Book of Memories,* 13–14. In *South and Southwest: Literary Essays and Reminiscences by Jay B. Hubbell,* 20–21, Hubbell writes that whenever someone complimented his editorial work, he recalled Edward Fitzgerald's words: "The power of writing one fine line transcends all the Able-Editor ability in the ably-edited Universe."

9. See Hubbell, *Lucinda,* 13–14.

10. See Hubbell, *Lucinda,* 15–17; see also "Zeek and Hubbell to Attend Meet," *Semi-Weekly Campus,* Dec. 18, 1926, 1; Bond and Sanders, "Jay Broadus Hubbell," 2–4.

11. See George Bond and Ottys Sanders, "A Tribute to a Giant among Men: In Memory of Jay B. Hubbell, 1885–1979," Hubbell Papers, 4. For infor-

mation on the history of the *Southwest Review,* see Thomas F. Gossett, "A History of the *Southwest Review:* 1915–1942" (master's thesis, Southern Methodist University, 1948), 14–38, 79–104. For a year after Hubbell left SMU, Louisiana State University (LSU) and SMU cosponsored the *Southwest Review* until philosophical differences between LSU editors Donald Davidson and Robert Penn Warren and the SMU staff brought an end to this cooperative venture.

12. See Bond and Sanders, "A Tribute." Additional information was taken from Robert Bond, telephone interview by author, June 26, 1996.

13. The stated objective of the Makers appears in "Poetry Club Organized," 1. For Hubbell's ulterior objective, see Hubbell, "The Makers," n.p. For information about the student contest, see the following articles: "Poems for Poetry Contest Come from All over Country," *Campus,* May 19, 1922, 4; "S. M. U. Prize Attracts Wide-Spread Notice," *Semi-Weekly Campus,* Apr. 20, 1922, 1; "Poetry Prizes to Be Offered by University," *Campus,* Mar. 9, 1922, 1; "National Poetry Contest Is Sponsored by 'Makers,'" *Semi-Weekly Campus,* Mar. 5, 1926, 1. These articles indicate that a national student poetry contest was uncommon. The quote is from Hilton Greer, "Poets of Texas: XXIV George Bond," *Dallas Journal,* Mar. 6, 1935, 8.

14. Quote from Bond and Sanders, "Jay Broadus Hubbell," 2. Information about Makers meetings was compiled from Hubbell, "The Makers," n.p.; "'Makers' Will Meet at Dinkey Den Wednesday," *Semi-Weekly Campus,* Nov. 4, 1925, n.p.; "Makers to Read Poems for National Contest," *Semi-Weekly Campus,* Mar. 14, 1925, 3; "Poetry Club Meet Held Wednesday," *Semi-Weekly Campus,* Feb. 18, 1928, 1.

15. Quote from Hubbell, "The Makers," n.p.

16. See the following articles in the *Semi-Weekly Campus:* "In the Limelight Today," Mar. 23, 1927, 1; "Poetic Eds and Co-eds Prepare for Poetry Society's National Contest in the Spring," Dec. 17, 1927, 1. In "Poetry Club Organized," 1, Mrs. Magnuson is called an "executive officer," but in Hubbell, "The Makers," n.p., Hubbell states that the club had no regular officers. In *Rotunda 1925,* Southern Methodist University, 205, the caption beneath a picture of the Makers indicates that membership was by invitation only.

17. Mildred Bond interview. Mildred Bond recalled meetings when fifteen to twenty casually dressed students and guests sat around the Hubbell living room, some on the floor, to discuss poetry and eat refreshments. See also "Makers Plan Meeting at Home of Sponsor," *Campus,* Oct. 17, 1923, 4; "Poetry Club Meet Held Wednesday," 4.

18. For comments by Bond and Sanders, see "A Tribute," 2–3, and "Jay Broadus Hubbell," 2. For Hubbell's comments, see Hubbell, "The Makers," n.p.

19. The original article appeared in the *Buccaneer* and is quoted in "The Makers," *Semi-Weekly Campus,* Dec. 3, 1924, 2.

20. For information about this contest, see "Poems for Poetry Contest," 4; see also Hubbell, "The Makers," n.p.; Ruth Patterson Maddox, *Building SMU 1915–1957,* 128; Ima H. Herron, "A Backward Glance," *Mustang,* May/June, 1964, 6.

21. For George Bond's accomplishments, see Florence Elbert Barnes, *Texas Writers of Today,* 83, 367, 449, 475; "Bond Becomes Editor of Review," *Semi-Weekly Campus,* Oct. 3, 1925, 1; "Bond, Dr. George D., Death and Funeral Announcements," *Dallas Morning News,* May 26, 1986, D:7. For information about Dr. Bond's students, see "On Student Writers and Writing," *Mustang,* Jan./Feb., 1963, 6–7.

22. For information about winners of other contests, see *Announcement of Awards: Prizes for Original Poems,* 1922; *Announcement of Awards: Prizes for Original Poems,* 1923; *Announcement of Awards: Prizes for Original Poems,* 1924. For information about later activities of these winners, see Goldie Capers Smith, *The Creative Arts in Texas: A Handbook of Biography,* 38–39, 43.

23. See Bond and Sanders, "A Tribute"; see also "Poems for Poetry Contest," 4; *Announcement of Awards,* 1922; *Announcement of Awards,* 1923; *Announcement of Awards,* 1924; *Bulletin of Southern Methodist University,* 1925; *Bulletin of Southern Methodist University,* 1926; *Bulletin of Southern Methodist University,* 1927.

24. Information about invited speakers was compiled from Bond and Sanders, "Jay Broadus Hubbell," 2; "Vachel Lindsay Gives Readings Here May 11," *Campus,* May 19, 1922, 1; "Sandburg Gives Recital-Lecture," *Semi-Weekly Campus,* Apr. 2, 1925, 1; "Harriet Monroe Gives Lecture," *Semi-Weekly Campus,* Apr. 18, 1925, 1. These articles indicate that tickets were sold to these literary events.

25. Judges' names were compiled from *Announcement of Awards,* 1922, 3; *Announcement of Awards,* 1923, 3; *Announcement of Awards,* 1924, 2; *Bulletin of SMU,* 1925, 2; *Bulletin of SMU,* 1926, 2; *Bulletin of SMU,* 1927, n.p.

26. Bynner's comment appears in Witter Bynner, "Foreword," in *Prairie Pegasus,* ed. Marie Hemke, George Bond, and Jay B. Hubbell, n.p. Hubbell tells of Sandburg's comments in Hubbell, "The Makers." For information about reviews of the Makers' poetry, see "Magazines Review 'Prairie Pegasus,'" *Semi-Weekly Campus,* Oct. 11, 1929, 1; "'The Makers' Publish SMU Student Poems," *Semi-Weekly Campus,* Sept. 24, 1924, 1.

27. George Bond, Charles Ferguson, Isaac Wade, and Roland Wilkinson were editors of the *Campus,* and Aubrey Burns, David Russell, and Mattie Lou Frye were on the staff. George Bond and Sarah Chokla were on the

staff of *Southwest Review*. For information about the Makers' speaking opportunities, see "Wade Gives Lecture Recital at Trinity," *Semi-Weekly Campus*, Apr. 18, 1925, 4; "Summarize Work of SMU Poets," *Semi-Weekly Campus*, Dec. 5, 1925, 4.

28. The quote by Hubbell is from *Lucinda*, 41.

29. Ibid.

30. The first quote is from "Dr. Hubbell," *Semi-Weekly Campus*, May 4, 1925, 1; the second quote, from Bond and Sanders, "A Tribute," 5.

31. See Jay B. Hubbell, "The Creative Writer and the University, with Special Reference to the 1920s," in *South and Southwest: Literary Essays and Reminiscences by Jay B. Hubbell*, 330–31. Indications that Hubbell continued to support the Makers appear in letters written by former Makers Ottys Sanders, Sarah Chokla, Charles Ferguson, Aubrey Burns, Dawson Powell, and George Bond, located in the Hubbell Papers.

32. Quote from Herron, "A Backward Glance," 9.

33. Quote from "Smith Says Makers Will Not Reorganize," *Semi-Weekly Campus*, Nov. 14, 1928, 1.

34. The quote by Vaida Montgomery is from Vaida Stewart Montgomery, "Dallas Poets," Montgomery Memorial Collection, MSS70, Box 2, FD69, DeGolyer Library, Southern Methodist University, Dallas, 2. The quote by Hilton Greer appears in Hubbell, "Southwest Review 1924–1927," 13.

35. See Hubbell, "The Makers"; see also "The Makers," *Semi-Weekly Campus*, 2. Internal evidence indicates that the author of this latter article was a member of the Makers.

36. For Hubbell's comments, see *Who Are the Major American Writers?*, 330–34. The quote is from Mildred Bond interview.

37. In telephone interviews, both Allen Maxwell and Mildred Bond indicated that they believe Loia Cheaney and Loia Magnuson were names used by the same person. Mildred Bond recalled that this individual married an explorer and made at least one excursion to the Arctic region. The name Loia Cheaney Magnuson appears in Isaac Wade, "Poets of the Future," *Semi-Weekly Campus*, Feb. 4, 1925, 1. Information about other Makers was taken from "Rites Monday for Ottys E. Sanders," A:43; "Charles W. Ferguson, Former Student of S. M. U.," *Semi-Weekly Campus*, Jan. 16, 1929, 1; "Madeline Roach Gets Job as Secretary to Essayist," *Semi-Weekly Campus*, Apr. 14, 1934, 2; Aubrey Burns, letter to Jay B. Hubbell, Apr. 9, 1969, Aubrey Burns file, Hubbell Papers.

38. Mildred Bond interview. For additional information, see Mabel Major and T. M. Pearce, *Southwest Heritage*, 105; "Poetry Club to Honor Member," *Semi-Weekly Campus*, Dec. 10, 1927, 1; Marvin Davis Winsett, "[I]n the

Space Age?" *Dallas Times Herald Magazine,* June 10, 1962, 19; "Sanders, Ottys, Death and Funeral Announcements," *Dallas Morning News,* Mar. 14, 1993, A:43; "Gross, Sarah Chokla," in *Contemporary Authors,* ed. Cynthia R. Fadool, 228; "Harriet Monroe Gives Lecture," 1. The reasons why these individuals returned to Texas could not be fully determined. Financial reversals and losses of jobs as a result of the stock market crash in 1929 and the Great Depression that ensued may have been factors.

39. Information about David Russell was compiled from Edwards, "David Russell," 37–42; Margaret Royalty Edwards, "Russell, David Riley," in *The New Texas Handbook in Six Volumes,* 5:729; "Ex-Texas Poet Laureate, David R. Russell, Dies," *Dallas Morning News,* Mar. 21, 1964, 1:12. In a telephone interview with the author, Mildred Bond stated that theater in Dallas at that time was superior to what the Makers who went to New York saw on Broadway, and they felt quite free to compare New York theater unfavorably to what they had seen in Dallas.

40. See "Gross, Sarah Chokla," 228; "Sarah C. Gross, 69, Editor, Reviewer," *New York Times,* July 21, 1976, A36; Barnes, *Texas Writers of Today,* 473; "Madeline Roach Gets Job as Secretary to Essayist," 2.

41. See "Co-eds Do Not Come Here for Pleasure, Mrs. Hay Says," *Semi-Weekly Campus,* Feb. 21, 1925, 1.

42. Only three editors of Texas anthologies published prior to 1997 list accomplishments of both male and female members of the Makers. All three of these editors are women: V. S. Montgomery, *A Century with Texas Poets;* Barnes, *Texas Writers of Today;* Major and Pearce, *Southwest Heritage.* For a comparison of death notices, see "Willis, Mattie Lou, Death and Funeral Announcements," *Dallas Morning News,* Oct. 25, 1990, A:40; "Harry, Elsie Marie, Deaths and Funeral Announcements," *Dallas Morning News,* July 25, 1993, A:40; "Ex-Texas Poet Laureate, David R. Russell, Dies," 1.12; "Sanders, Ottys, Death and Funeral Announcements," A:43; "Edyth Renshaw Rites Set Monday," *Dallas Morning News,* June 7, 1992, A:41; "Bond, Dr. George D., Death and Funeral Announcements," D7; "Sanders, Ruth Maxwell, Death and Funeral Announcements," *Dallas Morning News,* Sept. 25, 1985, A:26.

43. See Greer, "Poets of Texas: XXVII," 10; Hilton Greer, "Poets of Texas: XLVII Christopher O. Gill, *Dallas Journal,* Aug. 14, 1935, 6; Hilton Greer, "Poets of Texas: XXXV Fred Wilson," *Dallas Journal,* May 22, 1935, 8; Renshaw, *SMU Video Oral History;* Barnes, *Texas Writers of Today,* 199; Major and Pearce, *Southwest Heritage,* 99; "Winsett, Marvin Davis," in *Contemporary Authors,* 1015–16; "Services Set for Ruth Sanders," A.26; "Sanders, Ruth Maxwell, Death and Funeral Announcements," A:26; "Sanders, Ottys, Death and Funeral Announcements," A:43; "Harry, Elsie Marie, Deaths and Funeral Announcements," A:40.

44. Quote from Charles Ferguson, letter to J. B. Hubbell, Mar. 29, 1965, Charles Ferguson file, Hubbell Papers.

45. For information about Charles Ferguson's career, see "Ferguson, Charles W.," in *Contemporary Authors,* ed. Clare D. Kinsman, 265–66; Hilton Greer, "Prose Writers of Texas: XXXVII Charles W. Ferguson," *Dallas Journal,* June 17, 1936, 2.14; "Charles W. Ferguson, Ex-Magazine Editor," *New York Times,* Dec. 20, 1987, L:46; "Annual Awards Given by Texas Institute," *Dallas Morning News,* Mar. 19, 1972, n.p.

46. For information about Gill, see Greer, "Poets of Texas: XLVII," 6.

47. See "Rites Monday for Ottys E. Sanders," A:43; "Sanders, Ottys, Death and Funeral Announcements," A:43; Allen Maxwell interview, by author, July 2, 1996.

48. See: Ottys Sanders, letter to Aubrey Burns, Dec. 19, 1978, Aubrey Burns file, Hubbell Papers.

49. See Burns, letter to Dr. Jay B. Hubbell, Apr. 9, 1969, Hubbell Papers.

50. David Russell, *Sing with Me Now,* 48.

51. John Owen Beaty and Jay B. Hubbell, *An Introduction to Poetry,* 17.

Chapter 3. The Panhandle Pen Women of Amarillo

1. Much of the information that appears in this chapter was taken from personal interviews, telephone conversations, and information provided by Panhandle Pen Women (PPW) members: Nova Bair, Rosemary Kollmar, Ellen Richardson, and Doris Meredith. The quote in the first paragraph is from Laura Hamner, "A Word as to How It Happened," *Panhandle Pen-Points,* Mar. 9, 1922, 1; see also Phoebe K. Warner, "The County Federation," in *Selected Editorials,* 100–103. Warner recounts the history of the Wednesday Afternoon Club of Claude and remarks that women's clubs were "not the least bit popular."

2. Hamner, "A Word," 1.

3. Quote from Mildred J. Cheney, "Pen Women," *Amarillo Sunday News and Globe,* Aug. 14, 1938, n.p. A number of PPW members published work under pen names.

4. See Birdie N. Taylor, "The Women Writers of Texas," *Galveston Daily News,* June 18, 1893 and June 25, 1893, n.p. Taylor profiles sixty-three Texas women writers and lists an additional sixty names. For additional information about early women writers in Texas, see Grider and Rodenberger, *Texas Women Writers,* 5–9.

5. See Mrs. M. R. Walton, *A History of the Texas Woman's Press Association,*10. Walton indicates that female members of the Texas Press Association were literally and figuratively restricted to seats in the balcony. See also Texas State Historical Association, "Texas Press Women," notes in Texas Press Women file, The Woman's Collection, Texas Women's University Library. The Texas Women's Press Association, the first professional organization for women writers in the state, was open to all women writers until 1941, when membership was restricted to women engaged in newspaper work.

6. See Ruby Cook, letter to Mr. Ralph Edwards, Feb., 1959, Laura Hamner Papers, Kilgore Collection, Panhandle-Plains Historical Museum, Canyon. Cook includes the following quote by Hamner: "I was not allowed to go to public school. My father would not allow me to associate with girls who's [*sic*] families were not in our family's social standing. . . . I never knew a working girl until I became one." And PPW member Nova Bair stated in her interview with the author, June 19, 1996, that before Hamner came to the Panhandle, she "never so much as washed out a hanky" but soon learned that everyone in West Texas did things for themselves.

7. For information about the founding of Amarillo, see H. Allen Anderson, "Amarillo, Texas," in *The New Texas Handbook in Six Volumes*, 140–41. Information about Hamner's life was compiled from "Laura V. Hamner, 1871–1968," in *Panhandle Pen Women Golden Anniversary Plus Two: 1920–1972*, 2; Myra Hall, "Laura Hamner: A Woman before Her Time" (Ph.D. diss., University of Houston, 1988); Cook, letter to Mr. Ralph Edwards; Ruby Cook, letter to Mr. Ben Hibbs, Oct. 29, 1958, Hamner Papers.

8. Information about Phoebe K. Warner was compiled from the following sources: Loula Grace Erdman, "Foreword," in *Selected Editorials*, by Phoebe K. Warner, vii–viii; "Among the Outstanding Women in the Past," in *Panhandle Pen Women Golden Anniversary Plus Two: 1920–1972*, 3. Warner's social activism and her sympathy with feminist reformers are evident in editorials such as Warner, "The County Federation," 100–103.

9. See "Minutes of the Panhandle Pen Women Meeting, April 20, 1920," in *Panhandle Pen Women Minutes*, n.p. The names Dollie Buckley, Mrs. Davis, and Miss Marquis appear in these minutes but are omitted from later documents. The reason for this omission is unclear. See also Sophia Meyer, "The Little Things Make Her Life Overflow with Riches," *Amarillo Globe-News*, n.p.; Annette Barrett Dewey, "Panhandle Pen Women's Club," in *The Woman's Viewpoint*, Feb. 19, 1925, n.p.; "Among the Outstanding Women," 3. In "Light and Hitch No. 430," KGNC, Amarillo, July 29, 1951, Hamner writes about founding members: "None of them are writers of note, but all want to be; all feel the need of talking over writing problems with others who have the same unsolved questions."

10. Quote from Hamner, "A Word," 1. Information about Hamner's

terms as president appear in "Panhandle Pen Women, Panhandle Professional Writers Presidents." For additional information about the meeting, see "Minutes, Apr. 20, 1920," n.p.

11. See "Pen Women of Panhandle, New Club Organized," in *Panhandle Pen Women's History 1925–1955,* n.p.

12. Information was compiled from S. Meyer, "Little Things," n.p.; Dewey, "Panhandle Pen Women's Club," n.p.; "Among the Outstanding Women," 3.

13. Quote from Erdman, "Foreword," vii. For information about Hamner, see Laura Hamner, "Talks to Teens," Hamner Papers, n.p. For information about Meyer, see "Miss Meyer Rites Today," *Amarillo Daily News,* Nov. 20, 1968, n.p.

14. Information was compiled from Cheney, "Pen Women"; S. Meyer, "Little Things," n.p.; Dewey, "Panhandle Pen Women's Club," n.p.; "Among the Most Outstanding Women," 3.

15. Information was compiled from "Panhandle Pen Women Perfect Organization," *Amarillo Daily News,* May 2, 1920, n.p.; "Pen Women of Panhandle, New Club Organized," n.p.; "Women Writers of the Panhandle Have Inspiring Motto," *Amarillo Globe-News,* May 12, 1921, n.p.; "Spring Meeting Panhandle Pen Women on Tuesday," *Amarillo Globe-News,* Apr. 19, 1925, n.p.

16. See "Quarterly Convention Held by Panhandle Pen Women," *The Woman's Viewpoint,* Feb., 1925, 19; see also Cheney, "Pen Women," n.p.

17. Quote from "Laura V. Hamner, 1871–1968," 2; see also Hamner, "A Word," 1; "Amarillo Society: Many Persons Attend Meeting of Panhandle Pen Women and Interesting Program Rendered," unattributed article, *Amarillo Globe-News,* Oct., 1922, n.p.; "Panhandle Penwomen's Meeting Is Largely Attended," unattributed article, *Amarillo Globe-News,* n.p.

18. See "Pen Women of Panhandle to Meet," *Fort Worth Star Telegram,* Mar. 2, 1922, n.p.; see also Hamner, "A Word," 1.

19. Information on club proceedings was compiled from "Pen Women Elect New Officers," unattributed article, *Amarillo Globe-News,* n.p.; Alvah F. Meyer, "Panhandle Pen Women Gather for Quarterly Convention," 1921 article, *Amarillo Globe-News,* n.p.; "Spring Meeting," n.p.; "Karle Wilson Baker of Nacogdoches Is Guest of Pen Women Saturday," unattributed article, Mar. 18, 1923, in *Panhandle Pen Women's History,* n.p.; "Spring Convention Is Held by Panhandle Penwomen," 1922 unattributed article, n.p.

20. Information was compiled from "History of the Panhandle Pen Women," in *Pen-Points,* "Quarterly Convention," 19; "Pen Women Plan Quarterly Meet," unattributed article, *Amarillo Globe-News,* n.p.; "Pen Women Elect New Officers," unattributed article, *Amarillo Globe-News,* n.p.

21. See *Constitution and By-Laws of the Panhandle Pen Women 1925,* Panhandle Pen Women Collection, Amarillo Public Library, Amarillo. In personal interviews with the author, June 19, 1996, Pen Women Rosemary Kollmar and Nova Bair stated that, in their opinions, the most successful PPW members in terms of sales have not produced the finest work in terms of literary quality.

22. Quote from Hamner, "A Word," p.1.

23. Ibid. Hamner's words were confirmed by PPW members Kollmar and Bair in personal interviews.

24. See "Bulletin of Meeting of Panhandle Pen Women: July 18, 1950," Panhandle Pen Women Collection, Amarillo Public Library, n.p.

25. See *Constitution and By-Laws.*

26. See "Amarillo Society," n.p.; "Panhandle Pen Women Hold Best Meeting of Year," *Amarillo Daily News,* Oct. 22, 1924, n.p.; Cheney, "Pen Women," n.p.

27. Quote from Sophia Meyer, "College to Take Over Course Founded by Pen Women Here," n.p.

28. Information about the club motto was taken from "Women Writers of Panhandle Have Inspiring Motto," *Amarillo Globe-News,* May 12, 1921, n.p. Information about other contests was compiled from the following: "Short Story Contest to Close Soon," unattributed article, *Amarillo Globe-News,* n.p.; "Pen Women Hold Meeting," n.p.; "Writers Round-Up Slated Next Month," *Amarillo Daily News,* May 29, 1949, n.p.; A. Meyer, "Panhandle Pen Women Gather," n.p.; "Strict Rules Will Govern Contests," unattributed article, in *Panhandle Pen Women History: 1925–1955,* n.p. See also Frederic Nelson Litton, letter to Mrs. Minnie Tims Harper, June 27, 1949, Panhandle Pen Women Collection, Amarillo Public Library; Dewey, "Panhandle Pen Women's Club," n.p.

29. See "January Meeting: Jan. 17, 1933," in *Panhandle Pen Women's History,* n.p.; "History of the Panhandle Pen Women," 6; see also Cheney, "Pen Women," n.p.; "Pen Women Elect New Officers," n.p.; "Pen Women Plan Quarterly Meet," n.p. At some point in the club's history, the number of words required to maintain active member was reduced to 22,500 or twenty-two poems.

30. Quote from Kollmar interview. See also "Bulletin of Meeting: July 18, 1950," n.p.

31. See "Some Milestones in the History of Panhandle Pen Women," in *Panhandle Pen Women Golden Anniversary,* 4–5; see also Cheney, "Pen Women," n.p.; "History of the Panhandle Pen Women," 6.

32. See Cheney, "Pen Women," n.p.; see also *Panhandle Pen Women Golden Anniversary,* 4.

33. Quote from Cheney, "Pen Women," n.p. Additional information was taken from Bair interview.

34. Hamner's quote is from Laura Hamner, "Light and Hitch #431," KGNC, Amarillo, Aug. 5, 1951, 6. For biographical information about Erdman, see "Erdman, Loula Grace," in *Contemporary Authors,* ed. Barbara Harte and Crolyn Riley, 159. See also "Autograph Party Planned Monday," *Amarillo Globe-News,* Sept. 19, 1949, n.p.; "Second Erdman Novel Puts Author in Select Circle," *Amarillo Globe-News,* Sept. 19, 1949, n.p.

35. For details about Erdman's career, see "Erdman, Loula Grace," 159. See also Loula Grace Erdman, *A Time to Write;* "Organization Names Distinguished Members," *Amarillo Globe-News,* n.d.; "Autograph Party Planned Monday," n.p.

36. See "Afternoon Session: April 18, 1933," unattributed article, in *Panhandle Pen Women's History,* n.p.; see also "Bulletin of Meeting of Panhandle Pen Women: July 1948," Panhandle Pen Women Collection, Amarillo Public Library, n.p.; *Panhandle Pen Women Golden Anniversary,* 4.

37. See *Panhandle Pen Women Golden Anniversary,* 5. Additional information was taken from Bair interview.

38. Information about discontinuation of workshops was compiled from Doris Meredith, "6 Women Founded Panhandle Professional Writers in 1920 at Hotel," *Amarillo Sunday News-Globe,* Apr. 16, 1995, 8D. See also Pauline Durrett Robertson, "Bits of History," *PPW Window,* Apr., 1995, 4; "Panhandle Professional Writers to Mark 75th Anniversary in 1995," *Amarillo Globe-News,* Apr. 27, 1994, n.p.

39. For information about Nace's writing career, see "Among the Outstanding Women," 3; Meredith, "6 Women Founded Panhandle Professional Writers," 8D.

40. See Erdman, *A Time to Write,* 33–44.

41. For information about Chinn, see "Chinn, Laurene Chambers," in *Contemporary Authors,* ed. James Elhridge and Barbara Kopala, 173. See also "Spelling Bee Is Now Story," Aug. 7, 1949, *Amarillo Globe-News,* 7; "Panhandle Woman Is Winner," *Amarillo Globe-News,* unattributed article, n.p.

42. See Erdman, *A Time to Write,* 33–44.

43. See Robertson, "Bits of History," 4; see also "Panhandle Writers to Mark 75th Anniversary," n.p. Some other writers who have spoken at Frontiers in Writing conferences are John M. Allen, Sam Brown, Thomas Clark, Ed Eakin, Wallace Exman, John Erickson, Peggy Fielding, Richard Lederer, Sharyn McCrumb, D. R. Meredith, Howard Nemerov, Mary Ann O'Rourk, Marcia Preston, Lee Pennington, Carol Sobieski, and Dwight Swain.

44. Community support of PPW is evident in "Amarillo Society"; "Minutes of Panhandle Pen Women Meeting, Feb. 23, 1921," in *Panhandle Pen Women Book One Reports, 1920–1926,* n.p.; "Writers Group to Mark 75th Birthday," *Amarillo Daily News,* Mar. 31, 1995, n.p.

45. For information about PPW's contributions to the community, see "Among the Outstanding Women," 3; "Minutes of the Panhandle Pen Women, Oct. 12, 1921," in *Panhandle Pen Women Book One Reports,* n.p.; "Quarterly Convention," 19; "Writers Round-Up Slated Next Month," n.p.; "Amarillo Society" n.p. Additional information was taken from Ellen Richardson, interview by author, June 20, 1996; and Jerry Bradley, interview by author, June 19, 1996.

46. For Hamner's contribution as historian, see Hall, "Laura V. Hamner," n.p.; "Laura V. Hamner 1871–1968," 2; Cook, letter to Mr. Ralph Edwards; Cook, letter to Mr. Ben Hibbs.

47. See Cook, letter to Mr. Ben Hibbs. The story of Hamner's efforts to get her first book adopted for use in Texas schools appears in a number of sources, but accounts vary as to her means of travel and the identity of state officials she visited. Most versions state that she traveled by car, but Cook tells that Hamner traveled by train, bus, wagon, caboose, and even rode atop a farmer's load of hay on one occasion to reach her destination. The officials she visited at their homes are variously identified as being from the State Board of Education, the Texas School Board, and eleven members from the State Textbook Committee. All sources are in agreement that, because of Hamner's efforts, the book was adopted as a seventh-grade text for use in public schools in Texas and she paid off the loan she took out to pay for publishing the book. Several sources indicate that she sold over thirty-nine thousand copies of *No Gun Man of Texas.*

48. See Hamner, *Light 'n Hitch,* 126–27.

49. Quote from Peggy Williamson, "Laura Hamner," *Light and Hitch,* KGNC, Amarillo, Dec. 31, 1950, 5. See also "Organization Names Distinguished Members," n.p.

50. Loula Grace Erdman, *The Edge of Time* (Fort Worth: Texas Christian Univ. Press, 1988), dedication page. See also Erdman, *A Time to Write,* 141–65, 186–96.

51. See *Panhandle Pen Women Golden Anniversary,* 5; Hamner, "Light and Hitch No. 430"; S. Meyer, "College to Take Over Course," n.p.

52. See *Panhandle Pen Women Golden Anniversary,* 5; see also *Panhandle Professional Writers: 1994,* Private Collection, Nova Bair, Amarillo, 2.

53. See Donna McGee, "75th Anniversary of the Panhandle Professional Writers," *Ranger,* Oct. 14, 1994, 4; see also *A Celebration of the Written Word: 75th Anniversary of Panhandle Professional Writers,* Apr. 22, 1995, Panhandle Pen

Women file, Panhandle-Plains Historical Museum, West Texas A&M University, Canyon, n.p. Additional information was taken from Kollmar interview; Richardson interview.

54. Quote from Bair interview.

55. As quoted in *Panhandle Pen Women Golden Anniversary*, 14.

56. Quote from Kollmar interview.

Chapter 4. The Border Poets of Kingsville

1. Much information in this chapter was provided by the following individuals who were Border Poets or children and friends of Border Poets: Robert Rhode, Frank Goodwyn, Elizabeth Goodwyn, Charlotte Baker Montgomery, Mrs. Nick Harold, J. S. Scarborough, III, and Sara Johnson. See "Poetry Society Holds Meet in Kingsville," *South Texan*, Feb. 25, 1933, 1, 4. Attendees include Mrs. Ethel Waddell, Mrs. Lucie Gill Price, Mrs. Grace McComb, Lela Wilson Johnson, Frank Goodwyn, Professor Reed, Frances Alexander, Loyce Adams, Gertrude Ray Plummer, and Mrs. Cleveland Wright. For additional information about early meetings, see "Poetry Society Meets in Corpus Christi," *South Texan*, May 13, 1933, 2; "Border Poets Have Meeting Saturday, " *South Texan*, Mar. 17, 1934, 1, 4; "Kingsville Poets Meet in Corpus Christi," Mar. 18, 1933, 2.

2. Quote from "Poetry Society Meets in Corpus Christi," 2. See also V. S. Montgomery, *A Century with Texas Poets*, 108. In 1934, Montgomery listed the Border Poets with seventeen members, both male and female, and the Southwest Poetry Society with eight members, all of them female.

3. See "Border Poets Have Meeting Saturday," 1, 4; see also "Poetry Society Holds Meet in Kingsville," 1, 4.

4. Elizabeth Goodwyn, telephone interview by author, Aug.5, 1997.

5. Daniel Webster is quoted in *Kleberg County History*, 14. See also Tom Lea, *The King Ranch*, 2:11; Frank Goodwyn, *Life on the King Ranch*, 3–7.

6. Frank Goodwyn, *The Magic of Limping John*, 3.

7. Lea, *The King Ranch*, 1:3–7; F. Goodwyn, *Life on the King Ranch*, 3–22.

8. See F. Goodwyn, *Life on the King Ranch*, 31, 70–85, 88, 94, 99–168. On page 31, Goodwyn writes, "Except for Mr. Caesar and Uncle Mack and a few others who came and went, we Goodwyns were the only English-speaking people on the place." Goodwyn tells that he was the only Anglo student in the school, and when one of the teachers committed suicide, finding enough English-speaking men for an inquest was a difficult task. See also Lea, *The King Ranch*, 1:507, 512, 523–24.

In a telephone interview by the author, May 18, 1996, J. S. Scarborough, III, said that it was not uncommon in prominent South Texas families for the females to have more refined interests and more positive attitudes than the males toward education. Scarborough's mother was a music teacher and a Border Poet, but he was "a common South Texas boy" who had little interest in anything literary. He would rather be "getting on his pony and riding across the prairie" than reading poetry.

9. See *Kleberg County History*, 16–20; Lea, *The King Ranch*, 2:473–79; F. Goodwyn, *Life on the King Ranch*, 23–31. For conformation of the Kleberg family's cultural pursuits, see Rosa Kleberg, "Some of My Early Experiences in Texas," *Texas Historical Association Quarterly* 1 (1897): 297–302. Rosa Kleberg writes: We had our pleasures, too." She tells that the family brought a piano and a collection of books to Texas from Germany. The piano was damaged in transport, but she still managed to play on it. When Santa Anna's army advanced across Texas, burning and looting settlers' possessions, the Klebergs buried their highly prized books before they fled.

10. See *Kleberg County History*, 19, 22, 177.

11. J. S. Scarborough III, interview. This retired sheriff of Kleberg County, who was the son and grandson of Kleberg County sheriffs, indicated the amount of control that the Kings and Klebergs exerted over life in Kingsville with the following statement: "The Klebergs raised their sheriffs like they raised their horses." See also Lea, *The King Ranch*, 2:545–57; *Kleberg County History*, 174.

12. See *Kleberg County History*, 15, 19–20, 174, 177, 185, 187, 206, 231, 233, 547, 676, 695, 698, 700, 737, 781. See also Lea, *The King Ranch*, 2:576–92.

13. For information about the founding of this college, see *Kleberg County History*, 206, 441–43, 451, 453, 677. See also Evans, *The Story of Texas Schools*, 274, 411. Discrepancies exist concerning the number of students admitted to Texas A&I College during the first year. Evans reports that the college opened its doors to 300 students, and that six years later the enrollment was 600, but in *Kleberg County History* a member of the original faculty says the total number of students the first year was 180 (p. 451).

14. For information about Frances Alexander's background and career, see Barnes, *Texas Writers of Today*, 43; "Alexander, Frances Laura," in *Contemporary Authors*, ed. James G. Lesniak, 11. For information about Alexander's activities in Kingsville, see "Students Enjoy Miss Alexander's Art Collection," *South Texan*, July 1, 1935, 1; "Texas Poet Presented at Sat. Program," *South Texan*, Mar. 28, 1936, 1; "Faculty Members to Return from Orient," *South Texan*, Jan. 9, 1932, 4. Additional information came from "Miss Frances Alexander: She Finds Fun in Writing Poetry," *Austin American Statesman*, Apr.

17, 1949, n.p.; Bill Warrin, "books," *Austin American Statesman,* Nov. 28, 1971, n.p. Warrin quotes Alexander: "I started off in math, but women weren't too easily accepted then as math teachers, so I switched to English." See also Frances Alexander, "My Sun-Dial Report," unpublished manuscript, private collection of Charlotte Baker Montgomery, Nacogdoches, 50–60. Alexander tells that she was recruited to teach at the new college in Kingsville by Dr. Cousins. Some discrepancy exists concerning the year Alexander received her degree from Columbia. Most references list the year as 1922, but Alexander gives the date as June, 1923.

    15. Alexander, "My Sundial Report," 59–60.

    16. Quote from *Kleberg County History,* 704. Mrs. Collins became a member of the Woman's Club and the Historical Association and was founder of the public library and the Bookmobile. She worked diligently to secure a college for Kingsville.

    17. Quote from Robert Rhode, interview with author, May 23, 1996.

    18. Quote from Charlotte Montgomery, letter to Betty Wiesepape, July 8, 1997. Information about Siddie Joe Johnson was taken from "Siddie Joe Johnson," in *The Junior Book of Authors,* ed. Stanley Kunitz and Howard Haycraft, 172–73. See also Mabel Carter Nicholson, "Siddie Joe Johnson: Her Contribution to Literature" (master's thesis, East Texas State Teachers College, Aug., 1950), 11; Linda Gayle Cole, "Siddie Joe Johnson," Siddie Joe Johnson file, Children's Library Department, Dallas Public Library, 69.

    19. Quote from Alexander, "My Sun-Dial Report," 60. See also "Students Enjoy Miss Alexander's Art Collection," 1; "Texas Poet Presented at Sat. Program," 1.

    20. See "Miss Frances Alexander: She Finds Fun in Writing Poetry," n.p.

    21. Ibid. See also "Alexander, Frances Laura," 11; "Frances Alexander," in *Southwestern American Literature: A Bibliography,* ed. John Q. Anderson, Edwin W. Gaston, Jr., and James W. Lee, 173.

    22. Quote from Rhode interview. Additional information was taken from "Border Poets Have Meeting Saturday," 1, 4; "Poetry Group Holds Organizational Meet," *South Texan,* Oct. 14, 1933, 4. See also Alexander, "My Sun-Dial Report," 50; Alexander states that this was not her first experience with a literary club. She was a member of the Woman's Culture Club when she lived in Port Arthur.

    23. See "Poetry Group Holds Organizational Meet," 4. Additional information was taken from Rhode interview.

    24. See "Border Poets Meet in Kingsville," *South Texan,* Mar. 21, 1936, 4; "Border Poets Have Meeting Saturday," 1, 4; Rhode interview.

    25. Rhode interview; Elizabeth Goodwyn interview.

26. Information about racial makeup of the club was compiled from V. S. Montgomery, *A Century with Texas Poets,* 108; "Baker Publishes Mystery Novel," *Kingsville Record,* May 14, 1941, 8; Rhode interview; Frank Goodwyn, telephone interview by author, Aug. 5, 1997; Elizabeth Goodwyn interview. Only three individuals of Hispanic descent are known to have been members of the Border Poets: Joel Acevedo, the son of a minister of a Mexican American Presbyterian Church in Kingsville and a public schoolteacher in one of the schools outside of Kingsville; Bertha Christine Acevedo, Joel Acevedo's wife; and Bertha Dominguez, a native of Mexico who was a student at Texas A&I College.

27. Rhode interview; Elizabeth Goodwyn interview.

28. Elizabeth Goodwyn, letter to Betty Wiesepape, Aug. 12, 1997; see also "Frank Goodwyn's Poems Voted First Place at Poets Meet," *Kingsville Record,* Mar. 12, 1941, 3.

29. Elizabeth Goodwyn interview; see also "Border Poets Meet in Bishop Saturday Night," *South Texan,* Feb. 15, 1936, 1; "Border Poets Hear Reading of Remarks by Texas Poet," *South Texan,* Feb. 17, 1939, 7.

30. Quote from Elizabeth Goodwyn interview. See also "Border Poets Hear Poems Read at Meeting," *Kingsville Record,* Feb. 18, 1942, 3. Additional information came from Rhode interview; Frank Goodwyn interview.

31. See "Dr. Chandler and Dr. Davis Are Poets' Hosts," *South Texan,* Apr. 18, 1936, 1; "Poetry Society Meets in Bishop," *South Texan,* Apr. 15, 1933, 1, 3; "Poetry Society Holds Kingsville Meeting," *South Texan,* Nov. 18, 1933, 1; "Border Poets Hold Opening Meeting of Season," *Kingsville Record,* Oct. 18, 1939, 5. The sale of liquor was prohibited in Kingsville by a clause that Mrs. Richard King inserted into land contracts when the town was established.

32. "Border Poets Choose Name for Magazine," *South Texan,* Aug. 3, 1935, 4.

33. Rhode interview. See also "Border Poets Choose Name for Magazine," 4; "Border Poets Have Meeting Saturday," 1, 4; "Frank Goodwyn's Poems Voted First Place," 3; "Border Poets Hold Opening Meeting," 5.

34. See "Border Poets Have Kingsville Meeting," *South Texan,* Feb. 17, 1934, 1; "Border Poets Meet at College," *South Texan,* June 23, 1934, 4; "Border Poets Have Meeting Saturday," 1, 4; "Poetry Society Meets in Corpus Christi," 2; "Poetry Book to Be Released from Press," *South Texan,* Oct. 7, 1933, 4; "Poetry Program Is Presented Friday," *South Texan,* Oct. 21, 1933, 4.

35. See Hilton Greer, "Poets of Texas: XXIII Siddie Joe Johnson A Facile Rhythmist," *Dallas Journal,* Feb. 27, 1935, 6.

36. See "Border Poets Meet at College," 4. Some sources report the year of Lena Johnson's death as 1933, but this article indicates that she was an active member of the Border Poets in 1934. Newspaper reports of early meetings of the Southwest Poetry Society and of the Border Poets list four Johnson women: Siddie Joe, Lena Agnes, Lena Williams, and Mrs. H. B. Johnson. When the split in the club occurred, Lena Williams Johnson and Mrs. H. B. Johnson remained in the Southwest Poetry Society. Lena Agnes was Siddie Joe's sister, and it is probable that the other two women were her mother and her sister-in-law.

37. See "Siddie Joe Johnson," in *The Junior Book,* 172–73. Children's Story Hour, book parades, puppet shows, children's rare book collections, children's circulating picture collections, and Creative Writing Club for children were some of the library activities initiated by Johnson. See also Nicholson, "Siddie Joe Johnson: Her Contribution to Literature," 1–10, 20–22, 69–77. Students who studied poetry writing from Siddie Joe Johnson published poems in youth magazines and won Texas Poetry Society awards; one earned a scholarship to college because of her poetry. See also Janice Fisher Giles, "Siddie Joe Johnson and Dallas Public Library: A History of Service to Children," *Journal of Youth Services in Libraries* 6, no. 1 (1992): 67–71; Allen Maxwell, "Remembering Siddie Joe Johnson," *Dallas Morning News,* Aug. 7, 1977, 5:G. In this article published shortly after Johnson's death, Texas librarians tell that Johnson was a role model.

38. See "Siddie Joe Johnson," *The Junior Book,* 172–73; Cole, "Siddie Joe Johnson," 74; Greer, "Poets of Texas: XXIII," 6; "Siddie Joe Johnson Receives Grolier Award," *Texas Library Journal* 30, no. 3 (1954): 151; Vann, *Texas Institute of Letters,* 98.

39. Information was taken from Rhode interview; Charlotte Baker Montgomery, letter to Betty Wiesepape, July 8, 1997. See also V. S. Montgomery, *A Century with Texas Poets,* 108.

40. C. B. Montgomery, letter to Betty Wiesepape, July 8, 1997.

41. "Baker, Charlotte," in *Contemporary Authors,* ed. Clare D. Kinsman, 46.

42. See "Everett Gillis," Obituaries/Metro, *Lubbock Avalanche-Journal,* Jan. 27, 1989, A.10; "Gillis, Everett Alden," in *Contemporary Authors,* ed. Linda Metzger, 147–48.

43. Rhode interview.

44. Information about J. V. Chandler was taken from *Kleberg County History,* 232, 442, 940; Frank Goodwyn interview; "Border Poets Meet at College," 4; Margaret Royalty Edwards, "Dr. J. V. Chandler," in *Poets Laureate of Texas,* 85–90.

45. Information was taken from Rhode interview; C. B. Montgomery, letter to Betty Wiesepape, July 8, 1997. See also V. S. Montgomery, *A Century with Texas Poets,* 108.

46. See Vann, *Texas Institute of Letters,* 23, 93.

47. Frank Goodwyn interview. See also F. Goodwyn, *Life on the King Ranch,* 207–19.

48. See "Border Poets Have Kingsville Meeting," 1; "Border Poets Meet at College," 4; "Border Poets Have Meeting Saturday," 1, 4; "Poetry Society Meets in Corpus Christi," 2; "Poetry Book to Be Released from Press," 4; "Poetry Program Is Presented Friday," 4.

49. Quote from Warrin, "books." Warrin quotes Alexander as saying that when her mother was told the book of poetry would sell for $1.50, she said, "Oh Frances, 50 cents would have been *plenty.*" See also Rhode interview.

50. Rhode interview. See also "Frances Alexander Wins Award of Border Poets Club," *South Texan,* Nov. 21, 1936, 1; "Kingsville Boy Publishes Poems," *South Texan,* Mar. 24, 1934, 1; "Baker Publishes Mystery Novel," 8.

51. Orlan Sawey quote is from "Sawey, Orlan Lester," in *Contemporary Authors,* ed. Linda Metzger, 421–22; Robert Rhode quote is from "Rhode, Robert David," in *Contemporary Authors,* ed. Frances Locher, 447; Alexander quote is from "Miss Frances Alexander," n.p.

52. Rhode interview. Robert Rhode said that the editorial board tried to include at least one poem by each active member in each published volume.

53. See "Poetry Book to Be Released from Press," 4; "Border Poets Volume Added to Library," *South Texan,* Oct. 30, 1937, 1.Rhode interview; Elizabeth Goodwyn interview.

54. See "Dr. Chandler and Dr. Davis Are Poets' Hosts," 1; "Border Poets Meet in Bishop Saturday Night," 1; "Gillis, Everett Alden," in *Contemporary Authors,* 147–48.

55. Rhode interview.

56. This information was compiled from Rhode interview; J. S. Scarborough, III, interview; *Kleberg County History,* 232; Alexander, "My Sun-Dial Report," 83; "English Club Hears Works of Local Poets," *South Texan,* Mar. 21, 1936, 4; "Goodwyn on English Club Program Fri.," *South Texan,* May 9, 1936, 3; "Famous Poet to Appear Here Soon," *South Texan,* Mar. 14, 1936, 1; "J. Frank Dobie to Lecture Here Soon," *South Texan,* Mar. 19, 1932, 1; "N.Y. Writer Is Guest of Border Poets," *South Texan,* Jan. 18, 1936, 1, 4.

57. Rhode interview. Dr. Rhode commented on the great amount of literary activity in South Texas during the years the Border Poets were in operation and the rivalry that existed between certain groups in recruiting members. Some Border Poets belonged to more than one writer's club. Robert Frost submitted an entry to one of these competitions, but his poem did not place. See also Barnes, *Texas Writers of Today,* 260–61.

58. Rhode interview. See also "Alexander, Frances Laura," 11; Barnes, *Texas Writers of Today,* 313, 260–61; Vann, *Texas Institute of Letters,* 3–4, 87–98;

Alexander, "My Sun-Dial Report," 108; Edwards, "Dr. J. V. Chandler," 85–87; "Everett Gillis," Obituaries/Metro, A.10.

59. See "Miss Frances Alexander: She Finds Fun in Writing Poetry," n.p.; Warrin, "books," n.p.

60. *Kleberg County History,* 677. Another factor in the decrease in membership may have been the closing of railroad shops and general offices, an event that precipitated a major economic setback for Kingsville in the mid-1950s.

61. See "Rhode, Robert David," in *Contemporary Authors,* 447.

62. See John Q. Anderson, Edwin W. Gaston, Jr., and James W. Lee, eds., *Southwestern American Literature, Chicago: Swallow, 1980;* Vaida Stewart Montgomery, *A Century with Texas Poets and Poetry* (Dallas: Kaleidograph, 1934); and *Notable Women of the Southwest: A Pictorial Biographical Encyclopedia of the Leading Women of Texas, New Mexico, Oklahoma, and Arizona* (Dallas: William T. Tardy, 1938).

63. "Cruel Beauty" appears in Siddie Joe Johnson, *Agarita Berry* (Dallas: The South-west Press, 1933), 29. "Siesta" appears in Frances Alexander, *Time at the Window* (Dallas: Kaleidograph Press, 1948), 75.

64. Frank Goodwyn, *The Devil in Texas,* ix.

65. Border Poets, *Silver Spur,* 7.

66. Quote from Alexander, "My Sun-Dial Report," 107.

Conclusion

1. For comments on the limitations of early Texas writers, see Hilton Greer, "Prose Writers of Texas XV James Thomas DeShields," *Dallas Journal,* Dec. 18, 1935, 8.

2. See William H. Vann, "The Early Years 1936–1938," in *The Texas Institute of Letters,* 3–12; Greer, "The Poetry Society of Texas," 23–24; Whitney Montgomery, "Poetry Journals in Texas," *A Century with Texas Poets,* 30–33; Gossett, "History of the *Southwest Review,*" 78.

3. Facts about the organization of the Manuscript Club of Wichita Falls are sketchy, and no information about who originated the idea to organize this club could be located.

4. Former Maker Charles Ferguson, former Border Poet Siddie Joe Johnson, and former Manuscript Club member Anne Pence Davis appeared on programs sponsored by the Panhandle Pen Women. Makers David Russell, William Russell Clark, and Charles Ferguson and Panhandle Pen Women member Loula Grace Erdman appeared at the Southwestern Writers Conference in Corpus, a conference that a number of Border Poet members helped

to arrange. Manuscript Club member Anne Pence Davis taught creative writing classes at SMU.

5. For proof that Texas writers who left the state aided other Texas writers, see Cook, letter to Mr. Ben Hibbs. In this letter PPW member Ruby Cook relates that Charles Ferguson, editor of *Reader's Digest,* is eager to publish her story on Laura Hamner. See also Sophia Meyer, "College to Take Over Course"; "Border Poets to Hear Poems Read at Meeting," *Kingsville Record,* Feb. 18, 1942, 3; Aubrey Burns, letter to Dr. Jay B. Hubbell, May 19, 1976. Burns tells Dr. Hubbell that Maker Sarah Chokla edited his volume of poetry.

6. *The Edge of Time* by Loula Grace Erdman is currently available from Texas Christian University Press. Frank Goodwyn's *Life on the King Ranch* was reissued by Texas A&M University Press in 1993, and *Windfall and Other Stories* by Winifred Sanford is available currently from Southern Methodist University Press.

7. See Vaida Stewart Montgomery, "Leave the Ladies Alone!" unpublished manuscript, Montgomery Memorial Collection, DeGolyer Library, Southern Methodist University, Dallas.

8. See Clara Edgar McClure, "Comment on Recent Fiction: Texas in the Cocoon," *Southwest Review* 9, no. 4 (1924): 218–20.

Appendix

1. Chapters of the National Association of Pen Women existed in Abilene, Austin, Brazoria, Corpus Christi, Dallas, Denton, Fort Worth, Galveston, and Houston. Chapters of this association may have existed in other Texas cities as well, but historical records of this organization reside in an uncatalogued collection in Washington, D.C., and were not available for research. To complicate matters further, some Pen Women clubs that met in Texas towns and cities were not associated with the National Association of Pen Women.

2. Five Texas universities had chapters of Sigma Tau Delta, an English fraternity in which membership was based on creative writing: Baylor, Texas A&I, Texas Christian University, Trinity University, and the University of Texas. Eight other Texas colleges or universities had independent creative writing clubs in the 1930s. The source that mentioned these clubs did not give their names.

3. At least three Standard Clubs were operating in Dallas.

BIBLIOGRAPHY

"Afternoon Session: April 18, 1933." Unattributed article. In *Panhandle Pen Women's History 1925–55*. Panhandle Pen Women Collection. Amarillo Public Library, Amarillo.

Agatha, Sister M. *Texas Prose Writings: A Reader's Digest*. Dallas: Banks Upshaw, 1936.

Alexander, Frances. *Chac, the Chachalaca*. Austin: Von Boeckman-Jones, 1969.

——. *Conversation with a Lamb*. Austin: Steck, 1955.

——. *The Diamond Tree*. Austin: Von Boeckman-Jones, 1970.

——. *Mother Goose on the Rio Grande*. Dallas: Banks Upshaw, 1944.

——. "My Sun-Dial Report." Unpublished manuscript, 1976. Private collection of Charlotte Baker Montgomery, Nacogdoches.

——. *Orphans on the Guadalupe*. Wichita Falls: Nortex Press, 1971.

——. *Pebbles from a Broken Jar: Fables and Hero Stories from Old China*. New York: Bobbs-Merrill, 1963.

——. *Seven White Birds*. Dallas: Kaleidograph, 1938.

——. *Time at the Window*. Dallas: Kaleidograph, 1948.

"Alexander, Frances L." In *Notable Women of the Southwest: A Pictorial Biographical Encyclopedia of the Leading Women of Texas, New Mexico, Oklahoma, and Arizona*. Dallas: William T. Tardy, 1938.

"Alexander, Frances Laura." Vol. 35 of *Contemporary Authors New Revision* series, edited by James G. Lesniak, 11. Detroit: Gale Research, 1992.

"Amarillo Society: Many Persons Attend Meeting of Panhandle Pen Women and Interesting Program Rendered." Unattributed article, October 1922. Panhandle Pen Women files, *Amarillo Globe-News* archives. Amarillo.

"Among the Outstanding Women in the Past." In *The Panhandle Pen Women Golden Anniversary Plus Two: 1920–1972*, 3. *Panhandle Penwomen 1972 Scrapbook*, Panhandle Pen Women Collection. Amarillo Public Library, Amarillo.

Amyett, Paddy Dion Westergard. "A History of Literary Societies at Baylor University." Master's thesis, Baylor University, 1963.

Anderson, H. Allen. "Amarillo, Texas." In *The New Texas Handbook in Six Volumes*, 140, 142. Vol. 1. Austin: Texas State Historical Society, 1996.

Anderson, John Q., Edwin W. Gaston, Jr., and James W. Lee, eds. *Southwestern American Literature: A Bibliography*. Chicago: Swallow, 1980.

"Anne Pence Davis Again Honored." Unattributed article. Anne Pence Davis

Collection. Manuscripts. Library of Special Collection, Western Kentucky University, Bowling Green.

Announcement of Awards: Prizes for Original Poems. Dallas: SMU, 1922.

Announcement of Awards: Prizes for Original Poems. Dallas: SMU, 1923.

Announcement of Awards: Prizes for Original Poems. Dallas: SMU, 1924.

Announcement of Awards: Prizes for Original Poems. Dallas: SMU, 1925.

Announcement of Awards: Prizes for Original Poems. Dallas: SMU, 1926.

Announcement of Awards: Prizes for Original Poems. Dallas: SMU, 1927.

"Annual Awards Given by Texas Institute." *Dallas Morning News,* March 19, 1972. Panhandle Penwomen file, *Amarillo Globe-News* archives. Amarillo.

"Autograph Party Planned Monday." September 19, 1949. Panhandle Pen Women files, *Amarillo Globe-News* archives. Amarillo.

Bair, Nova. Interview by author. Amarillo, June 19, 1996.

Baker, Charlotte. *The Best of Friends.* New York: McKay, 1966.

——. *Cocklebur Quarters.* Scarborough, N.Y.: Prentice-Hall, 1972.

——. *The Green Poodles.* New York: McKay, 1956.

——. *Hope Hacienda.* New York: Crowell, 1942.

——. *House of the Roses.* New York: Dutton, 1942.

——. *House on the River.* New York: Coward, 1948.

——. *Kinnery Camp.* New York: McKay, 1951.

——. *The Kittens and the Cardinals.* New York: McKay, 1969.

——. *Magic for Mary M.* New York: McKay, 1953.

——. *Necessary Nellie.* New York: Coward, 1942.

——. *Nellie and the Mayor's Hat.* New York: Coward, 1947.

——. *A Sombrero for Miss Brown.* New York: Dutton, 1941.

——. *Sunrise Island.* New York: McKay, 1952.

——. *Thomas, the Ship's Cat.* New York: McKay, 1958.

——. *The Venture of the Thunderbird.* New York: McKay, 1954.

"Baker, Charlotte." Vols. 17–20 of *Contemporary Authors First Revision,* edited by Clare D. Kinsman, 46. Detroit: Gale Research, 1976.

"Baker Publishes Mystery Novel." *Kingsville Record,* May 14, 1941, 8.

Baldwin, Dan. Review of *Windfall and Other Stories,* by Winifred Sanford. *Legacies I* 1 (1989): 39.

Bard, W. E. "An Aside to the Reader." In *Fountain Unsealed: A Collection of Verse by Texas Writers,* by the Barrington Fiction Club. Dallas: Clyde C. Cockrell, 1931.

Barker, Ruth Laughlin. "Club-Women." *Southwest Review* 12 (January, 1927): 154–58.

Barnes, Florence Elberta. *Texas Writers of Today.* Ann Arbor, Mich.: Grayphon Books, 1971.

Baym, Nina. "Melodramas of Beset Manhood." In *Feminism and American Literary History,* by Nina Baym, 3–18. New Brunswick, N.J.: Rutgers University Press, 1992.

Beasley, Edna Gertrude. *My First Thirty Years.* N.p.: The Book Club of Texas, 1989.

Beaty, John Owen, and Jay B. Hubbell, eds. *An Introduction to Poetry.* New York: Macmillan Co., 1922.

Blair, Karen J. *The Clubwoman as Feminist: True Womanhood Redefined, 1868–1914.* New York: Holmes & Meier, 1980.

———. Introduction to *The Woman's Club of El Paso: Its First Thirty Years,* by Mary Cunningham, vii–xii. El Paso: Texas Western, 1978.

"Bond Becomes Editor of Review." *Semi-Weekly Campus,* October 3, 1925, 1.

"Bond, Dr. George D., Death and Funeral Announcements." *Dallas Morning News,* May 26, 1986, D:7.

Bond, George D. Letter to Dr. Jay B. Hubbell, March 20, 1972. Jay Broadus Hubbell Papers. Rare Book, Manuscript, and Special Collections Library, Duke University, Durham.

———. Letter to Dr. Jay B. Hubbell, November 21, 1964. George Bond file, Jay Broadus Hubbell Papers. Rare Book, Manuscript, and Special Collections Library, Duke University, Durham.

———. "Sketches of the Texas Prairie." In *Prairie Pegasus,* edited by Marie Hemke, George Bond, and Jay B. Hubbell. Dallas: n.p., 1924.

Bond, George D., and Ottys Sanders. "Jay Broadus Hubbell, 1885–1979." Jay Broadus Hubbell Papers. Rare Book, Manuscript, and Special Collections Library, Duke University, Durham.

———. "A Tribute to a Giant Among Men: In Memory of Jay B. Hubbell, 1885–1979." Jay Broadus Hubbell Papers. Rare Book, Manuscript, and Special Collections Library, Duke University, Durham.

Bond, Mildred. Telephone interview by author. July 2, 1996.

Bond, Robert. Telephone interview by author. June 26, 1996.

"Bond Will Write for Guardian." *Semi-Weekly Campus,* March 11, 1925, 1.

Booth, Wayne C. "Who Is Responsible in Ethical Criticism, and for What?" In *The Company We Keep: An Ethics of Fiction,* 125–55. Berkeley and Los Angeles: University of California Press, 1988.

Border Poets. *Cantando.* Dallas: Kaleidograph, 1939.

———. *Cenizo Spray.* Dallas: Banks Upshaw, 1947.

———. *Serenata.* Dallas: Tardy, 1937.

———. *Silver Spur.* Santa Fe, N.Mex.: Seton Village, 1942.

———. *Silver Spur V: Yucca Trail.* Kingsville, Tex.: Kingsville Publishing Co., 1951.

———. *Silver Spur VI: Cactus Tongues*. Ann Arbor, Mich.: Edwards Brothers, 1955.

———. *Silver Spur VII: Buenos Dios*. Kingsville, Tex.: Kingsville Publishing Co., 1962.

"Border Poets Are Numerous in New Texas Collection." *South Texan*, August 3, 1935, 1.

"Border Poets Choose Name for Magazine." *South Texan*, August 3, 1935, 4.

"Border Poets Have Kingsville Meeting." *South Texan*, February 17, 1934, 1.

"Border Poets Have Meeting Saturday." *South Texan*, March 17, 1934, 1, 4.

"Border Poets Hear Poems Read at Meeting." *Kingsville Record*, February 18, 1942, 3.

"Border Poets Hear Reading of Remarks by Texas Poet." *South Texan*, February 17, 1939, 7.

"Border Poets Hold Opening Meeting of Season." *Kingsville Record*, October 18, 1939, 5.

"Border Poets Meet at College." *South Texan*, June 23, 1934, 4.

"Border Poets Meet in Bishop Saturday Night." *South Texan*, February 15, 1936, 1.

"Border Poets Meet in Kingsville." *South Texan*, March 21, 1936, 4.

"Border Poets Volume Added to Library." *South Texan*, October 30, 1937, 1.

Bradley, Jerry. Interview by author. Canyon, June 19, 1996.

"Bulletin of Meeting of Panhandle Pen Women: July 1948." Panhandle Pen Women Collection. Amarillo Public Library, Amarillo.

"Bulletin of Meeting of Panhandle Pen Women: April 18, 1950." Panhandle Pen Women Collection. Amarillo Public Library, Amarillo.

"Bulletin of Meeting of Panhandle Pen Women: July 18, 1950." Panhandle Pen Women Collection. Amarillo Public Library, Amarillo.

Bulletin of Southern Methodist University: Announcement of Awards Fifth Annual Poetry Contest. Dallas: SMU, 1926.

Bulletin of Southern Methodist University: Announcement of Awards First Annual Poetry Contest. Dallas: SMU, 1922.

Bulletin of Southern Methodist University: Announcement of Awards Fourth Annual Poetry Contest. Dallas: SMU, 1925.

Bulletin of Southern Methodist University: Announcement of Awards Second Annual Poetry Contest. Dallas: SMU, 1923.

Bulletin of Southern Methodist University: Announcement of Awards Sixth Annual Poetry Contest. Dallas: SMU, 1927.

Bulletin of Southern Methodist University: Announcement of Awards Third Annual Poetry Contest. Dallas: SMU, 1924.

Burns, Aubrey. "For The Makers." Aubrey Burns file, Jay Broadus Hubbell

Papers. Rare Book, Manuscript, and Special Collections Library, Duke University, Durham.

———. Letter to Dr. Jay B. Hubbell, May 19, 1976. Aubrey Burns file, Jay Broadus Hubbell Papers. Rare Book, Manuscript, and Special Collections Library, Duke University, Durham.

———. Letter to Dr. Jay B. Hubbell, April 9, 1969. Aubrey Burns file, Jay Broadus Hubbell Papers. Rare Book, Manuscript, and Special Collections Library, Duke University, Durham.

———. *Out of a Moving Mist.* Fairfax, Calif.: Tamal Land, 1978.

Bynner, Witter. "Foreword." In *Prairie Pegasus,* edited by Marie Hemke, George Bond, and Jay B. Hubbell. Dallas: Southwest, 1924.

A Celebration of the Written Word: 75th Anniversary of Panhandle Professional Writers. Panhandle Professional Writers, Panhandle Pen Women file. Panhandle-Plains Historical Museum, West Texas A&M University, Canyon, April 22, 1995.

Chandler, Jesse Van Buren. *Night Alone.* Kingsville, Tex.: Kingsville Publishing Co., 1947.

———. Petals Fall. Kingsville, Tex.: Kingsville Publishing Co., 1959.

"Charles W. Ferguson, Ex-Magazine Editor." *New York Times,* December 20, 1987, L:46.

"Charles W. Ferguson, Former Student of S. M. U." *Semi-Weekly Campus,* January 16, 1929, 1.

Cheney, Mildred J. "Pen Women." *Amarillo Sunday News and Globe,* August 14, 1938. Panhandle Pen Women files, *Amarillo Globe-News* archives. Amarillo.

"Chinn, Laurene Chambers." Vols. 1–4 of *Contemporary Authors First Revision,* edited by James Elhridge and Barbara Kopala, 173. Detroit: Gale Research, 1962.

Christensen, Paul. Telephone interview by author. May 10, 1995.

"Co-eds Do Not Come Here for Pleasure, Mrs. Hay Says." *Semi-Weekly Campus,* February 21, 1925, 1.

Cole, Linda Gayle. "Siddie Joe Johnson." Siddie Joe Johnson file. Children's Library Department, Dallas Public Library, Dallas.

Constitution and By-Laws of the Panhandle Pen Women 1925. Panhandle Pen Women Collection. Amarillo Public Library, Amarillo.

Cook, Ruby. Letter to Mr. Ben Hibbs, October 29, 1958. Laura Hamner Papers. Kilgore Collection. Panhandle-Plains Historical Museum, Canyon, Texas.

———. Letter to Mr. Ralph Edwards, February, 1959. Laura Hamner Papers. Kilgore Collection. Panhandle-Plains Historical Museum, Canyon, Texas.

——. Unpublished manuscript. Laura Hamner Papers. Kilgore Collection. Panhandle-Plains Historical Museum, Canyon, Texas.

Croly, Mrs. J. C. *The History of the Woman's Club Movement in America*. New York: Henry G. Allen, 1898.

Cunningham, Mary S. *The Woman's Club of El Paso: Its First Thirty Years*. El Paso: Texas Western, 1978.

Davis, Anne Pence. Papers. Anne Pence Davis Collection. Manuscripts. Library of Special Collections, Western Kentucky University, Bowling Green.

——. *The Customer Is Always Right*. New York: Macmillan, 1940.

——. "Designing a Novel." *The Writer,* November, 1940, 323–26.

——. *Every Girl's Mystery and Adventure Stories*. Chicago: Goldsmith, 1935.

——. *Mimi at Camp*. Chicago: Goldsmith, 1935.

——. *Mimi at Sheridan School*. Chicago: Goldsmith, 1935.

——. *Mimi's House Party*. Chicago: Goldsmith, 1936.

——. *Money from the Juvenile*. Wichita Falls: N.p., 1937.

——. *So Swift the Stone: Collected Poems of Anne Pence Davis*. Wichita Falls: N.p., 1978.

——. *Top Hand of Lone Tree Ranch*. New York: Crowell, 1960.

——. *Wishes Are Horses*. Dallas: Mathis Van Nert, 1938.

Davis, Natalie Zemon. *Fiction in the Archives: Pardon Tales and Their Tellers in Sixteenth-Century France*. Stanford, Calif.: Stanford University Press, 1987.

——. *Women on the Margins: Three Seventeenth-Century Lives*. Cambridge, Mass.: Harvard University Press, 1995.

Dewey, Annette Barrett. "Panhandle Pen Women's Club." *The Woman's Viewpoint,* February 19, 1925, 19. Panhandle Pen Women Collection. Amarillo Public Library, Amarillo.

"Diamond Anniversary: Celebration of the Written Word." Panhandle Professional Writers. Private Collection. Ellen Richardson, Amarillo, 1995.

"Diploma Exercises of the National Shakespeare Club." *South Texan,* June 8, 1935, 3.

Dobie, J. Frank. *A Guide to Life and Literature of the Southwest*. Dallas: Southern Methodist University Press, 1952.

——. Letter to William H. Vann, September 28, 1936. Texas Institute of Letters Records. Southwestern Writers' Collection. Southwest Texas State University, San Marcos.

"Dr. Chandler and Dr. Davis Are Poets' Hosts." *South Texan,* April 18, 1936, 1.

"Dr. Hubbell." *Semi-Weekly Campus,* May 4, 1925, 1.

"Dr. J. DeWitt Davis Lists Vocational Aims of A&I Department of Education." *South Texan,* September 21, 1935, 2.

"Dr. Orlan Sawey." Unattributed article. Orlan L. Sawey folder, South Texas Archives & Special Collections. Texas A&M University, Kingsville.

Dvorken, Margaret. Interview by author. Wichita Falls, February 6, 1991.

Eagleton, Davis Foute. "Survey of the Field." In *Writers and Writings of Texas,* 7–15. New York: Broadway Publishing Co., 1913.

Edwards, Margaret Royalty. "David Russell." In *Poets Laureate of Texas: 1932–1966,* 37–42. San Antonio: Naylor, 1966.

——. "Dr. J. V. Chandler." In *Poets Laureate of Texas 1932–1966,* 85–90. San Antonio: Naylor, 1966.

——. "Russell, David Riley." In *The New Texas Handbook in Six Volumes,* 728–29. Austin: Texas State Historical Society 5, 1996.

"Edyth Renshaw Rites Set Monday." *Dallas Morning News,* June 7, 1992, A:41.

"English Club Hears Works of Local Poets." *South Texan,* March 21, 1936, 4.

"English Club Holds Initial Meeting." *South Texan,* October 8, 1932, 1.

"Erdman, Loula Grace." Vol. 10 of *Contemporary Authors,* edited by Barbara Harte and Carolyn Riley, 159. Detroit: Gale Research, 1962.

Erdman, Loula Grace. *The Edge of Time.* New York: Dodd, Mead, 1950.

——. *The Far Journey.* New York: Dodd, Mead, 1955.

——. "Foreword." In *Selected Editorials,* by Phoebe K. Warner, vii–viii. San Antonio: Naylor, 1964.

——. *Life Was Simpler Then.* New York: Dodd, Mead, 1948.

——. *Lonely Passage.* New York: Dodd, Mead, 1948.

——. *Separate Star.* New York: Longmans, Green, 1944.

——. *The Sky Is Blue.* New York: Longmans, Green, 1953.

——. *A Time to Write.* New York: Dodd, Mead, 1969.

——. *The Wind Blows Free.* New York: Dodd, Mead, 1952.

——. *A Wonderful Thing and Other Stories.* New York, Dodd, Mead, 1940.

——. *The Year of the Locust.* New York: Dodd, Mead, 1947.

Evans, C. E. *The Story of Texas Schools.* Austin: Speck, 1955.

"Everett Gillis." Obituaries/Metro. *Lubbock Avalanche-Journal,* January 27, 1989, A10.

"Ex-Editor Writes for Bookman." *Semi-Weekly Campus,* May 5, 1928, 5.

"Ex-Texas Poet Laureate, David Russell Dies." *Dallas Morning News,* March 21, 1964, 1.12.

Ezell, Margaret. *Writing Women's Literary History.* Baltimore: Johns Hopkins University Press, 1993.

"Faculty Members to Return from Orient." *South Texan,* January 9, 1932, 4.

"Famous Novelist Addresses Crowd." *South Texan,* April 2, 1932, 1.

"Famous Poet to Appear Here Soon." *South Texan,* March 14, 1936, 1.

Fehrenbach, T. R. *Lone Star: A History of Texas and Texans.* New York: American Legacy, 1983.

Ferguson. Charles W. *A Is for Advent.* Boston: Little, Brown, 1968.

———. *The Abecedarian Book.* Boston: Little, Brown, 1964.

———. *The Confusion of Tongues: A Review of Modern Isms.* New York: Doran, 1927.

———. *Fifty Million Brothers: A Panorama of American Lodges and Clubs.* New York: Farrar & Rinehart, 1937.

———. *Getting to Know the U.S.A.* New York: Coward, 1963.

———. *I, the Witness.* Boston: Little, Brown, 1975.

———. Letter to J. B. Hubbell, March 29, 1965. Charles Ferguson file, Jay Broadus Hubbell Papers. Rare Book, Manuscript, and Special Collections Library, Duke University, Durham.

———. *A Little Democracy Is a Dangerous Thing.* New York: Association Press, 1948.

———. *The Male Attitude.* Boston: Little, Brown, 1966.

———. *Naked to Mine Enemies: The Life of Cardinal Wolsey.* London, New York, and Toronto: Longmans, Green, 1958.

———. *Organizing to Beat the Devil: Methodists and the Making of America.* New York: Doubleday, 1971.

———. *Pigskin.* Garden City: Doubleday, Doran, 1928.

———. *Say It with Words.* New York: Knopf, 1959.

"Ferguson, Charles W." Vols. 13–16 of *Contemporary Authors First Revision,* edited by Clare D. Kinsman, 265–66. Detroit: Gale Research, 1965.

"Ferguson, Charles W." Vol. 124 of *Contemporary Authors New Revision* series, edited by Hal May and Susan M. Trosky, 147. Detroit: Gale Research, 1988.

"'First Novels Are Easy to Sell,' Says Famous Grad." *College Heights Herald.* Unattributed article. Anne Pence Davis Collection. Manuscripts. Library of Special Collections, Western Kentucky University. Bowling Green.

Flexner, Eleanor. *A Century of Struggle: The Woman's Rights Movement in the United States.* 4th ed. Cambridge: Belknap, 1975.

Forrester-O'Brien, Esse. *Art and Artists of Texas.* Dallas: Tandy, 1935.

"Former Student Wins Essay Prize." *Semi-Weekly Campus,* November 25, 1925, 1.

"Former Student Wins Society Poetry Prize." *Campus,* January 24, 1923, 3.

"Former Yell Leader's Humor Dominates Book on Religions." *Semi-Weekly Campus,* November 21, 1928, 2.

"Forty Girls Are Practicing for New Football Squad." *Semi-Weekly Campus,* November 4, 1925, 1.

"Frances Alexander." In *Southwestern American Literature: A Bibliography,* edited by John Q. Anderson, Edwin W. Gaston, Jr., and James W. Lee, 173. Chicago: Swallow, 1980.

"Frances Alexander." Unattributed article. Francis Alexander. Vertical files. Barker Center for American History, University of Texas at Austin.

"Frances Alexander Wins Award of Border Poets Club." *South Texan,* November 21, 1936, 1.

"Frances L. Alexander." In *Notable Women of the Southwest: A Pictorial Biographical Encyclopedia of the Leading Women of Texas, New Mexico, Oklahoma, and Arizona,* 3. Dallas: William T. Tardy, 1938.

"Frank Goodwyn's Poems Voted First Place at Poets Meet." *Kingsville Record,* March 12, 1941, 3.

Gilbert, Sandra M., and Susan Gubar. *No Man's Land: The Place of the Woman Writer in the Twentieth Century.* New Haven, Conn.: Yale University Press, 1988.

Giles, Janice Fisher. "Siddie Joe Johnson and Dallas Public Library: A History of Service to Children." *Journal of Youth Services in Libraries* 6, no. 1 (1992): 67–71.

Gillette, Michael L. *Texas in Transition.* Austin: Lyndon B. Johnson School of Public Affairs, 1986.

Gillis, Everett. *Angels of the Wind.* Dallas: Kaleidograph, 1954.

———. *Heart Singly Vowed.* Burnet: Nortex Press, 1980.

———. *Hello the House!* Dallas: Kaleidograph, 1944.

———. *South by West: A Galaxy of Southwestern and Western Scenes and Portraits.* Lubbock: Pisces Press, 1981.

———. *Sunrise in Texas.* N.p.: Fotolith, 1949.

———. *Who Can Retreat?* West Los Angeles: Wagon & Star, 1944.

"Gillis, Everett Alden." Vol. 15 of *Contemporary Authors New Revision* series, edited by Linda Metzger, 147–48. Detroit: Gale Research, 1985.

Gillis, Everett. Papers. Southwest Collection. Texas Tech University, Lubbock.

Goodwyn, Elizabeth. Letter to Betty Wiesepape, August 12, 1997.

———. Telephone interview by author. August 5, 1997.

Goodwyn, Frank. *Behind the Scenes: A Book of Emotions.* Boston: Christopher Publishing, 1935.

———. *The Black Bull.* Garden City: Doubleday, 1958.

———. *The Devil in Texas.* Dallas: Dealey & Lowe, 1936.

———. *Life on the King Ranch.* 1951. Reprint, College Station: Texas A&M University Press, 1993.

———. *Lone Star Land: Twentieth Century Texas in Perspective.* New York: Alfred A. Knopf, 1955.

——. *The Magic of Limping John: A Story of the Mexican Border Country.* New York: Farrar & Rinehart, 1944.

——. *Poems about the West.* Washington, D.C.: Potomac Corral, The Westerners, 1975.

——. Telephone interview by author. August 5, 1997.

"Goodwyn on English Club Program Fri." *South Texan,* May 9, 1936, p.3.

Gordon, Mary. Telephone interview by author. April 22, 1991.

Gossett, Thomas F. "A History of the *Southwest Review:* 1915–1942." Master's thesis, Southern Methodist University, 1948.

Gould, Joseph E. *The Chautauqua Movement: An Episode in the Continuing American Revolution.* Albany: New York State University Press, 1961.

Graham, Don B. "Literature." In *The New Texas Handbook in Six Volumes,* 225–26. Vol. 4. Austin: Texas State Historical Society, 1996.

——. "Second Reader's Report." Southern Methodist University Press, Dallas, March 31, 1987.

——. "The Short Story in Texas." In *South by Southwest: 24 Stories from Modern Texas,* edited by Don Graham, xi–xix. Austin: University of Texas Press, 1986.

Graham, Don, James Ward Lee, and William T. Pilkington. *The Texas Literary Tradition.* Austin: University of Texas Press, 1983.

Greene, A. C. *The Fifty Best Books on Texas.* Dallas: Pressworks, 1982.

Greer, Hilton Ross. "The Poetry Society of Texas." In *A Century with Texas Poets and Poetry,* edited by Vaida Stewart Montgomery, 23–24. Dallas: Kaleidograph, 1934.

——. "Poets of Texas: XXIII Siddie Joe Johnson A Facile Rhythmist." *Dallas Journal,* February 27, 1935, 6.

——. "Poets of Texas: XXIV George Bond." *Dallas Journal,* March 6, 1935, 8.

——. "Poets of Texas: XXVI Fay M. Yauger Distinguished Ballad-Maker." *Dallas Journal,* March 20, 1935, 1.6.

——. "Poets of Texas: XXVII William Russell Clark." *Dallas Journal,* March 27, 1935, 10.

——. "Poets of Texas: XXXV Fred Wilson." *Dallas Journal,* May 22, 1935, 8.

——. "Poets of Texas: XXXVII Fania Kruger Different and Effective." *Dallas Journal,* June 5, 1935, 2.2.

——. "Poets of Texas: XLIV David Russell." *Dallas Journal,* August 28, 1935, 11.

——. "Poets of Texas: XLVII Christopher O. Gill." *Dallas Journal,* August 14, 1935, 6.

——. "Poets of Texas: XLX Conclusion." *Dallas Journal,* September 4, 1935, 7.

——. "Prose Writers of Texas: XV James Thomas DeShields." *Dallas Journal,* December 18, 1935, 8.

——. "Prose Writers of Texas: XXXVII Charles W. Ferguson. *Dallas Journal,* June 17, 1936, 2.14.

——. "Prose Writers of Texas: XXXX Winifred Sanford Distinguished Realist." *Dallas Journal,* July 8, 1936, 2.1.

——. *Voices of the Southwest: A Book of Texan Verse.* New York: Macmillan, 1923.

Grider, Sylvia Ann, and Lou Halsell Rodenberger, eds. *Texas Women Writers: A Tradition of Their Own.* College Station: Texas A&M University Press, 1997.

Gross, Sarah Chokla. *Every Child's Book of Verse.* New York: Watts, 1968.

"Gross, Sarah Chokla." Vol. 61–64 of *Contemporary Authors,* edited by Cynthia R. Fadool, 128. Detroit: Gale Research, 1976.

Guestbook and History 1947–48. Panhandle Pen Women Collection. Amarillo Public Library, Amarillo.

Hall, Myra Dorris Collie. "Laura V. Hamner: A Woman before Her Time." Ph.D. diss., University of Houston, 1988.

Hamner, Laura V. "Frustrations." In *Prairie Vagabonds,* 2. San Antonio: Naylor, 1952.

——. "Light and Hitch #430." July 29, 1951. Radio Script. KGNC. Private Collection of Ellen Richardson, Amarillo.

——. "Light and Hitch #431." August 5, 1951. Radio Script. KGNC. Private Collection of Ellen Richardson, Amarillo.

——. *Light 'n Hitch: A Collection of Historical Writing Depicting Life on the High Plains.* Dallas: American Guild Press, 1958.

——. *No Gun Man of Texas: A Century of Achievement, 1835–1929.* Amarillo: N.p., 1935.

——. Papers. Kilgore Collection. Panhandle Plains Historical Museum, Canyon, Texas.

——. *Prairie Vagabonds.* San Antonio: Naylor, 1955.

——. *Short Grass & Longhorns.* Norman: University of Oklahoma Press, 1943.

——. "Talks to Teens." Laura V. Hamner Papers. Kilgore Collection. Panhandle Plains Historical Museum, Canyon, Texas.

——."A Word as to How It Happened." *Panhandle Pen-Points,* March 9, 1922, 1. Panhandle Pen Women Collection. Amarillo Public Library, Amarillo.

"Harriet Monroe Gives Lecture." *Semi-Weekly Campus,* April 18, 1925, 1.

"Harry, Elsie Marie, Deaths and Funeral Announcements." *Dallas Morning News,* July 25, 1993, A:40.

"Heads Fine Arts." *Kingsville Record,* September 20, 1939, B.2.

Hemke, Marie D., George D. Bond, and Jay B. Hubbell. *Prairie Pegasus.* Dallas: Southwest Printing, 1924.

Herron, Ima H. "A Backward Glance." *Mustang,* May/June 1964, 6.

Hindman, Jenny Louise. Interview by author. Wichita Falls, February 6, 1991.

"History of the Panhandle Pen Women." In *Pen-Points.* Brooklyn: Polygon, 1941.

Hoffmann, Leonore, and Deborah Rosenfelt. *Teaching Women's Literature from a Regional Perspective.* New York: Modern Language Association of America, 1992.

Hubbell, Jay B. "The Creative Writer and the University, with Special Reference to the 1920s." *South and Southwest: Literary Essays and Reminiscences by Jay B. Hubbell,* 330–64. Durham: Duke University Press, 1965.

———. *Lucinda, a Book of Memories.* Privately published, 1975.

———. "The Makers." In *Prairie Pegasus,* edited by Marie D. Hemke, George Bond, and Jay B. Hubbell. Dallas: Southwest, 1924.

———. "The New Southwest." *Southwest Review* 1 (October, 1924): 91–99.

———. Papers. Rare Book, Manuscript, and Special Collections Library, Duke University, Durham.

———. "Southwest Review 1924–1927." In *South and Southwest: Literary Essays and Reminiscences by Jay B. Hubbell,* 3–21. Durham: Duke University Press, 1965.

———. *Who Are the Major American Writers?* Durham, Duke University Press, 1972.

"In the Limelight Today." *Semi-Weekly Campus,* March 23, 1927, 1.

"January Meeting: Jan. 17, 1933." Unattributed article. *Panhandle Pen Women's History 1925–1955.* Panhandle Pen Women Collection. Amarillo Public Library, Amarillo.

"J. Frank Dobie to Lecture Here Soon." *South Texan,* March 19, 1932, 1.

Johnson, Siddie Joe. *Agarita Berry.* Dallas: South-west Press, 1933.

———. *Cat Hotel.* New York: Longmans, Green, 1955.

———. *Cathy.* New York: Longmans, Green, 1945.

———. *Gallant the Hour.* Dallas: Kaleidograph, 1945.

———. *A Month of Christmases.* New York: Longmans, Green, 1952.

———. *New Town in Texas.* New York: Longmans, Green, 1942.

———. *Rabbit Fires.* Boerne: Highland Press, 1951.

———. *Susan's Year.* New York: Longmans, Green, 1948.

———. *Texas: The Land of the Tejas.* Dallas: Cokesbury, 1943.

"Johnson, Siddie Joe." Vol. 106 of *Contemporary Authors,* edited by Frances Locher, 276. Detroit: Gale Research, 1982.

"Karle Wilson Baker of Nacogdoches Is Guest of Pen Women Saturday." Unattributed article, March 18, 1923. *Panhandle Pen Women's History 1|925–1955.* Panhandle Pen Women Collection. Amarillo Public Library, Amarillo.

"Kingsville Boy Publishes Poems." *South Texan,* March 24, 1934, 1.

"Kingsville Poets Meet in Corpus Christi." *South Texan,* March 18, 1933, 2.

Kleberg County History. Kingsville: Kleberg County Historical Commission, 1979.

Kleberg, Rosa. "Some of My Early Experiences in Texas." *Texas Historical Association Quarterly* 1 (1897): 297–302.

Kollmar, Rosemary. Interview by author. Amarillo, June 19, 1996.

Kruger, Fania. *Cossack Laughter.* Dallas: Kaleidograph, 1937.

———. Papers. Harry Ransom Humanities Research Center, University of Texas at Austin.

———. *Selected Poems.* Austin: American Universal Artforms Corp., 1973.

———. *The Tenth Jew.* Dallas: Kaleidograph, 1949.

———. "'The Tenth Jew,' Fania Kruger's Second Volume of Poetry." *Texas Jewish Press,* December, 1949. Fania Kruger Papers. Harry Ransom Humanities Research Center, University of Texas at Austin.

"Kruger, Fania." In *Who's Who of American Women.* Wilmette, Ill.: Marquis Who's Who, 1961.

"Kruger, Fania." In *Who's Who in World Jewry.* New York: Pitman, 1972.

LaCapra, Dominick. *Rethinking Intellectual History: Texts, Contexts, Language.* Ithaca, N.Y.: Cornell University Press, 1983.

"Laura Faye Yauger." Unattributed article. Yauger folder. Vertical files. Texas/Dallas History and Archives. Dallas Public Library, Dallas.

"Laura V. Hamner, 1871–1968." In *Panhandle Pen Women Golden Anniversary Plus Two: 1920–1972,* 2. Panhandle Pen Women Collection. Amarillo Public Library, Amarillo.

Law, Robert Adger. "Points of View — Education Should Not Be Provincial." *Southwest Review* 14 (July, 1929): 480.

Lea, Tom. *The King Ranch.* 2 vols. Boston and Toronto: Little, Brown, 1957.

Lee, James Ward. *Classics of Texas Fiction.* Dallas: E-Heart, 1987.

"Lewis, Willie Newberry, 1886–1896." *History of the Dallas Shakespeare Club: 1886–1970,* 1–16. Dallas: Dallas Shakespeare Club, 1956. Available at Dallas Public Library.

"Lillian Loyce Adams." In *Notable Women of the Southwest: A Pictorial Biographical Encyclopedia of the Leading Women of Texas, New Mexico, Oklahoma, and Arizona.* Dallas: William T. Tardy, 1938.

Lindenberg, Myra. "Fania Kruger Returns to School; Goal: U. N. Translator." *Justice,* 4. Fania Kruger Papers. Harry Ransom Humanities Research Center, University of Texas at Austin.

Litton, Frederic Nelson. Letter to Mrs. Minnie Tims Harper, June 27, 1949.

Maddox, Ruth Patterson. *Building SMU 1915–1957: A Warm and Personal Look at the People Who Started SMU.* N.p.: Oldenwald, 1995.

"Madeline Roach Gets Job as Secretary to Essayist." *Semi-Weekly Campus,* April 14, 1934, 2.

"Magazines Review 'Prairie Pegasus.'" *Semi-Weekly Campus,* October 11, 1929, 1.

Major, Mabel, and T. M. Pearce, eds. *Southwest Heritage: A Literary History with Bibliographies.* 3d ed. Albuquerque: University of New Mexico Press, 1972.

"The Makers." *Semi-Weekly Campus,* December 3, 1924, 2.

"Makers Plan Meeting at Home of Sponsor." *Campus,* October 17, 1923, 4.

"'The Makers' Publish SMU Student Poems." *Semi-Weekly Campus,* September 24, 1924, 1.

"Makers to Read Poems for National Contest." *Semi-Weekly Campus,* March 14, 1925, 3.

"Makers' Verse." *Semi-Weekly Campus,* February 19, 1927, 2.

"'Makers' Will Meet at Dinkey Den Wednesday." *Semi-Weekly Campus,* November 4, 1925.

"Manuscript Club Proves Methods by Successes." Unattributed article. *Wichita Daily Times,* n.d. Scrapbook of Peggy Schachter.

Manuscript: Published by and for the Wichita Falls Penwomen's Club I. January 22, 1925. Winifred Sanford Papers. Sanford Family, Dallas.

Martin, Theodora Penny. *The Sound of Our Own Voices: Women's Study Clubs 1860–1910.* Boston: Beacon, 1987.

Maxwell, Allen. "Remembering Siddie Joe Johnson." *Dallas Morning News,* August 7, 1977, 5G.

——. Telephone interview by author. July 2, 1996.

McClure, Clara Edgar. "Comment on Recent Fiction: Texas in the Cocoon." *Southwest Review* 9, no. 4 (1924): 218–20.

McGee, Donna. "75th Anniversary of the Panhandle Professional Writers." *Ranger,* October 14, 1994, 4.

McMurtry, Larry. "Afterword." In *My First Thirty Years,* by Edna Gertrude Beasley, 332–40. N.p.: Book Club of Texas, 1989.

Medina, David D. "Reading in the Margins." *Sallyport* (Rice University, spring, 1995): 27–31.

Meinig, D. W. *Imperial Texas: An Interpretive Essay in Cultural Geography.* Austin: University of Texas Press, 1969.

Mencken, H. L. Letters to Winifred Sanford, various dates. Winifred Sanford Papers. Sanford Family, Dallas.

Meredith, Doris. "6 Women Founded Panhandle Professional Writers in 1920 at Hotel." *Amarillo Sunday News-Globe,* April 16, 1995, 8D.

——. Telephone interview by author. June 20, 1997.

Meyer, Alvah F. "Panhandle Pen Women Gather for Quarterly Convention." 1921. Panhandle Pen Women Collection. *Amarillo Globe-News* archives, Amarillo.

Meyer, Sophia. "College to Take Over Course Founded by Pen Women Here." In *Guestbook and History 1947–48.* Panhandle Pen Women Collection. Amarillo Public Library, Amarillo.

——. "The Little Things Make Her Life Overflow with Riches." Panhandle Pen Women files, *Amarillo Globe-News* archives. Amarillo.

——. "Panhandle Pen Women Perfect Organization." *Amarillo Daily News,* May 2, 1920. *Panhandle Pen Women's History 1925–1955.* Panhandle Pen Women Collection. Amarillo Public Library, Amarillo.

Miles, Emerett Sanford. Telephone interview by author, February 14, 1991.

"Minutes of the Panhandle Pen Women Meeting, April 20, 1920." *Panhandle Pen Women Minutes.* Panhandle Pen Women Collection. Amarillo Public Library, Amarillo.

"Minutes of the Panhandle Pen Women Meeting, February 23, 1921." *Panhandle Pen Women Book One Reports, 1920–1926.* Panhandle Pen Women Collection. Amarillo Public Library, Amarillo.

"Minutes of the Panhandle Pen Women, May 13, 1921." *Panhandle Pen Women Book One Reports, 1920–1926.* Panhandle Pen Women Collection. Amarillo Public Library, Amarillo.

"Minutes of the Panhandle Pen Women Meeting, Oct. 12, 1921." *Panhandle Pen Women Book One Reports, 1920–1926.* Panhandle Pen Women Collection. Amarillo Public Library, Amarillo.

"Miss Frances Alexander: She Finds Fun in Writing Poetry." *Austin American Statesman,* April 17, 1949. Frances Alexander. Vertical files. Barker Center for American History. University of Texas, Austin.

"Miss Meyer Rites Today." *Amarillo Daily News,* November 20, 1968. In *PPW Scrapbook 1966–1975.* Panhandle Pen Women Collection. Amarillo Public Library, Amarillo.

Montgomery, Charlotte Baker. Letter to Betty Wiesepape, July 8, 1997.

——. Letter to Betty Wiesepape, July 17, 1997.

Montgomery, Vaida Stewart. "Are Women Poets Inferior to Men Poets." Montgomery Memorial Collection. MSS70, Box 2, FD69. DeGolyer Library, Southern Methodist University, Dallas.

——. *A Century with Texas Poets and Poetry.* Dallas: Kaleidograph, 1934.

——. "Dallas Poets." Montgomery Memorial Collection. MSS70, Box 2, FD69. DeGolyer Library, Southern Methodist University, Dallas.

——. "Foreword." In *A Century with Texas Poets and Poetry,* edited by Vaida Stewart Montgomery, vii–viii. Dallas: Kaleidograph, 1934.

———. "Leave the Ladies Alone!" Unpublished manuscript. Montgomery Memorial Collection. MSS70, Box 2, FD69. DeGolyer Library, Southern Methodist University, Dallas.

———. "Texas Poets of the Past." In *A Century with Texas Poets and Poetry,* edited by Vaida Stewart Montgomery, 19–22. Dallas: Kaleidograph, 1934.

Montgomery, Whitney. "Poetry Journals in Texas." In *A Century with Texas Poets and Poetry,* edited by Vaida Stewart Montgomery, 30–33. Dallas: Kaleidograph, 1934.

Moorty, S. S. "Stories Reveal the Twenties as More Than Gin and Flappers." Review of *Windfall and Other Stories,* by Winifred Sanford. *Texas Books in Review* 9, no. 2 (1989): 14–15.

"National Poetry Contest Is Sponsored by 'Makers.'" *Semi-Weekly Campus,* March 5, 1926, 1.

Nicholson, Mabel Carter. "Siddie Joe Johnson: Her Contribution to Literature." Master's thesis. East Texas State Teachers College, 1950.

"N.Y. Writer Is Guest of Border Poets." *South Texan,* January 18, 1936, 1, 4.

Olmsted, Frederick Law. *A Journey through Texas: Or a Saddle-Trip on the Southwestern Frontier.* 1857. Reprint, Austin: University of Texas Press, 1978.

Olsen, Tillie. *Silences.* 1978. Reprint, New York: Dell, 1989.

"On Student Writers and Writing." *Mustang,* January/February 1963, 6–7.

"Organization Names Distinguished Members." N.d. Panhandle Pen Women files, *Amarillo Globe-News* archives. Amarillo.

"Panhandle Pen Women Bulletin Jan. 21, 1947." In *Panhandle Pen Women Bulletins 1922–1950.* Panhandle Pen Women Collection. Amarillo Public Library, Amarillo.

"Panhandle Pen Women Gather for Quarterly Convention." Unattributed article, 1921. *Amarillo Globe-News* archives, Amarillo.

Panhandle Pen Women Golden Anniversary Plus Two: 1920–1972. Panhandle Pen Women, n.d.

"Panhandle Pen Women Hold Best Meeting of Year." *Amarillo Daily News,* October 22, 1924. Panhandle Pen Women files, *Amarillo Globe-News* archives. Amarillo.

Panhandle Pen Women Minutes Book One Reports 1920–1926. Panhandle Pen Women Collection. Amarillo Public Library, Amarillo.

"Panhandle Pen Women, Panhandle Professional Writers Presidents." Unpublished list. Private Collection of Nova Bair, Amarillo.

"Panhandle Pen Women Perfect Organization." May 2, 1920. Panhandle Pen Women files, *Amarillo Globe-News* archives. Amarillo.

Panhandle Pen Women's History 1925–55. Panhandle Pen Women Collection. Amarillo Public Library, Amarillo.

"Panhandle Penwomen's Meeting Is Largely Attended." Unattributed article. Panhandle Pen Women files, *Amarillo Globe-News* archives. Amarillo.

Panhandle Penwomen Scrapbooks—1920–1976. Panhandle Pen Women Collection. Amarillo Public Library, Amarillo.

Panhandle Professional Writers: 1994. Amarillo: PPW, 1994. Private Collection of Nova Bair, Amarillo.

"Panhandle Professional Writers to Mark 75th Anniversary in 1995." Unattributed article, April 27, 1994. Panhandle Pen Women files, *Amarillo Globe-News* archives. Amarillo.

"Panhandle Woman Is Winner." Unattributed article. Panhandle Pen Women files, *Amarillo Globe-News* archives. Amarillo.

"Pen Women Elect New Officers." Unattributed article. Panhandle Pen Women files, *Amarillo Globe-News* archives. Amarillo.

"Pen Women Hold Meeting." Unattributed article. Panhandle Pen Women files, *Amarillo Globe-News* archives. Amarillo.

"Pen Women of Panhandle, New Club Organized." Unattributed article. In *Panhandle Pen Women's History 1925–1955.* Panhandle Penwomen Collection. Amarillo Public Library, Amarillo.

"Pen Women of Panhandle to Meet." *Fort Worth Star Telegram,* March 2, 1922. Panhandle Pen Women Collection. Amarillo Public Library, Amarillo.

"Pen Women Plan Quarterly Meet." Unattributed article. Panhandle Pen Women files, *Amarillo Globe-News* archives. Amarillo.

Pilkington, William T. "First Reader's Report." Dallas, Southern Methodist University Press, n.d.

"Poems for Poetry Contest Come from All Over Country." *Campus,* May 19, 1922, 4.

"Poetic Eds and Co-eds Prepare for Poetry Society's National Contest in the Spring." *Semi-Weekly Campus,* December 17, 1927, 1.

"Poetry Book to Be Released from Press." *South Texan,* October 7, 1933, 4.

"Poetry Club Holds Meet Wednesday." *Semi-Weekly Campus,* February 7, 1925, 3.

"Poetry Club Meet Held Wednesday." *Semi-Weekly Campus,* February 18, 1928, 1.

"Poetry Club Organized on Last Friday." *Campus,* April 6, 1922, 1.

"Poetry Club to Be Reorganized." *Semi-Weekly Campus,* October 10, 1928, 1.

"Poetry Club to Honor Member." *Semi-Weekly Campus,* December 10, 1927, 1.

"Poetry Group Holds Organizational Meet." *South Texan,* October 14, 1933, 4.

"Poetry League Holds Kingsville Meet." *South Texan,* November 18, 1933, 1.

"Poetry Prizes to Be Offered by University." *Campus,* March 9, 1922, 1.

"Poetry Program Is Presented Friday." *South Texan,* October 21, 1933, 4.

"Poetry Society Elects Members." *Semi-Weekly Campus,* April 29, 1925, 3.

"Poetry Society Holds Kingsville Meeting." *South Texan,* November 18, 1933, 1.

"Poetry Society Holds Meet in Kingsville." *South Texan,* February 25, 1933, 1, 4.

"Poetry Society Meets in Bishop." *South Texan,* April 15, 1933, 1, 3.

"Poetry Society Meets in Corpus Christi." *South Texan,* May 13, 1933, 2.

Potter, Fannie C. *History of the Texas Federation of Women's Clubs, 1918–1938.* N.p.: Texas Federation of Women's Clubs, 1941.

"Quarterly Convention Held by Panhandle Pen Women." *Woman's Viewpoint,* February 1925, 19.

Ragsdale, Crystal. *Women of Texas: Their Lives, Their Experiences, Their Accomplishments.* Austin: State House, 1992.

Raines, Cadwell Walton. *Bibliography of Texas: Being A Descriptive List of Books, Pamphlets, and Documents Relating to Texas in Print and Manuscript since 1536.* Austin: Gammel, 1896.

"Renshaw, Dr. Edyth, Death and Funeral Announcements." *Dallas Morning News,* June 6, 1992, A:40.

Renshaw, Dr. Edyth. *SMU Video Oral History Interview.* With Judy Mohraz. SMU, June 20, 1983. Fondren Library, Southern Methodist University, Dallas.

Reynolds, Clay. Review of *Windfall and Other Stories,* by Winifred Sanford. *Western American Literature* 25, no. 2 (1989): 177–78.

Rhode, Robert. Interview by author. Kingsville, May 23, 1996.

"Rhode, Robert David." Vols. 93–96 of *Contemporary Authors,* edited by Frances Locher, 447. Detroit: Gale Research, 1980.

Richardson, Ellen. Interview by author. Amarillo, June 20, 1996.

"Rites Monday for Ottys E. Sanders." *Dallas Morning News,* March 14, 1993, A:43.

Robertson, Pauline Durrett. "Bits of History." *PPW Window,* April 1995, 4.

Romain, Mrs. P. W., Mrs. Leon Simpson, Mrs. Jack Akin, and Mrs. C. A. Bickley, eds. Vol. 3 of *History of the Texas Federation of Women's Clubs 1938–1988.* Seagraves, Tex.: Pioneer Book Publishing, 1988.

Romberg, Annie. "A Texas Literary Society of Pioneer Days." *Southwestern Historical Quarterly* 60 (1947–48): 61–65.

Rossbach, Mabel L. "Department Store." Review of *The Customer Is Always Right,* by Anne Pence Davis. *New York Times,* March 24, 1940. Anne Pence Davis Collection. Manuscripts. Library of Special Collections, Western Kentucky University, Bowling Green.

Rothman, Sheila M. *Woman's Proper Place: A History of Changing Ideals and Practices 1870 to the Present.* New York: Basic Books, 1978.

Rotunda. Dallas: SMU, 1922.

Rotunda. Dallas: SMU, 1924.

Rotunda. Dallas: SMU, 1925.

Rundell, Walter, Jr. *Early Texas Oil: A Photographic History, 1866–1936.* College Station: Texas A&M University Press, 1977.

Russell, R. David. "From the Incoming President." Book 20 of *A Book of the Year 1941.* Dallas: Poetry Society of Texas, 1941.

———. *The Incredible Flower.* Dallas: Kaleidograph, 1953.

———. *Sing with Me Now.* Dallas: Kaleidograph, 1945.

———. *There Is No Night.* Dallas: Kaleidograph, 1943.

"Sandburg Gives Recital-Lecture." *Semi-Weekly Campus,* April 2, 1925, 1.

"Sanders, Ottys, Death and Funeral Announcements." *Dallas Morning News,* March 14, 1993, A:43.

Sanders, Ottys. Letter to Aubrey Burns, December 19, 1978. Aubrey Burns file, Jay Broadus Hubbell Papers. Rare Book, Manuscript, and Special Collections Library, Duke University, Durham.

———. Letter to Jay B. Hubbell, June 12, 1974. Ottys Sanders file, Jay Broadus Hubbell Papers. Rare Book, Manuscript, and Special Collections Library, Duke University, Durham.

"Sanders, Ruth Maxwell, Death and Funeral Announcements." *Dallas Morning News,* September 25, 1985, A:26.

Sanford, Helen. Interview by author. Dallas, February 14, 1991.

———. Letter to Betty Wiesepape, July 3, 1993.

Sanford, Winifred. Letter to Margaret Cousins, October 5, 1945. Winifred Sanford Papers. Sanford Family, Dallas.

———. Letter to Mrs. M. L. Toulme, March 31, 1925. Winifred Sanford Papers. Sanford Family, Dallas.

———. Letter to Whitelaw Saunders, n.d. Winifred Sanford Papers. Sanford Family, Dallas.

———. "Letter to William H. Vann," n.d. Texas Institute of Letters Records. Southwestern Writers' Collection. Southwest Texas State University, San Marcos.

———. "Letter to William Kane [internal evidence indicates February 1928]. Winifred Sanford Papers. Sanford Family, Dallas.

———. "The Method of Irony." *Editor,* March 6, 1926, 150–51.

———. Papers. Sanford Family. Dallas.

———. "Two Junes." *Household,* November, 1931, 4–5.

———. *Windfall and Other Stories.* Dallas: Southern Methodist University Press, 1988.

———. "Writing the Short Story." *Southwester* 1 (1935): 26–27.

"Sarah C. Gross, 69, Editor, Reviewer." *New York Times,* July 21, 1976, A:36.

Sawey, Orlan. *Bernard DeVoto.* New York: Twayne, 1969.

——. *Charles A. Siringo.* Boston: Twayne, 1981.

——. "A Cowman's Autobiography." *Southwestern Historical Quarterly* 61 (1957): 317–18.

——. "Regional Histories Draw Their Readers." Unattributed published article, May 1975. Orlan Sawey folder. South Texas Archives and Special Collections. Texas A&M University, Kingsville.

"Sawey, Orlan Lester." Vol. 12 of *Contemporary Authors New Revision* series, edited by Linda Metzger, 421–22. Detroit: Gale Research, 1963.

Sawey, Orlan, and Nina Sawey, eds. *She Hath Done What She Could: Reminiscences of Hetti Lee Ewing.* Dallas: Gospel Teachers Publishing, 1974.

Scarborough, J. S., III. Telephone interview by author, May 18, 1996.

Schachter, Peggy. Interview by author. Dallas, February 11, 1991.

——. Telephone interview by author. January 2, 1991.

"Scores Another Hit." Unattributed article. Anne Pence Davis Collection. Manuscripts. Library of Special Collections, Western Kentucky University, Bowling Green.

"Second Erdman Novel Puts Author in Select Circle." September 19, 1949. Panhandle Pen Women files, *Amarillo Globe-News* archives. Amarillo.

"Services Set for Ruth Sanders." *Dallas Morning News,* September 25, 1985, A:26.

Shockley, Martin. *Southwest Writers Anthology.* Austin: Steck-Vaughn, 1962.

"Short Story Contest to Close Soon." Unattributed article. Panhandle Pen Women files, *Amarillo Globe-News* archives. Amarillo.

Showalter, Elaine. *A Literature of Their Own.* Princeton: Princeton University Press, 1977.

——. *Sister's Choice: Tradition and Change in American Women's Writing.* Oxford: Clarendon, 1991.

"Siddie Joe Johnson." *The Junior Book of Authors.* 2d ed., rev. Edited by Stanley Kunitz and Howard Haycraft, 172–73. New York: H. W. Wilson Co., 1951,

"Siddie Joe Johnson Receives Grolier Award." *Texas Library Journal* 30, no. 3 (1954): 151.

Smith, Bert Kruger. Telephone interview by author, January 30, 1991.

——. Telephone interview by author, July 6, 1993.

Smith, Goldie Capers. *The Creative Arts in Texas: A Handbook of Biography.* Dallas: Cokesbury, 1926.

Smith, Rebecca. "Minutes of the 1936 Meeting." Texas Institute of Letters Records. Southwestern Writers' Collection. Southwest Texas State University, San Marcos.

——. "Minutes of the 1937 Meeting." Texas Institute of Letters Records. Southwestern Writers' Collection. Southwest Texas State University, San Marcos.

——. "Minutes of the 1938 Meeting." Texas Institute of Letters Records. Southwestern Writers' Collection. Southwest Texas State University, San Marcos.

Smith-Rosenberg, Caroll. *Disorderly Conduct*. New York: Knopf, 1985.

"Smith Says Makers Will Not Reorganize." *Semi-Weekly Campus,* November 14, 1928, 1.

"S. M. U. Prize Attracts Wide-Spread Notice." *Semi-Weekly Campus,* April 20, 1922, 1.

"Some Milestones in the History of Panhandle Pen Women." In *The Panhandle Pen Women Golden Anniversary Plus Two: 1920–1972,* 4–5. Panhandle Pen Women Collection. Amarillo Public Library, Amarillo.

Sonnichsen, C. L. *The Southwest in Life and Literature*. New York: Devin Adair, 1962.

"Spelling Bee Is Now Story." August 7, 1949. Panhandle Pen Women files, *Amarillo Globe-News* archives. Amarillo.

"Spring Convention Is Held by Panhandle Penwomen." Unattributed article, 1922. Panhandle Pen Women Collection. Amarillo Public Library, Amarillo.

"Spring Meeting Panhandle Pen Women on Tuesday." April 19, 1925. Panhandle Pen Women files, *Amarillo Globe-News* archives. Amarillo.

"Stanley E. Babb Reads Original Poems before S. M. U. Poetry Society." *Semi-Weekly Campus,* December 13, 1924, 1.

Stewart, Rick. *Lone Star Regionalism: The Dallas Nine and Their Circle, 1928–1945*. Austin: Texas Monthly, 1985.

"Strict Rules Will Govern Contests." Unattributed article. In *Panhandle Pen Women History 1925–1955*. Panhandle Pen Women Collection. Amarillo Public Library, Amarillo.

"Students Enjoy Miss Alexander's Art Collection." *South Texan,* July 1, 1935, 1.

"Summarize Work of SMU Poets." *Semi-Weekly Campus,* December 5, 1925, 4.

Taylor, Birdie N. "The Women Writers of Texas." *Galveston Daily News,* June 18, 1893, and June 25, 1893. Barker Center for American History, University of Texas at Austin.

"Texas Federation of Women's Clubs: Contributions to the Humanities — Library and Literacy." Texas Federation of Women's Clubs Inventory. MSS20. Texas Foundation for Women's Resources. Women's Collection. Blagg-Huey Library, Texas Women's University, Denton.

"Texas Poet Presented at Sat. Program." *South Texan,* March 28, 1936, 1.

"Texas Poet Will Be Guest Artist." Unattributed article. Yauger folder. Vertical files. Dallas Public Library, Dallas.

"Texas Press Women." Texas State Historical Association. Notes in Texas Press Women file, The Woman's Collection. Texas Women's University, Denton.

Tinkle, Lon. *An American Original: The Life of J. Frank Dobie.* Boston: Little, Brown, 1978.

Turner, Victor. *From Ritual to Theatre: The Human Seriousness of Play.* New York: PAJ Publications, 1982.

Vann, William H. "The Early Years 1936–1938." In *The Texas Institute of Letters 1936–1966,* 3–12. Austin: Encino, 1967.

———. *The Texas Institute of Letters 1936–1966.* Austin: Encino, 1967.

"Vachel Lindsay Gives Readings Here May 11." *Campus,* May 19, 1922, 1.

"Viola Wheless McKinney." In *Notable Women of the Southwest: A Pictorial Biographical Encyclopedia of the Leading Women of Texas, New Mexico, Oklahoma, and Arizona,* 217. Dallas: William T. Tardy, 1938.

"Wade Gives Lecture Recital at Trinity." *Semi-Weekly Campus,* April 18, 1925, 4.

Wade, Isaac W. "Poets of the Future." *Semi-Weekly Campus,* February 4, 1925, 1.

Waerenskjold, Elise. *The Lady with the Pen: Elise Waerenskjold in Texas.* Edited by C. A. Clausen. New York: Arno, 1979.

Walton, Mrs. M. R. *A History of the Texas Woman's Press Association.* N.p., 1908. Texas Women's Collection. Texas Women's University, Denton.

Warner, Phoebe K. "The County Federation." In *Selected Editorials,* 100–103. San Antonio: Naylor, 1964.

Warren, Bill. "Mrs. Anne Pence Davis Is Inspired to Write Her First Book after Conversing with Young Bookworm." *Park City Daily News,* February 16, 1936, n.p. Anne Pence Davis Collection. Manuscripts. Library of Special Collections, Western Kentucky University, Bowling Green.

Warrin, Bill. "books." *Austin American Statesman,* November 28, 1971. Frances Alexander. Vertical files. Barker Center for American History, University of Texas at Austin.

"Welcome College Students." *Kingsville Record,* September 20, 1939, 1.4.

Williams, Anne Lee. "Distinguished Writer to Teach Creative Writing Courses at SMU." *Wichita Falls Times,* January 11, 1970, C15.

Williamson, Peggy. "Laura Hamner." In *Light and Hitch.* With Warren Hart and Bob Watson. KGNC, Amarillo, December 31, 1950. Private collection of Ellen Richardson, Amarillo.

"Willis, Mattie Lou, Death and Funeral Announcements." *Dallas Morning News,* October 25, 1990, A:40.

"Winsett, Marvin Davis." Vols. 1–4 of *Contemporary Authors First Revision,* edited by James Ethridge and Barbara Kapala, 1015–16. Detroit: Gale Research, 1965.

Winsett, Marvin Davis. "[I]n the Space Age?" *Dallas Times Herald Magazine,* June 10, 1962, 19.

"Woman's Reading Society Formed at Salado College Believed First in State." *Dallas Morning News,* May 7, 1928, n.p.

"Women Writers of the Panhandle Have Inspiring Motto." Unattributed article, May 12, 1921. *Panhandle Pen Women's History 1925–1955.* Panhandle Pen Women Collection. Amarillo Public Library, Amarillo.

"Writers Group to Mark 75th Birthday." *Amarillo Daily News,* March 31, 1995, n.p. Panhandle Pen Women files, *Amarillo Globe-News* archives. Amarillo.

"Writers Round-Up Slated Next Month." *Amarillo Daily News,* May 29, 1949, n.p. Panhandle Pen Women files, *Amarillo Globe-News* archives. Amarillo.

Yaeger, Patricia. *Honey-Mad Women: Emancipatory Strategies in Women's Writing.* New York: Columbia University Press, 1988.

Yauger, Laura Faye. Letter to Betty Wiesepape, February 3, 1991.

———. Letter to Betty Wiesepape, December 27, 1991.

———. Letter to William Vann, July 7, 1936. Texas Institute of Letters Records. Southwestern Writers' Collection. Southwest Texas State University, San Marcos.

———. *Planter's Charm.* Dallas: Kaleidograph, 1935.

"Yauger, Laura Faye." Yauger folder. Vertical files. Dallas Public Library, Dallas.

Yergan, Daniel. *The Prize: The Epic Quest for Oil, Money, and Power.* New York: Simon & Schuster, 1991.

"Zeek and Hubbell to Attend Meet." *Semi-Weekly Campus,* December 18, 1926, 1.

INDEX

Photos are indicated with *italic* page numbers.

ISBN 1-58544-324-7

90000